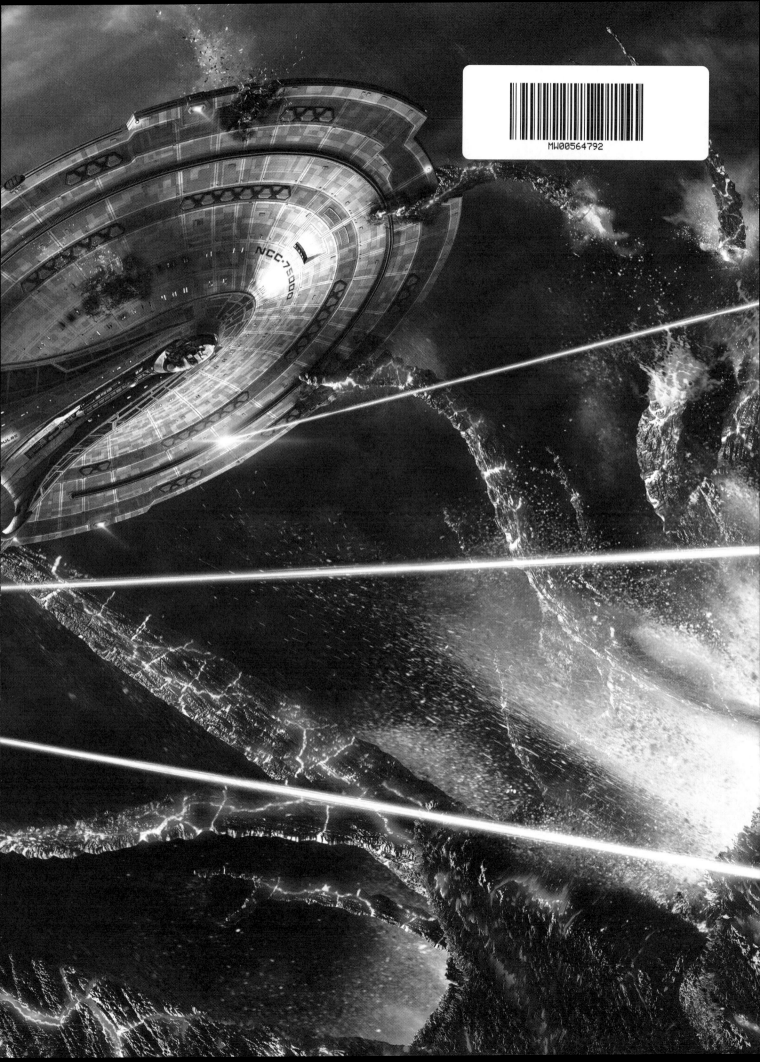

CREDITS

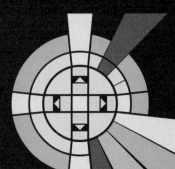

273920

193820

283220

SYSTEM DESIGN
NATHAN DOWDELL

LINE DEVELOPMENT
SAM WEBB AND JIM JOHNSON

WRITING
FRED LOVE, MARCO RAFALÀ, AARON M. POLLYEA, JOE RIXMAN, CHRISTOPHER L. BENNETT, ANDREW PEREGRINE, IAN LEMKE, SPRING NETTO, SAM WEBB, JASON BULMAHN, AND JIM JOHNSON

EDITING
JIM JOHNSON

PROOFREADING
MATEUSZ PŁOSZCZYCA, JIM JOHNSON, RICHARD L. GALE, AND VIRGINIA PAGE

INTERNAL ARTWORK
WAYNE MILLER, NICK GREENWOOD, VINCENT LAIK, MARTIN SOBR, DAVID METLESITS, JOHN EAVES, FRED PIENKOS, D.M. PHOENIX, JOHN M. TESKA

COVER ARTWORK
RODRIGO GONZALEZ

ART DIRECTION
RICHARD L. GALE, SAM WEBB, KATYA THOMAS, AND JIM JOHNSON

GRAPHIC DESIGN
MATTHEW COMBEN

LAYOUT
RICHARD L. GALE AND MICHAL E. CROSS

PUBLISHING DIRECTOR
CHRIS BIRCH

OPERATIONS DIRECTOR
RITA BIRCH

BUSINESS MANAGER
CAMERON DICKS

HEAD OF DEVELOPMENT
ROB HARRIS

HEAD OF RPG DEVELOPMENT
SAM WEBB

PUBLIC RELATIONS
PANAYIOTIS LINES

SOCIAL MEDIA MANAGER
SALWA AZAR

PRODUCTION MANAGER
PETER GROCHULSKI

SCHEDULING
STEVE DALDRY

VIDEO PRODUCTION
STEVE DALDRY

PUBLISHING ASSISTANT
VIRGINIA PAGE

ASSISTANT ART DIRECTOR
KATYA THOMAS

SALES AND MARKETING MANAGER
RHYS KNIGHT

ASSISTANT SALES MANAGER
COLE LEADON

COMMUNITY SERVICE MANAGER
LLOYD GYAN

CUSTOMER SUPPORT
SHAUN HOCKING

FOR CBS STUDIOS
BILL BURKE, JOHN VAN CITTERS, MARIAN CORDRY, VERONICA HART, BRIAN LADY, AND KEITH LOWENADLER

AUX SYS

MODIPHIUS™ ENTERTAINMENT 2d20™

Published by Modiphius Entertainment Ltd.
2nd Floor, 39 Harwood Road, London, SW6 4QP, England.
Printed by Standartų Spaustuvė, UAB, Vilnius, Lithuania.

INFO@MODIPHIUS.COM
WWW.MODIPHIUS.COM
STARTREK.COM

Modiphius Entertainment Product Number: MUH051763
ISBN: 978-1-912743-26-1

CONTENTS

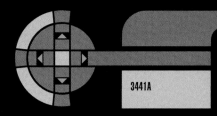

3441A

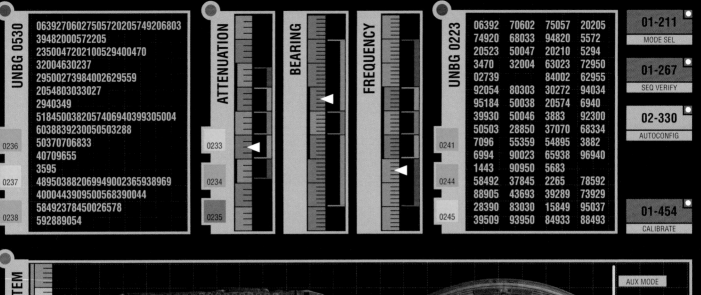

UNBG 0530

0639270602750572020574920680339482000572205
2350047202100529400470
32004630237
29500273984002629559
2054803033027
2940349
5184500382057406940399305004
6038839230050503288
50370706833
40709655
3595
4895038820699490023659389694000443909500568390044
58492378450026578
592889054

0236
0237
0238

ATTENUATION
0233
0234
0235

BEARING

FREQUENCY

UNBG 0223

06392	70602	75057	20205
74920	68033	94820	5572
20523	50047	20210	5294
3470	32004	63023	72950
02739		84002	62955
92054	80303	30272	94034
95184	50038	20574	6940
39930	50046	3883	92300
50503	28850	37070	68334
7096	55359	54895	3882
6994	90023	65938	96940
1443	90950	5683	
58492	37845	2265	78592
88905	43693	39289	73929
28390	83030	15849	95037
39509	93950	84933	88493

0241
0244
0245

01-211 MODE SEL
01-267 SEQ VERIFY
02-330 AUTOCONFIG
01-454 CALIBRATE

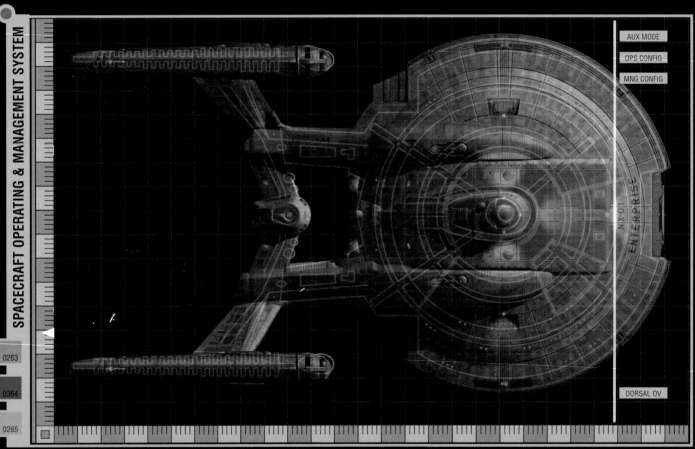

SPACECRAFT OPERATING & MANAGEMENT SYSTEM

AUX MODE
OPS CONFIG
MNG CONFIG

DORSAL OV

0263
0364
0265

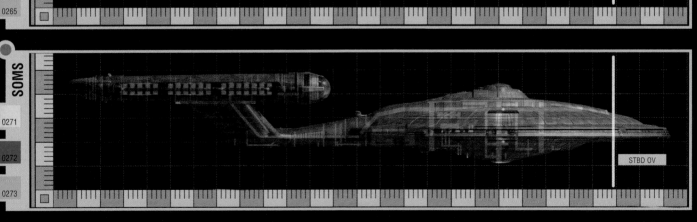

SOMS

STBD OV

0271
0272
0273

03-225 SUBSYS SEL
03-367 AUX MODE
04-275 SECONDARY
07-388 AUTOCONFIG
01-455 ROOT DIR
01-745 SUBSYS SEL

CHAPTER 01

INTRODUCTION

49816529318672
3021239494

INTRODUCTION
STRANGE NEW WORLDS

"THIS IS WHERE THE ADVENTURE IS. THIS IS WHERE HEROES ARE MADE."

— DR. JULIAN BASHIR

One of Starfleet's core mandates issued by the Federation Council is to expand the boundaries of known space and explore the incredibly diverse array of planets, planetoids, artificial constructions, and strange artifacts all across the Galaxy where sentient beings of all types live, work, interact, or exist. "Exploring strange new worlds" is a key component of every *Star Trek* series, and it should be equally important in any *Star Trek Adventures* campaign or standalone mission. Discovering and exploring new worlds are ways for humanity to learn, grow, and innovate for a better future.

This compendium provides the Gamemaster of *Star Trek Adventures* the means to further those themes of discovery and exploration. *Strange New Worlds, Mission Compendium, Volume 2* contains nine full-length missions for use with the *Star Trek Adventures* roleplaying game. Each mission details some form of strange new world and has been designed to provide at least 4-5 hours of gameplay for the average group consisting of a Gamemaster and one or more Players. The missions offer a range of experiences, from investigating the return of a deadly viral plague on a massive artificial ring built around a planet, exploring an ancient doomsday seed vault on an ice-bound world, investigating a self-aware sentient planet, and more.

HOW TO USE THIS BOOK

Each mission presented in this compendium may be used as the starting point for a new *Star Trek Adventures* campaign or dropped into an existing campaign with a minimum of revision. They also work well as standalone missions. None of them require an encyclopedic understanding of the *Star Trek* universe, and all have been designed to stand independent of any episode or movie in the *Star Trek* canon (i.e., you don't need to have watched a specific television episode or movie to understand the events portrayed in each mission).

The missions are presented in rough chronological order and grouped by eras of play. While all of the missions

were written to fit into a specific *Star Trek* era, guidance is included within each to help Gamemasters modify them for use in any era of play.

We hope you enjoy the missions contained within this compendium. We encourage you to share your experiences playing these missions with us and with the ever-expanding *Star Trek Adventures* gaming community online.

And now, gather your crew, select a mission, grab some dice, and explore these strange new worlds!

A CURE WORSE THAN THE DISEASE [ENT]

This mission presents a mystery involving the suspicious resurgence of a viral plague among a population of aliens who attempted to rid themselves of the virus generations ago by constructing a mammoth artificial ring around their planet. The Players receive a plea for help from the planet Fosstarian II and move to investigate. They must deal with high levels of radiation, explore a massive artificial planetary ring, and deal with a duplicitous corporation and its minions.

PLATO'S CAVE [TOS]

The Players are sent to Tanghal IV, an ice-age world, to resupply a remote Federation archaeological outpost. Finding no life signs on the planet, they beam down to investigate. They find the lead archaeologist dead – the only clue a disturbing message in which he appears mad. Searching for the outpost's other personnel, the Players explore a doomsday seed vault and missile silo that was converted into a survival bunker some 10,000 years before. Inside, they soon realize that they are not alone. They must deal with a sentient quantum computer driven insane by isolation and existential

crisis. The mission requires Players to confront issues of survival and morality.

DRAWING DEEPLY FROM THE WELL [TOS]

Players are sent to investigate strange occurrences at a newly operational alien megastructure nicknamed 'The Big Dipper.' This facility is a massive structure consisting of a central hub the size of a small outpost and two tethers stretching outwards from the hub. The tethers end in huge ramscoops that dip down into layers of the planet, scooping out common heavy metals and a significant amount of dilithium. Players will discover there is intelligent life here known as the 'Free' and that they are being destroyed by the dilithium mining. Can the Players find a way to protect the aliens from the dilithium mining?

NO GOOD DEED [TOS]

The Players intercept a call for help and track the signal to a star system. They discover a beautiful world devoid of sentient life and a space station, its orbit decaying. Upon investigating the station, the Players find desiccated corpses from what appear to be both avian and arthropod species. The Players learn that the avians were at war with the arthropods, which led to an extinction event due to an airborne virus that killed off over 99% of the avian population within a matter of weeks. The crew learns the virus had been artificially created by the arthropods and that the virus was spread by vents in the planet's crust through natural, volcanic activity. When they discover frozen embryos from both species stored within a cryochamber, they must decide what to do.

WHOLE OF THE LAW [TNG]

The Players come upon an exotic object in space: a large, flat disk of hyperdense matter generating its own gravitational field. The structure resists scans, but the ship receives a friendly hail inviting it to dock. The disk habitat is called Thelema, and its builders belong to a race of enlightened anarchists. The habitat is subdivided into a Light Face for relatively wholesome indulgences and a Dark Face for more extreme entertainment – with the strict provision that everyone who enters does so voluntarily. During shore leave on Thelema, several Players are abducted to the Dark Face. The Thelemans refuse to believe the officers were taken against their will, so the Players must investigate their abduction and try to prove it to Thelema's administrator, while also attempting to pierce the habitat's privacy shielding to locate and rescue their crew.

and storms form in the skies. It becomes apparent that the ocean itself is a life-form that has not taken kindly to the intrusion. The Players must contend with the Ferengi and make contact with the alien entity before it destroys the refinery and its hundreds of residents.

FOOTFALL [TNG]

The characters are ordered to Ashgrave IV, a colony considered a holy place by many different species. The planet is a place of pilgrimage to people from many different cultures, and therein lies the problem. With all of them believing the place is sacred, there are several tensions due to the differences in various faiths. Recently, the usual tensions have grown worse. A more militant group of pilgrims has taken to violence. The Players will discover that the planet is actually a powerfully telepathic self-aware entity, which has come to the conclusion that it must be the 'god' the inhabitants believe in and that a holy apocalypse might help to resolve its crisis of faith. Can the Players convince the entity it is not a god, even when it seems to match the description of one?

DARKNESS [TNG]

This mission takes place on the frontier of explored space, in response to a distress call from a Vulcan Expeditionary Group on the planet of Trax Episilon 1. The Players' vessel arrives in the Trax Episilon system to find the Class-H planet the Vulcans were studying is now a black void in the sky. The characters must don EV suits and descend into the thick black atmosphere to investigate. On the planet, Players investigate what happened to the missing doomed expedition and encounter a vast alien mind terraforming the planet and attempting to make telepathic contact with anyone it can reach.

THE ANGSTROM OPERATION [TNG]

The Players are ordered to the Dran'Ankos system near the Cardassian Demilitarized Zone. A small research facility sent out a distress signal and then was silenced. The Players are ordered to go to the base, restore it if possible, but to retrieve the research at all costs. Upon arrival, they discover the planet's sun is inexplicably losing stellar mass. They investigate the damaged facility and attempt to piece together what happened. Along the way, they'll encounter crazed scientists, lethal neural parasites, and a contingent of war-hungry Cardassians.

A CRY FROM THE VOID [TNG]

Players discover a living world – an entity that shifts from oceanic to crystalline form. They encounter a renegade Ferengi female and her illegal latinum processing plant and assist in searching for some of her missing workers. After undertaking a search and rescue operation, the Players recover the missing workers just as the oceans become violent with seemingly no apparent cause. Massive waves begin pounding the shores where the refinery is located,

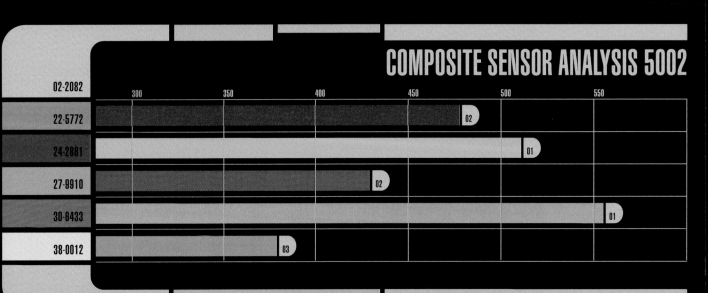

COMPOSITE SENSOR ANALYSIS 5002

	300	350	400	450	500	550
02-2082						
22-5772				02		
24-2881					01	
27-9910			02			
30-8433						01
38-0012		03				

A CURE WORSE THAN THE DISEASE

BY FRED LOVE

AD ASTRA PER ASPERA

A CURE WORSE THAN THE DISEASE
SYNOPSIS

Set around the year 2155, this mission for a United Earth Starfleet vessel presents Player Characters with a mystery: Why has plague returned to a planet encircled by a mammoth artificial ring constructed to rid the population of the virus generations ago?

Act 1 opens with the crew receiving a plea for help from the planet Fosstarian II. The distress call asks for help to combat a viral outbreak. As the Player Characters approach Fosstarian II, they notice the planet is surrounded by a mechanical ring containing photonic crystals that bombard the planet with radiation. The Player Characters will have to invent some means of coping with this radiation before visiting the planet's surface.

The regent leading the Fosstarian planetary government invites the crew to the capital city, where she explains that her people are battling a deadly plague on several continents. The planet's leading scientists confirmed the virus is virtually identical to one that ravaged the planet two centuries ago after the Fosstarian's first interplanetary expeditions returned from deep space carrying the extra-terrestrial disease. The Fosstarians learned that highly focused radiation could suppress the virus, so a Fosstarian mega corporation called ImmutiCorp manufactured medication to allow Fosstarians to cope with radiation

01-202
MODE SEL

01-478
SEQ VERIFY

02-346
AUTOCONFIG

sickness. ImmutiCorp then built the artificial ring to saturate the entire planet, thus eliminating the disease. The only catch is that Fosstarians must receive regular doses of radiation meds or become sickened.

The current CEO of the corporation, Valastra Th'lacen, warns against accepting the help of the Player Characters. The virus came from off world, and working with offworlders will lead to another calamity, she argues. The regent overrules her, however, and asks the Player Characters to help cure the current outbreak.

In Act 2, the Player Characters analyze the virus and discover that it has mutated to develop a resistance to the radiation generated by the artificial ring. They also learn that synthesizing an antigen for the virus isn't particularly difficult. Their research uncovers clues that ImmutiCorp once developed a vaccine but suppressed the breakthrough after concluding the corporation would earn a greater long-term profit by selling anti-radiation medication on an ongoing basis. Soon after this discovery, the crew comes under attack from a corporate starship secretly housed in the artificial ring, in an effort to keep ImmutiCorp's money-hungry scheme secret.

Act 3 begins as the Player Characters come into direct conflict with the corporate forces, who will try to run the Player Characters' vessel out of the system. If the Player Characters fend off the ImmutiCorp attack, they can pursue Th'lacen, who makes her last stand in a stronghold in the artificial ring. If ImmutiCorp's scheme is revealed, the Fosstarians can begin distributing the vaccine that will permanently rid them of the virus.

ADAPTING THIS MISSION
TO OTHER ERAS

This scenario takes place in the mid-2150s, during the *Star Trek: Enterprise* era, and is ideal for NX-class vessels and other starships from that timeframe. The planet Fosstarian II should be located near the Federation core worlds due to the limitations of Starfleet's warp engines at the time. However, because the events of the scenario involve an original planet and species, Gamemasters can run this scenario in later eras with minimal modification. In such cases, Gamemasters may consider relocating the scenario to a more distant region of space and substituting more advanced technology and weaponry for that used by the Fosstarians to present Players with an era-appropriate threat. For instance, switching the phase cannons of the ImmutiCorp strike ship for phaser arrays may be more fitting for campaigns set during later eras.

DIRECTIVES

In addition to the Prime Directive, the Directives for this mission are:

- Investigate all credible distress signals

- Render aid to all sufficiently advanced species who request help in dealing with humanitarian crises

The Gamemaster begins this mission with 2 points of Threat for each Player Character in the group.

A CURE WORSE THAN THE DISEASE
ACT 1: RENDERING AID

SCENE 1: PREPARATIONS

This scene should allow the crew to make any preparations they wish as they approach Fosstarian II, where they expect to find a plague-ravaged population in need of help. Any character who checks the library computer for additional information on Fosstarian II or its inhabitants will find only one brief mention in the database, an 80-year-old log entry from a Vulcan survey vessel.

As the Starfleet vessel approaches Fosstarian II, science and medical personnel may wish to formulate a plan to analyze the plague as well as set up mobile hospitals to treat the sick. Engineering and tactical officers may assist in working out the logistics of responding to a pandemic.

Once the Starfleet vessel is within visual distance of Fosstarian II, it will become clear to anyone looking at the viewscreen that the planet's ring is not a natural feature. Rather, the ring appears artificially constructed. A **Reason + Engineering or Science** Task with a of Difficulty 1, aided by the ship's **Sensors + Science**, reveals that

CAPTAIN'S STARLOG
FEBRUARY 6, 2155

We've received a distress signal from the planetary government of Fosstarian II, a Class-M world boasting a major population of humanoids. The automated message, recorded by a planetary regent named Tresta Zammeline, asked for urgent help in responding to a virulent plague sweeping the planet. The Fosstarians are known to be a technologically advanced race, though they follow a strict policy of isolationism, making this plea for off-world help highly irregular. We've set course and intend to render aid if possible.

massive sheets of duranium compose the outside of the ring, while the inner surface features rows of photonic crystals that bombard the planet's surface with continuous, low-level waves of gamma radiation. Spending a point of

SHIP'S LOG
VULCAN SURVEY VESSEL *T'MIRA*

We approached the Fosstarian star system as part of our survey mission of this sector. However, before we could enter the system and commence in-depth scans, we received an audio-only subspace radio transmission from an individual identifying himself as the planetary leader of Fosstarian II. The Fosstarian leader struck a rather threatening tone before demanding that we keep our distance and respect his civilization's wish to remain isolated. We were allowed only a brief conversation before the regent cut the transmission. Rather than risk a botched first contact, we decided to comply with the Fosstarian's demand and rerouted our course to avoid the area.

Judging by the Fosstarians' ability to detect our approach and their use of subspace radio, it seems logical to conclude they possess some form of advanced technology. We had time to conduct only a cursory sensor sweep, which confirmed the Fosstarian transmission originated from the system's second planet, a ringed *Minshara*-class world. Perhaps, in time, we will be able to learn more of this hermit civilization. End recording and file with the Vulcan Science Directorate.

03-225 — SUBSYS SEL
03-367 — AUX MODE
04-275 — SECONDARY
07-388 — AUTOCONFIG

Momentum to improve the quality of success for the sensor scan reveals the interior of the ring contains numerous compartments and life-signs.

As the Player Characters approach Fosstarian II, they will receive a hail from Regent Tresta Zammeline, the current planetary leader. Zammeline voices her gratitude for Starfleet's concern and invites the Player Characters to her palace in the capital city for a full briefing on the pandemic. If the Player Characters hesitate to travel to the planet for fear of contracting the infection, Zammeline assures them the virus has not yet spread to the continent on which the capital is located. Or, if the Player Characters express concern about the planet's high levels of surface radiation, Zammeline offers them anti-radiation innoculations upon their arrival. Additionally, Player Characters may fashion their own inoculation to stave off radiation sickness with a successful **Reason + Medicine** Task with a Difficulty of 1.

If this does not allay the Player Characters' concerns, Zammeline will consent to a meeting on the Player Characters' vessel and submit to any biosecurity measures beforehand, so long as she can be accompanied by one of her chief advisors.

Gamemaster Note: Regent Zammeline will not show all her cards in this first encounter with the Player Characters. She will explain that a deadly virus has swept across two of the planet's continents and that her world's scientists have failed to slow its spread, but she won't elaborate further until she's

CONTRACTING THE OUTLANDER VIRUS

Characters run the risk of contracting the Outlander Virus at various points during this scenario. The virus travels through the air and can infect most humanoid species through respiration. Player Characters can avoid infection by wearing EV suits in environments where the virus is present or by fashioning a respirator capable of filtering out the virus. The construction of such a respirator would require study of the virus and completion of an appropriate Task. Characters that visit the surface of Fosstarian II should make use of a decontamination chamber, such as those installed on NX-class starships, where topical gels applied to the skin and ultraviolet radiation eradicate contaminants before landing parties resume normal contact

with crewmates. During later eras, transporters routinely filter out dangerous biological agents.

Despite these precautions, the possibility of infection remains. Players whose Characters enter an environment where the virus is present without a means of protecting themselves must roll 1▲. If an effect is rolled, that Character gains the **Infected** Trait. They immediately start to show symptoms such as a high fever, skin discoloration and intense pain. Roughly 24 hours after infection, a Character takes 8▲ Stress damage. From that point on, Characters with the **Infected** Trait take an additional 8▲ Stress damage each day they remain infected (normal rules for Injuries apply). Infected

Characters cannot regain Stress until they receive a cure for the virus. However, Characters that suffer an Injury due to the virus can be stabilized with a successful **Daring + Medicine** Task with a Difficulty of 1. Stabilized Characters will not die from the virus, but remain badly sickened and unable to attempt Tasks until they receive a cure. Characters that take on the **Infected** Trait also become carriers of the virus, capable of spreading it to others.

Whenever possible, Gamemasters should allow Players whose Characters suffer an Injury due to the Outlander Virus to take over Supporting Cast Characters so they can continue to participate in the mission.

had a chance to size up the crew in person. Her culture displays a deep suspicion of aliens and blames offworlders for the presence of the virus in the first place. However, she's desperate to avoid the massive casualties inflicted by the virus two centuries ago and has pinned her hope on receiving help from the Player Characters. She will attempt to mask her desperation, but characters with telepathic abilities or an aptitude for diplomacy or negotiation may pick up on her state of mind with an appropriate Task.

SCENE 2: A RESURGENT VIRUS

If the Player Characters agree to Regent Zammeline's invitation, they may travel to the planet's capital in a shuttlepod. If, however, the Player Characters insist on a meeting on their vessel, Zammeline, accompanied by ImmutiCorp CEO Valastra Th'lacen and a small honor guard, boards a similar short-range craft and docks with their vessel. This text assumes this scene takes place on the planet's surface, but it will play out similarly if set elsewhere.

To start this scene, Gamemasters should read or paraphrase the following:

> *"Planetary Regent Tresta Zammeline welcomes you into an expansive hall under a clear dome. Looking skyward through the dome, the massive artificial ring towers overhead. An orbital tether snakes down from the underside of the ring and connects to the planet's surface somewhere nearby. Zammeline, her face hidden behind a radiation visor decorated with an intricate gold design, thanks you for your willingness to help and introduces you to her advisor, ImmutiCorp CEO Valastra Th'lacen."*

Zammeline explains that two continents on the planet are experiencing an outbreak of a plague that closely resembles the Outlander Virus, thought to have been eradicated centuries ago by the ring. If history repeats itself, the virus will spread to every continent on the planet and could wipe out millions. She asks for the Player Characters' help in finding a cure to the virus and suggests they work with ImmutiCorp researchers to pool resources. Zammeline explains that several infected Fosstarians have been sent to ImmutiCorp's most advanced medical laboratory housed inside the ring where, protected by quarantine fields, researchers are studying the virus. Zammeline will suggest the Starfleet medical and science personnel begin their work in the ImmutiCorp medical research lab.

Th'lacen, for her part, bristles at the presence of the Starfleet crew. Player Characters who size her up with telepathy or diplomacy-related Tasks will notice that she's radiating hostility and is doing little to hide it. If confronted, Th'lacen explains that offworlders were

responsible for the virus in the first place, and asking for the help of non-Fosstarians invites further catastrophe. Observant Player Characters, may notice that she seems to be hiding something during this conversation. However, she eventually will consent to working with the Player Characters and will invite Starfleet science and medical personnel to ImmutiCorp's research facility inside the ring.

Gamemaster Note: *This scene requires the Gamemaster to play two NPCs with opposing viewpoints. Zammeline wants Starfleet help; Th'Lacen does not. If the Gamemaster is comfortable playing up this confrontation, it could give command officers a chance to demonstrate their diplomatic prowess as they thread the needle between these two viewpoints. However the scene plays out, Th'lacen will agree to work with Starfleet, even though it should be clear she has misgivings.*

REGENT TRESTA ZAMMELINE

Zammeline is the planetary leader of Fosstarian II, and possesses a keen intellect and skill in diplomatic situations. Her main objective is to save her people from the Outlander Virus, but she knows her own power and influence pale in comparison to that of ImmutiCorp.

TRAITS: Fosstarian, Planetary Regent

VALUE: My People are What Matters Most

ATTRIBUTES

CONTROL	08	FITNESS	07	PRESENCE	10
DARING	08	INSIGHT	09	REASON	09

DISCIPLINES

COMMAND	03	SECURITY	01	SCIENCE	02
CONN	02	ENGINEERING	01	MEDICINE	–

FOCUSES: Diplomacy, Rhetoric, Law

STRESS: 8   **RESISTANCE:** 0

ATTACKS:

- Unarmed Strike (Melee, 2▲ Knockdown, Size 1H, Non-lethal)
- Phase Pistol (Ranged, 4▲, Size 1H)

SPECIAL RULES:

- **Advisor:** Whenever Zammeline assists another character using her Command Discipline, the character being assisted may re-roll one d20.
- **Keen Rhetoric:** when attempting a Persuasion Task using her Presence Attribute, Zammeline may add 1 bonus d20.

0222

0223

05-440
SEQ VERIFY

02-488
CALIBRATE

VALASTRA TH'LACEN, IMMUTICORP CEO

FOCUSES: Economics, Brand Management, Virology, Radiobiology, Orbital Engineering, Planetary Security Policy

Believing ImmutiCorp to be Fosstarian II's supreme institution, Th'lacen will try to keep the viral vaccine a secret at all costs.

STRESS: 9 **RESISTANCE:** 0

TRAITS: Fosstarian, CEO

ATTACKS:
- Unarmed Strike (Melee, 3▲ Knockdown, Size 1H, Non-lethal)
- Phase Pistol (Ranged, 4▲, Size 1H)
- Escalation: Particle Rifle (Ranged, 6▲, Size 2H, Accurate)

VALUES:
- The Bottom Line is Everything
- All Offworlders are a Threat

SPECIAL RULES:
- **Ruthless and Determined:** Th'lacen may spend 2 Threat, rather than 3, to gain the effects of a point of Determination.
- **Supreme Authority:** Whenever an ImmutiCorp employee attempts a Task to resist persuasion or intimidation, Th'lacen may spend 1 Threat to allow that employee to re-roll, even if Th'lacen is not present in the scene herself.
- **Expects Success:** Whenever Th'lacen uses the Direct or Assist Task to aid a subordinate, that Task may always Succeed at Cost.
- **Immune to Outlander Virus:** Th'lacen and the highest-placed ImmutiCorp officials received doses of the top-secret Outlander vaccine, so cannot have the **Infected** Trait.

ATTRIBUTES

| CONTROL | 10 | FITNESS | 07 | PRESENCE | 10 |
| DARING | 09 | INSIGHT | 11 | REASON | 12 |

DISCIPLINES

| COMMAND | 04 | SECURITY | 02 | SCIENCE | 02 |
| CONN | 01 | ENGINEERING | 03 | MEDICINE | 04 |

0225
0226
0227

FOSSTARIAN II AND ITS INHABITANTS

The Class-M world Fosstarian II supports plant and animal life, including an intelligent humanoid species. The Fosstarians developed warp capability ahead of humanity and launched a deep space exploratory expedition. It returned with knowledge of surrounding space, yet the crew unwittingly carried a virus back home. The resulting plague, referred to as the Outlander Virus, ravaged the population for years, until ImmutiCorp, a massive conglomerate, discovered concentrated gamma radiation could halt its spread. ImmutiCorp at first produced small-scale, localized radiation generators to fight the virus.

ImmutiCorp also discovered an effective vaccine for the virus, but the company's leaders decided to disavow all knowledge of the project and allow only the company's most senior officials access to the vaccine. The corporation determined that there was less profit in vaccinating every Fosstarian against the virus

once than there was in selling anti-radiation medications to the entire population in perpetuity.

Accordingly, ImmutiCorp proposed a radical solution: an artificial ring that would surround and saturate the planet with radiation, providing a permanent cure. Taking decades to complete, the ring represents the single greatest work of engineering in Fosstarian history, and dominates the skyward view anywhere near the planet's equator. The inside of the ring is composed of photonic crystals that amplify the radiation and direct it at the planet, while the outside houses thousands of ImmutiCorp employees. Magnetic lifts inside orbital tethers connect the ring to governmental and corporate facilities on the planet.

All Fosstarians use anti-radiation meds and protective clothing to protect against the radiation bombardment. The constant radiation resulted in mass

extinctions of a range of native species and laid waste to vast sections of the planet's surface. Anticipating this, ImmutiCorp built massive domed structures on the planet's continents where crops and food animals are raised and processed. ImmutiCorp's control of both the ring and food production grants the company near-limitless power. The planetary government ostensibly creates public policy but seldom without the consent of the ImmutiCorp CEO. The virus's origins on a distant planet cemented an attitude of xenophobia among the Fosstarians, who have isolated themselves from interstellar affairs.

Fosstarians are rarely seen in public without radiation masks – as much a fashion accessory as a radiation filter. Without masks, Fosstarians largely resemble humans. Fosstarians grow little hair as a result of the planet's ambient radiation levels, and most choose to shave their heads and exposed skin.

ACT 2: THE OUTLANDER VIRUS

Act 2 provides the Player Characters with an opportunity to study the Outlander Virus and to uncover ImmutiCorp's deceit. This act focuses on science and medical personnel but also provides suggestions for how other characters may get involved later. The Player Characters will have to complete a Gated Challenge to piece together the truth about the virus. This investigation will provoke an aggressive response by ImmutiCorp to suppress the Player Characters' discoveries, which will lead into Act 3.

ImmutiCorp CEO Valastra Th'lacen has granted Starfleet medical and science personnel access to the company's research facility inside the ring. Th'lacen will greet the Player Characters herself in order to keep a close eye on them. The Player Characters can travel to the ring either via the orbital tethers connected to the planet's surface or by traveling over in a small craft and docking with an airlock.

SCENE 1: INSIDE THE RING

Read or paraphrase the following to begin this scene:

"Th'lacen leads you into a large laboratory filled with advanced scientific instruments and computers. An enormous window takes up an entire wall of the lab, granting a sweeping view of the planet below. Armed security guards stand watch at all the lab's entrances, and a handful of technicians work at several of the computer consoles. Three Fosstarians clad in hospital gowns sit on cots placed behind a shimmering force field."

The three Fosstarians behind the quarantine field are infected with the Outlander Virus and were transferred from the planet's surface so ImmutiCorp scientists could study them. These infected Fosstarians – an elderly man named Jaylem, a middle-aged woman named Nelvia, and a young boy named Xanodel – are suffering from high fevers and excruciating pain, and lapse in and out of consciousness. The infected Fosstarians originate from different regions of the planet and were selected to give the ImmutiCorp scientists a broad spectrum of variables to study.

The infected Fosstarians cannot attempt Tasks, but they may, at the Gamemaster's discretion, speak to the Player Characters. Xanodel, in particular, acts frightened after

CAPTAIN'S STARLOG
SUPPLEMENTAL

We've made contact with Regent Tresta Zammeline, the planetary leader of Fosstarian II. She's asked for our help in finding a cure to a viral plague that threatens the planet's entire population. To do so, we'll need to work with researchers at ImmutiCorp, a private company that constructed the artificial ring that bombards the planet with radiation. The ring was built centuries ago to eradicate the Outlander Virus, but it appears the remedy is no longer effective.

06-388

SAVE ENTRY

having been separated from his family and taken to the ring. The Player Characters also can run scans of the infected Fosstarians. Any diagnostic procedures that require physical contact may be run through the use of holo-technology that projects an image of a "doctor" into the quarantined area. This projection can carry out pre-programmed tasks, such as taking tissue samples from the infected Fosstarians, but it must be controlled directly by someone in the laboratory and possesses no intelligence of its own. In this manner, the Player Characters may conduct whatever research they like to investigate the virus, though Th'lacen keeps a close eye on the Starfleet personnel the entire time.

If the Player Characters conduct a medical scan of Th'lacen, a **Reason + Medicine or Science** Task with a Difficulty of 1 confirms that she is currently unaffected by the virus. Spending a point of Momentum to *Obtain Information* shows that Th'lacen's blood stream carries antibodies capable of fighting off the Outlander Virus, an indication that she's received a vaccine to make her immune. If confronted about this, Th'lacen will become angry and deny the existence of any such vaccine.

*Gamemaster Note: Should it become necessary for the Gamemaster to have game statistics for the Fosstarian viral carriers or for the ImmutiCorp lab technicians, simply use the statistics provided for ImmutiCorp guards in Act 3. That same stat block should work for virtually any other Fosstarian NPC required for this scenario. Any character suffering from the Outlander Virus takes on the **Infected** Trait.*

CHALLENGE: FINDING A CURE

Identifying an effective treatment for the Outlander Virus presents the Player Characters with a Gated Challenge, or a series of Key Tasks that require a few steps to complete. The Player Characters must begin by isolating and sequencing the virus from one of the three carriers inside the quarantine field. This requires a **Reason + Medicine or Science** Task with a Difficulty of 2. The Player Characters may attempt this Task more than once until a successful result is achieved. However, a failed attempt causes the viral carrier being studied to worsen. In this case, someone must attempt a **Daring + Medicine** Task with a Difficulty of 1 to use the holographic interface to stabilize the viral carrier. If the viral carrier is not stabilized, he or she will die at the end of the scene.

Successfully isolating the virus satisfies the first Key Task and gives the Player Characters the following information:

- The current strain of the Outlander Virus is highly contagious, fast-acting, and potentially fatal for virtually all mammalian humanoid species.

- It's similar to the virus that causes Anchilles Fever, a virulent disease capable of wiping out millions in a matter of days.

- However, while Anchilles fever requires rare materials that are difficult to synthesize to produce a vaccine, the Outlander Virus should respond to conventional anti-viral medications.

Having completed the first Key Task, the Player Characters can move onto the two remaining Key Tasks in any order they wish.

Key Task: Comparing the genome of the current viral strain to the one that decimated Fosstarian II during the previous pandemic requires a **Reason + Science or Engineering** Task with a Difficulty of 2. A successful attempt turns up one important answer but also poses a new mystery. It appears the current strain of the virus developed, through natural selection, a resistance to the radiation that suppressed older viral strains. That explains why the virus has resurfaced now after 200 years of dormancy. However, the genomic data contained in ImmutiCorp's archive conspicuously lacks several key genetic sequences that would play a key role in developing a treatment.

If asked about these missing sequences, Th'lacen insists it's due to the limited capabilities of older sequencing technology. The real reason, as will become clear in Act 3, is that ImmutiCorp intentionally redacted the genomic data to keep anyone from discovering a permanent cure to the Outlander Virus.

Key Task: Having gathered the information from the previous Key Tasks, it's now possible to identify a treatment to the current strain of the Outlander Virus. Doing so requires a **Reason + Medicine** Task with a Difficulty of 3. A success means the Player Characters discover an antigen capable of provoking an immune response in humanoids that will fight off the disease. All that remains is to synthesize the treatment and administer it via hypospray to infected Fosstarians. Failing this final Key Task triggers the Success at Cost rule. In this case, the Player Characters successfully discover an antigen to treat the virus, but they also suffer a Complication. A suggested Complication would be for the antigen to require periodic modification from medical researchers to keep up with mutations in the viral genome. The Gamemaster can substitute a different Complication or gain 2 additional Threat.

Suggested Threat Spends: Gamemasters may spend Threat in various ways to heighten the tension as the Player Characters investigate the Outlander Virus.

- Gamemasters may spend 2 Threat at any point during the Challenge to cause a **Medical Emergency** Complication for any of the three viral carriers behind the quarantine field. This means the viral carrier's condition has worsened, and the Player Characters must render emergency medical assistance or the viral carrier will die at the end of the scene. Providing such assistance requires a **Daring + Medicine** Task with a Difficulty of 1. A success stabilizes the viral carrier's condition, while a failure allows the disease to intensify, increasing the Difficulty of the next attempt by 1.

- Gamemasters may spend 2 Threat at any point to cause a **Viral Evolution** Complication in which the new strain of the Outlander Virus swaps genetic material

with its current host to mutate at an accelerated rate. This makes the virus more resistant to treatment and increases the Difficulty of any attempts to isolate the virus or identify a cure in individuals affected by this Complication by one step. This increases the Difficulty of the third Key Task from 3 to 4. Additionally, Gamemasters may use this Threat Spend at any time during this scenario when Player Characters administer antigen to infected individuals, requiring the creation of a modified version of the antigen with a **Reason + Medicine** Task with a Difficulty of 3 for that particular viral carrier.

▪ Gamemasters may spend 2 Threat for each Player Character present in the scene to trigger a Reversal in which an unexpected power surge causes the quarantine field in the medical laboratory to fail, exposing everyone present to the Outlander Virus. This will not affect Th'lacen, as she has received a secretly developed vaccine. Everyone else runs the risk of taking the **Infected** Trait, as described in the "Contracting the Outlander Virus" section of Act 1.

Th'lacen will immediately downplay the importance of any breakthroughs that point toward a permanent cure

and insist the treatment must undergo extensive testing before it can be distributed to the population. She will urge the Player Characters to consider the possibility of intensifying or modifying the radiation produced by the ring to address the mutated virus, though Characters who analyze the mutations present in the current viral strain will deduce that the ring has outlived its usefulness as a remedy. Th'lacen also tells the Player Characters not to report their findings to Regent Zammeline so as not to inspire "false hope" in a cure. Of course, Th'lacen's real motivation is to obstruct the discovery of a permanent cure so ImmutiCorp can continue to enjoy its monopoly on anti-radiation medication. If this discussion grows too hostile, Th'lacen will order a handful of ImmutiCorp guards to escort the Player Characters off the ring.

SCENE 2: EMERGENCY RELIEF

While science and medical personnel research the Outlander Virus, the crisis worsens on the planet's surface. The virus has sparked panic on multiple continents, and the planetary government struggles to manage the situation. Regent Zammeline will contact the Player Characters to ask for help in restarting a water treatment facility near a major city called Peldrinar. ImmutiCorp, which owns and operates virtually all water treatment and food production facilities, pulled out its employees when the virus broke out in the city. Over the following days, the machinery that purifies the city's water supply of radiation shut down. Now, clean water is in short supply, and citizens are drinking irradiated water, which eventually will cause even more public health problems. Zammeline warns that the away team should take precautions to avoid contracting the virus, since they'll be visiting an area that has experienced an outbreak. This scene will give engineering and security personnel an opportunity to shine, should they accept Zammeline's plea for aid.

Player Characters can take a small craft to the Peldrinar water treatment facility or they can transport if they have access to reliable transporter technology. To begin the scene, read the following:

> *"Several industrial buildings near a reservoir form the water treatment complex just outside the city of Peldrinar. The complex appears abandoned, and the enormous pumps used to purify irradiated water stand silent and motionless. The ImmutiCorp logo, a stylized*

illustration of the planet surrounded by a thick ring, emblazons many of the buildings".

Five infected Fosstarians suffering the early stages of the virus roam the far side of the massive complex looking for potable water. These Fosstarians don't notice the arrival of the Player Characters and will remain at extreme distance for most of the scene. Any scans of the complex conducted by the Player Characters will pick up the Fosstarians unless the Gamemaster spends 2 Threat to create a **Radiation Interference** Complication, which causes sensors and tricorders to return inconclusive readings. Player Characters can counteract this Complication by spending 2 Momentum or succeeding on a **Reason + Science** Task with a Difficulty of 2 to cut through the interference. Additionally, the Player Characters can deduce the Fosstarians carry the Outlander Virus by spending Momentum to improve the outcome of any successful sensor scans.

Studying the water treatment machinery allows the Player Characters to locate a central control room where they learn that the pumps channel water from the reservoir through a biomatter membrane that neutralizes the radiation from the ring. Water that passes through the membrane becomes safe for consumption. However, the membrane must be replaced regularly to remain effective. The facility's main computer sensed the membrane was worn out and automatically shut down the pumps. Running the facility's membrane replacement subroutine requires a **Reason or Control + Engineering** Task with a Difficulty of 2. Successful completion of the Task causes the pumps to whir back to life and restores Peldrinar's water supply for the time being. A failure causes a malfunction in the pumping mechanism, increasing the Difficulty of a follow-up attempt by one step.

However the Task is resolved, working on the pumps makes enough noise to attract the attention of five infected Fosstarians lurking in the facility.

ENCOUNTER: INFECTED FOSSTARIANS

Five infected Fosstarians, all of whom are in the early stages of the sickness, converge on the Starfleet personnel and beg for help. They have no clean food or water, and their symptoms are worsening. They've grown desperate and plead with the Starfleet crew to take them back to their starship. If refused, one of the Fosstarians may even make an unarmed attack against one of the Player Characters. If such an attack is successful against a Character wearing an EV suit or respirator, the Gamemaster may spend 2 Threat to rule that the altercation causes the EV suit or respirator to be torn or fall off, potentially exposing that Player Character to the virus as described in Act 1's "Contracting the Outlander Virus" section.

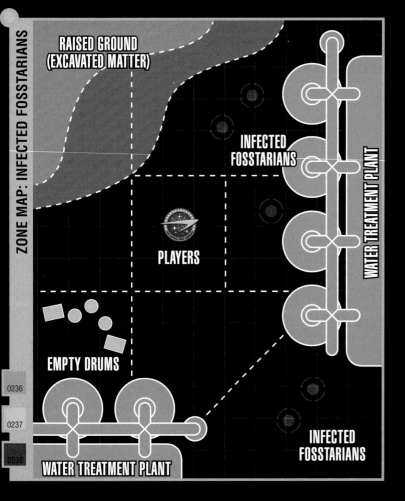

RAISED GROUND (EXCAVATED MATTER)

INFECTED FOSSTARIANS

WATER TREATMENT PLANT

PLAYERS

EMPTY DRUMS

0236

0237

0238

WATER TREATMENT PLANT

INFECTED FOSSTARIANS

02.40
LOAD FILE

0241

0242

A CURE WORSE THAN THE DISEASE
ACT 3: THE CORPORATE AGENDA

Act 3 opens with ImmutiCorp CEO Valastra Th'lacen contacting the Starfleet vessel and offering a bribe to convince the Player Characters to cease their efforts to find a cure to the Outlander Virus. Refusing Th'lacen's offer will put the Player Characters into direct conflict with ImmutiCorp's agenda, and how this conflict plays out will determine the fate of millions of Fosstarians who could be exposed to the virus as it spreads across the planet.

SCENE 1: HUSH MONEY

Following the departure of the Starfleet medical and science personnel from the ring, Th'lacen hails the Player Characters' vessel and demands to speak with the commanding officer. Th'lacen intends to convince the Player Characters to abandon their mercy mission before word of a potential cure can spread among the Fosstarian populace. She'll begin her effort by commending the Player Characters on their progress in researching the new strain of the Outlander Virus. She says ImmutiCorp researchers are standing by to take possession of Starfleet's research and see it through to completion. Accordingly, Starfleet's presence in the system is no longer necessary, she argues.

If Th'lacen's logic doesn't persuade the Player Characters to leave, Th'lacen then offers a bribe to get them to leave the region. She describes the bribe as a sign of her company's appreciation for Starfleet's contribution to the viral response, but she asks the commanding officer to respect her people's adherence to isolation and let them sort out the rest of the crisis. This bribe takes the form of an offer for Starfleet to use some of ImmutiCorp's latest advancements in viral engineering. Th'lacen will even offer to waive the licensing fee that usually accompanies such transactions.

Refusing this offer will anger Th'lacen. "I'm sorry that you don't know a good deal when you see one. It appears I'll have to end your meddling in my planet's affairs via more direct means," she spits before cutting off the communication.

A moment later, a section of the ring will detach from the main structure, revealing itself to be a starship with

CAPTAIN'S STARLOG
SUPPLEMENTAL

Our science team has made some progress in analyzing the viral strain that threatens Fosstarian II. However, the Fosstarian corporation we're working with to study the disease has responded with less enthusiasm than we anticipated.

03-225	03-367	04-275	07-388
SAVE ENTRY	AUX MODE	SECONDARY	AUTOCONFIG

warp-capable engines and defensive and offensive systems. Although the Fosstarians embraced isolationism generations ago, ImmutiCorp leaders viewed interstellar travel as a potentially profitable venture and secretly invested in the construction of the strike ship. This strike ship will attack the Starfleet vessel.

ENCOUNTER: IMMUTICORP STRIKE SHIP

The ImmutiCorp strike ship, under direct orders from CEO Th'lacen, who remains in her office on the ring, will attempt to run the Starfleet vessel from the system and will attack aggressively to achieve that end. If the Player Characters flee, the strike ship will not pursue. The commander of the strike ship is an ImmutiCorp security officer who is not authorized to negotiate or deviate from his orders in any way. The strike ship will not retreat, though it may cease hostilities if it sustains enough breaches to cripple its major systems. If the Starfleet vessel suffers heavy damage, the commander of the strike ship may offer to hold fire long enough to allow the Player Characters to limp away if they promise never to return to Fosstarian II. Gamemasters should use their judgment to make sure this starship combat encounter doesn't drag on if it becomes clear one side or the other is going to claim victory.

IMMUTICORP STRIKE SHIPS

TRAITS: Fosstarian Starship, Detachable from the ring

SYSTEMS

COMMS	05	ENGINES	06	STRUCTURE	08
COMPUTERS	06	SENSORS	06	WEAPONS	08

DEPARTMENTS

COMMAND	02	SECURITY	03	SCIENCE	02
CONN	02	ENGINEERING	04	MEDICINE	02

0243

POWER: 6   **SCALE:** 3
SHIELDS: 12   **RESISTANCE:** 3

ATTACKS:
- Pulse Cannons (Energy, Close range, 8▲, Versatile 1)
- Spatial Torpedoes (Torpedo, Medium range, 5▲)

SPECIAL RULES:
- **Fast Targeting Systems:** The ship does not suffer the normal Difficulty increase for targeting a specific System on an enemy ship.
- **Improved Damage Control:** When a Character takes the Damage Control Task aboard this ship, they may re-roll a single d20. If the repairs require an Extended Task, then the characters also gain Progression 1, adding +1 to Work done for each Effect rolled.
- **Detachable:** The ship is designed to detach and reattach to the ring as needed. Separating is a **Control + Conn** Task with Difficulty 0, assisted by the ship's **Structure + Engineering**. Reattaching requires the same Task with Difficulty 1.

02-048	03-204	03-256
MODE SEL	SECONDARY	AUTOCONFIG

This encounter takes place in five zones, as outlined below:

- **Zone 1** is the area of space immediately surrounding the K-class orange star at the center of the Fosstarian system. Starships that enter this zone suffer a +1 to the Difficulty of all Tasks that require the use of sensors due to the gravimetric and radiation interference given off in close proximity to the star.

- **Zone 2** is the area near Fosstarian I, a frigid and lifeless Class-K world. Starships in this zone receive 2▲ Cover as the planet can be used to shield a vessel from hostile fire.

- **Zone 3** is the area near Fosstarian II and includes the ring. The ImmutiCorp strike ship will spend most of its time defending this zone. Starships in this zone also enjoy 2▲ Cover, but the proximity to the radiation produced by the ring poses a difficulty to the Starfleet vessel. Any Complication rolled by a Player Character while in this zone causes a breach to an appropriate ship system as a result of a radiation flare-up from the ring. The Fosstarian strike ship is immune to this effect.

- **Zone 4** is the remaining space within the Fosstarian system.

- **Zone 5** is interstellar space beyond the confines of the Fosstarian system.

Gamemasters may consider using Threat to ramp up the tension of this encounter in any of the ways listed in the **Star Trek Adventures** core rulebook. Additionally, 2 Threat may be spent to create a Complication that causes weapons fire to strike the ring, instead of an

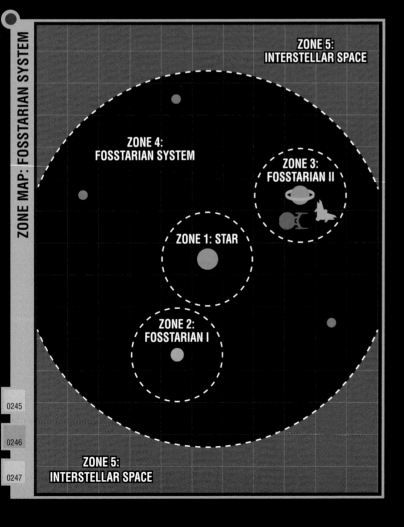

ZONE MAP: FOSSTARIAN SYSTEM
ZONE MAP: FOSSTARIAN SYSTEM

ZONE 5: INTERSTELLAR SPACE

ZONE 4: FOSSTARIAN SYSTEM

ZONE 3: FOSSTARIAN II

ZONE 1: STAR

ZONE 2: FOSSTARIAN I

ZONE 5: INTERSTELLAR SPACE

0245

0246

0247

intended target. In this case, debris breaks off from the ring's superstructure and hurtles toward the surface of Fosstarian II, where it threatens to level a populated area. The Player Characters have a single round to defuse the situation, either by using grappler cables or other means devised by the crew, or thousands of Fosstarians will die.

If the Player Characters defeat the ImmutiCorp strike ship, Regent Zammeline, who monitored the battle with sensor technology from the planet's surface, will contact the Starfleet commanding officer and demand an explanation for the conflict. If the Player Characters explain that they've made progress toward a cure for the Outlander Virus, she asks them to deliver the antigen to her in the capital.

Zammeline also explains that all the mag lifts leading from the planet's surface to the ring have shut down, and Th'lacen has not been heard from since hostilities broke out between ImmutiCorp and the Starfleet vessel. Since Zammeline has no means of getting aboard the ring, she asks the Player Characters to find Th'lacen and bring her to the planet's surface to answer accusations that her company deceived the planetary government in order to profit from the Outlander Virus.

ENCOUNTER: THE RING ADMINISTRATION

If the Player Characters comply with Zammeline's request to find Th'lacen, they'll discover that the ring will not respond to hails. This means the Player Characters will have to force their way onto the ring. This can be done by docking with the ring in a small craft or using transporters.

Gamemaster's Note: Some starships had access to transporter technology during the 2150s, though they were used more commonly for cargo than for biomatter. Gamemasters may consider increasing the Complication Range for any Tasks that require the use of a transporter during this era. If a Complication is rolled, perhaps the Characters rematerialize in a prone position or transport someplace other than the intended beam-down location.

The Player Characters will have to make their way to the main administration section of the ring to find CEO Th'lacen. Following the battle with the ImmutiCorp strike ship, she's holed herself up in her office with a squad of six guards to protect her. These guards have been ordered to shoot on sight any non-ImmutiCorp personnel who try to reach Th'lacen. If the Player Characters don't immediately return to their ship, the guards will open fire.

This encounter takes place in two zones. One is in Th'lacen's private office and the other is a lobby connected to the office with an automatic door, which is locked and requires a Task to open. Three of the guards have taken

IMMUTICORP GUARD

These statistics may be used for ImmutiCorp guards as well as any other Fosstarian Minor NPCs. If the NPC has been infected with the Outlander Virus, Gamemasters should assign them a Trait to that effect, which acts like an injury and prevents the Character from attempting Tasks. Some infected Characters may remain conscious, however, and may speak or otherwise interact with Player Characters during dramatically appropriate moments.

TRAITS: Fosstarian

ATTRIBUTES

CONTROL	09	FITNESS	09	PRESENCE	07
DARING	08	INSIGHT	07	REASON	08

DISCIPLINES

COMMAND	–	SECURITY	02	SCIENCE	–
CONN	02	ENGINEERING	01	MEDICINE	01

STRESS: 11   RESISTANCE: 0

ATTACKS:
- Unarmed Strike (Melee, 3🅰 Knockdown, Size 1H, Non-lethal, Vicious 1)
- Phase Pistol (Ranged, 5🅰, Size 1H)
- Escalation Particle Rifle (Ranged, 6🅰, Size 2H, Accurate)

SPECIAL RULES:
Mean Right Hook: Unarmed Strike Attack has the Vicious 1 Damage Effect.

0248

0249

up position in the lobby area while the remaining three guards stay close to Th'lacen inside her office and act as bodyguards. The Player Characters may either fight their way into Th'lacen's office, requiring them to bypass the door's locking mechanism with a **Control + Engineering** Task with a Difficulty of 2. Or, they may simply beam directly into Th'lacen's office. In this case, the guards in the lobby will immediately rush into the office area to defend Th'lacen. Both the office and the lobby feature heavy furniture that may be upturned to provide 2🅰 cover. Both the ImmutiCorp personnel and the Player Characters may take cover in this manner.

Gamemasters may consider spending Threat in the following ways during this encounter:

- Escalation: Gamemasters that wish to make this fight more dangerous can spend 1 Threat to equip Th'lacen with a particle rifle rather than a phase pistol. Similarly,

05-451
AUX SYBSYS

07-270
SEQ VERIFY

1 Threat may be spent to equip all of the guards with particle rifles as well.

■ **Viral weapon:** The Gamemaster may spend 2 Threat to trigger an emergency defense mechanism Th'lacen designed to release a viral agent based on the Outlander Virus into the air of her office. This fast-acting bioweapon sickens anyone who inhales it within moments, doing 8▲ stress damage upon exposure. Exposed Characters take on the **Infected** trait and will die at the end of the scene unless they receive medical attention. Infected Characters can be stabilized with a **Daring + Medicine First Aid** Task with a Difficulty of 1. Stabilized characters will not die at the end of the scene, but they still suffer severe symptoms until they receive a permanent cure. Th'lacen is immune to this virus, having taken the corporation's secret vaccine years ago. Her guards, however, are susceptible. Player Characters may have concocted an antigen or vaccine to the Outlander Virus at this point in the adventure.

If so, they also may be immune to the viral weapon if they took the precaution of administering the cure to themselves before entering the ring.

If Th'lacen deploys her viral weapon, she will try to use the ensuing confusion to escape. She'll flee to a mag lift and attempt to travel to the planet's surface, where she will go into hiding. Whatever her fate, the Player Characters can gather extensive incriminating evidence from Th'lacen's personal computer database to convince the Fosstarian population that ImmutiCorp is guilty of a massive deception to suppress the discovery of a permanent cure to the Outlander Virus in the name of profit.

Regent Zammeline will eagerly accept the Player Characters' research into a cure for the virus and offer her gratitude for their role in uncovering the ImmutiCorp plot. She'll also ask for Starfleet's help in the widespread delivery of a cure to rid her people of the Outlander Virus once and for all.

A CURE WORSE THAN THE DISEASE
CONCLUSION

The outcome of this scenario will have sweeping repercussions for Fosstarian society, necessitating long-term and difficult change. ImmutiCorp's influence colored virtually every aspect of life on Fosstarian II, from health care to food production to fashion. If the Player Characters exposed ImmutiCorp's scheme, the Fosstarian population, led by Regent Zammeline, will arrest and incarcerate the corporation's leaders, seize the ring, and shut down its constant barrage of radiation. If the Player Characters managed to capture Th'lacen, she can be brought before Regent Zammeline to face justice.

Any research the Player Characters conducted into the Outlander Virus leads to a vaccine that will rid the planet of the disease forever. However, the planet's ecosystems will remain devastated by the ring's heavy radiation bombardment for generations. The Fosstarian people will have to rebuild their food production and infrastructure to function in a new, post-ImmutiCorp age.

CONTINUING VOYAGES...

Gamemasters that wish to follow up on the events contained in this scenario may wish to start with setting up a means of distributing the new viral cure to the millions of Fosstarians who need it. This likely will require extensive medical and engineering expertise to set up new laboratories to synthesize the medicine and new hospitals in plague-ravaged areas of the planet. Fosstarian II is suffering a humanitarian crisis and will need a range of other essential supplies that Starfleet may help provide. The planet also could benefit from Starfleet's expertise in terraforming after centuries of widespread radiation damage have devastated most of the planet's ecosystems. Aid from Earth and its allies also may convince Fosstarian II to abandon its isolationist bent and join the community of worlds in the Alpha and Beta Quadrants that will one day become the United Federation of Planets.

BY MARCO RAFALÁ

22

25

43

147

PLATO'S CAVE
SYNOPSIS

The Player Characters are sent to Tanghal IV, an ice-age world harboring the remains of a long dead Earth-like civilization, to resupply a remote Federation archaeological outpost. Finding no life signs on the planet, they beam down to investigate. They find the lead archaeologist dead – the only clue a disturbing message in which he appears mad. Searching for the outpost's other personnel, the Player Characters explore a doomsday seed vault and missile silo that was converted into a survival bunker some 10,000 years before. Inside, they soon realize that they are not alone.

The bunker's original inhabitants uploaded their minds into a quantum computer. Over millennia these minds merged into one consciousness, driven insane by isolation and existential crisis. Desperate, the consciousness now sees a chance to reclaim its corporeal form. After failed attempts

to download into the bodies of the outpost personnel, it sets its sights on the Player Characters – and takes their ship hostage to get what it wants. But the Player Characters find an unexpected ally: a boy whose mind has survived intact inside the quantum computer and who is willing to sacrifice his own existence – and the machine consciousness – to save them.

The mission requires Player Characters to confront issues of survival and morality. The boy's solution goes against everything the Federation stands for, but do they have another choice?

DIRECTIVES

In addition to the Prime Directive, the Directives for this mission are:

► Resupply the Federation science outpost on Tanghal IV and support the seven-member team's general well-being.

► Uphold Starfleet Order 2, which prohibits the killing of intelligent life-forms.

The Gamemaster begins this mission with 2 points of Threat for each Player Character in the group.

PRELUDE

Prior to playing your first session, discuss with your Players ideas about their characters that might make the story richer. What subplots can tie the narrative more directly into the characters' personal lives? What personal challenges might affect how the mission unfolds?

Since the mission includes visiting renowned archaeologist Jannick Stoltz, this presents several character opportunities. Perhaps Stoltz mentored a character who studied archaeology, a father figure who disapproved when his promising student joined Starfleet. What sort of relationship might they have? Is the character nervous about seeing Stoltz? Alternately, a character could have a personal passion for archaeology and idolize Stoltz.

Set up a short opening scene, perhaps in the briefing room reviewing Stoltz's last report, where the Player Characters discuss their relationship to Stoltz and trepidation or excitement at seeing him (see the Archaeological Report in the Multipurpose Laboratory in **Act 1, Scene 2** for this information).

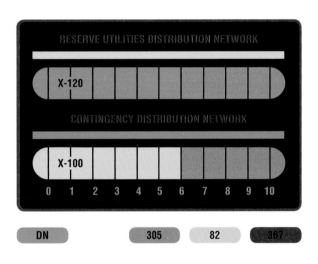

ADAPTING THIS MISSION TO OTHER ERAS

While this mission is set during The Original Series era, it can easily fit into other *Star Trek* eras without modification. Missions set during *The Next Generation* era may benefit from Player Characters' familiarity with the work of Doctor Ira Graves from the episode, "The Schizoid Man." His research into uploading a mind into a computer never captured the Human equation, but he did successfully transfer his consciousness into Lieutenant Commander Data. Records of these events could be accessed on their ship or at the outpost. On a successful Task researching this topic, Players can spend two Momentum to Create an Advantage, reducing the Difficulty of related Tasks by 1.

03.20

PLATO'S CAVE

ACT 1: THE SCIENCE OUTPOST

SCENE 1: HAILING FREQUENCIES OPEN

This mission begins on the bridge of the Player Characters' ship. To set the scene, read or paraphrase the following:

Tanghal IV – a Class-M world – fills the lower half of your viewscreen. Approximately the size of Earth, the planet is a frozen wasteland. Thick sheets of ice cover the two large continents and swaths of the oceans. Magnifying the viewscreen reveals the barely visible ruins of a lost civilization – shards of once towering cities protrude from the ice. A whole people forever gone.

Hailing the science outpost is a **Control + Engineering** Task, assisted by the ship's **Communications + Engineering**, with a Difficulty of 0.

▶ Success opens the channel and sends the signal. The outpost does not respond.

CAPTAIN'S LOG

Captain's Log, Stardate 1513.2. We have assumed a standard orbit around Tanghal IV, an Earth-like planet in the throes of an ice age. For the last five years, it has also been home to a team of archaeologists and paleoclimatologists. Their last report indicated a remarkable find beneath the ice: a collection of this world's crop diversity stored in a doomsday seed vault. Our mission is to resupply and check in on the outpost's personnel.

At this point, Player Characters may conduct a **Sensor Sweep** of the outpost and planet surface. They may even wish to scan for interference or other phenomena that may be obstructing communications. This is a

Reason + Science Task, assisted by the ship's **Sensors + Science**, with a Difficulty of 0. Success reveals:

▶ There are no spatial phenomena interfering with communications, no other vessels in the vicinity, and no evidence of signal jamming.

▶ There are no intelligent life signs on the planet.

▶ There are no power readings from the science outpost.

The Players can spend Momentum to *Obtain Information*, asking one question for every point spent. Possible answers include:

▶ It is -52 degrees inside the outpost.

▶ The outpost is modular, but schematics in the library computer do not match its current configuration. A new section extends over the excavated seed vault sight. This module was constructed approximately five months ago, which matches the discovery of the seed vault as detailed in the team's last report.

▶ Sensors detect a second massive structure – appearing to be a missile silo – beneath the outpost. There is a very faint, intermittent power signature within.

With no response from the outpost, the Player Characters must send a landing party to investigate. The Players may ignore the **Opportunity Cost** to obtain cold-weather gear since it is needed for their survival. They will also need at least one beacon as a light source. The Opportunity Cost for each beacon is 1.

USING THE TRANSPORTER
Transporting to the outpost is a **Control + Engineering** Task with a Difficulty of 2, assisted by the ship's **Sensors + Engineering**. This Task should Succeed at Cost, adding 2 Threat in place of the Complication.

SCENE 2: THE INVESTIGATION
The landing party materializes in the outpost's transporter and storage module. When they exit to the corridor umbilical, read or paraphrase the following:

The corridor is deserted, with sealed doors on either end. A thin layer of frost covers everything. Motes of dust float through beams of light from your handheld beacons. Through small, round windows you glimpse the frozen world outside and the remains of wind turbines, excavated out of the ice. There are no signs of life inside or out. It is as if the entire scientific team vanished into thin air.

If they have not already, inform the Players they can pull up the outpost's schematics on a tricorder. There are seven modules: control, hydroponics, habitat, multipurpose laboratory, seed vault module, infirmary, and reactor. Corridor umbilicals connect the modules and, unless otherwise noted, Player Characters can manually open the doors to each module using an emergency hand actuator located in a nearby panel.

CONTROL
At the center of the facility, the Player Characters find the main computer systems. Read or paraphrase the following:

The doors are partially open but not wide enough for someone to squeeze through. A wall panel to the left of the door has been blasted open with a phaser. It contains a mechanism meant to crank open the doors in the event of a power failure, but the mechanism is broken.

Forcing open the doors is a **Fitness + Security** Task with a Difficulty of 2. As they enter, read or paraphrase the following:

The frozen body of archaeologist, Jannick Stoltz, sits at a terminal with a power cable coiled around his neck. His stiff arms reach for the cable in a desperate bid to save himself. The expression on his face – a look of horror – captures his last agonizing moments. A patch of shaved hair on the back of his head reveals a treated wound, suggesting the doctor suffered from a recent head injury.

A scan with a medical tricorder is an **Insight + Medicine** Task, with a Difficulty of 1. Success reveals:

▶ Stoltz did not suffer an injury, but rather a device was implanted into his brain and later removed. Without the device, it is impossible to tell what function it served.

HYDROPONICS
This module provided the scientists with fresh fruits and vegetables. Since the power went out, the plants have all died.

HABITAT
This module contains the mess hall and living quarters for the five scientists, the medical doctor, and engineer.

MULTIPURPOSE LABORATORY
This module contains archaeological and climatology laboratories. Once power is restored, Player Characters can review the personnel's findings.

CLIMATOLOGY REPORT
For several centuries, during Tanghal IV's industrial age, greenhouse gas emissions built up in the atmosphere. As revealed in the geological record, this brought about

a catastrophic warming of the planet with devastating impact on its ecology and biodiversity, including ocean deoxygenation. This deoxygenation led to a major mass extinction event – the end of all marine life, a major food supply for the humanoid populace. Thousands of years after the fall of Tanghal IV's civilization, natural changes in solar insolation thrust the planet into its present ice age.

ARCHAEOLOGICAL REPORT

Excavations in the ice revealed large cities and industrial areas dating back 10,000 years. Artifacts show a humanoid civilization remarkable for its similarities to Earth's past. Like Humanity in its technological infancy, the people of Tanghal IV ventured into their solar system in primitive rockets, waged war upon one another, and burned fossil fuels for energy. The recent discovery of an intact seed vault was a remarkable find. Using the outpost's reactor to restore power to its systems brought its vast database back online – a treasure trove of records.

SEED VAULT MODULE

This newest section of the outpost does not appear on the schematics available to the Player Characters. If they haven't learned this already, a simple tricorder scan will tell them that it was constructed approximately five months ago and that it extends over the excavated site containing the seed vault.

Read aloud the following:

> *The door is sealed. The emergency mechanism to open the door in the event of a power failure has been sabotaged. A trail of blood leads from the door down a corridor umbilical to the infirmary.*

The Player Characters will need to restore power to enter this module.

INFIRMARY

When the Player Characters enter, read or paraphrase the following:

> *The small infirmary is in disarray. Medicine and equipment are scattered on the floor around the frozen body of the outpost's engineer. A large, dark stain mars the front of his red tunic. His left arm holds the edge of a biobed, as if he had been trying to hoist himself up. His other arm clutches a hypospray.*

A Player Character within reach can scan the body with a medical tricorder. This is an **Insight + Medicine** Task with a Difficulty of 1. Success reveals:

▶ The officer suffered from severe abdominal wounds. There are multiple lead fragments inside his abdominal cavity. Cause of death: sepsis.

AUTONOMOUS DRONE
MINOR NPC

TRAITS: Tracked Robot, Primitive AI

ATTRIBUTES

CONTROL	08	FITNESS	09	PRESENCE	08
DARING	09	INSIGHT	07	REASON	07

DISCIPLINES

COMMAND	02	SECURITY	02	SCIENCE	–
CONN	01	ENGINEERING	01	MEDICINE	–

FOCUSES: Combat Tactics

STRESS: 11   **RESISTANCE:** 1

ATTACKS:
▶ Machine Gun (Ranged, 4⬩ Intense, Vicious 1, Size 2H, Debilitating)

SPECIAL RULES:
▶ Machine 1

REACTOR

As the Player Characters enter, read or paraphrase the following:

> *The doors to the reactor module are partly open. Scorch marks and holes cover the computer consoles on the far wall. Conduits snake across the ceiling from the terminals to a fusion reactor. The reactor itself is intact but powered down. Due to the computer failure, its failsafe mechanism activated, preventing the reactor from going critical. The emergency batteries used as a backup power supply have been destroyed.*

RESTORING POWER

To restore power, the Player Characters will need to beam down two 203-R control consoles from their ship's stores. This has an Opportunity Cost of 2. Installing the 203-Rs while in a cold-weather suit is delicate work. This is a Linear Challenge requiring three Tasks completed in order:

▶ **Disconnect Damaged 203-R Control Consoles:** This is a **Control + Engineering** Task with a Difficulty of 2. Allow this Task to Succeed at Cost, increasing the Difficulty of the next Task by 1. Success Creates Advantage on the next Task.

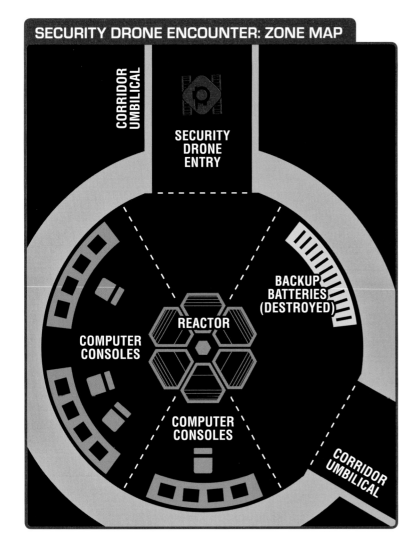

CORRIDOR UMBILICAL

SECURITY DRONE ENTRY

BACKUP BATTERIES (DESTROYED)

REACTOR

COMPUTER CONSOLES

COMPUTER CONSOLES

CORRIDOR UMBILICAL

TANGHAL IV
SCIENCE OUTPOST

TRAITS: Federation Science Outpost, Modular

SYSTEMS

COMMS	08	ENGINES	05	STRUCTURE	07
COMPUTERS	10	SENSORS	10	WEAPONS	–

DEPARTMENTS

COMMAND	02	SECURITY	01	SCIENCE	05
CONN	01	ENGINEERING	01	MEDICINE	02

POWER: 5   SCALE: 3
SHIELDS: 8   RESISTANCE: 3

▶ **Install Replacements:** This is a **Control + Engineering** Task, with a Difficulty of 2. If the previous Task Succeeded at Cost, this Difficulty increases by 1. Advantage created in the previous Task reduces the Difficulty to 1.

▶ **Bypass Damaged Circuits:** Couple the 203-R consoles to the GNDN relays to bypass the damaged circuits. This is a **Daring + Engineering** Task with a Difficulty of 2.

ENCOUNTER: SECURITY DRONE

While the Player Characters are restoring power, a primitive security drone approaches from the corridor umbilical. A whine of gears alerts the Player Characters. Read aloud the following:

A tracked military robot moves down the corridor. Similar to early 21st century Earth autonomous drones, it is 1.2 meters tall and tank-like in appearance. A 360-degree camera perches atop the machine. A crackly computerized voice repeats the same word: 'In-in-in-truuuu-der.'

Scanning the drone with a tricorder is an **Insight + Science** or **Engineering** Task with a Difficulty of 0. The scan reveals the drone to be a primitive AI construct with a damaged voice system. It is armed with a primitive rapid-fire projectile weapon with 400 rounds of ammunition. A laser sight appears on the nearest Player Character's chest and a round drops into the weapon's chamber.

When combat begins, each Task made to restore power counts as the Player's Task in their turn. The doors to the reactor module provides 2▲ of Cover for two Player Characters. Anyone working on the reactor is exposed to fire from the drone.

WHEN POWER IS RESTORED

With repairs complete, the reactor begins start-up procedures. Read or paraphrase the following:

Life-support systems come on as warm air begins circulating through the vents. Lights and computer consoles flicker to life. Jannick Stoltz appears on every monitor. Disheveled and sleep-deprived, he grips the edges of the computer terminal. 'They're all dead.' He glances over his shoulder. 'What was that?' The screen goes to static. The recording starts again. Companels hum and indecipherable voices begin whispering over the open channel. A hiss of air echoes down the corridor as the door to the seed vault module opens.

To replay Stoltz's complete message and examine the communications systems the Player Characters will need to return to the control module. If they access the message, read or paraphrase the following:

Jannick Stoltz runs his hand through his mess of hair and slams his fist on the console. 'It never stops. The voices. At first, we thought – no, not we, they – they thought it was a malfunction. Communications systems playing all logs at once. But there's something else here, buried in the ice.' He looks down, presses buttons, slams the console again. 'Is anyone reading this? Anyone at all! We're all dead.' He glances over his shoulder. 'What was that?'

If the Player Characters suspect a virus affected the outpost personnel, a scan with a medical tricorder confirms no known pathogens in the air. This is a **Reason + Medicine** Task with a Difficulty of 0.

Running a diagnostic on the communication systems is a **Control + Engineering** Task assisted by the outpost's **Communications + Engineering** with a Difficulty of 2. Success reveals:

▶ The computer is simultaneously broadcasting audio from every recorded log in the outpost at low volume.

▶ There are no identifiable system malfunctions.

▶ The following are answers to potential questions should the Players spend Momentum to *Obtain Information*:

  ▶ It appears someone has remote access to the system from within the missile silo.

  ▶ You isolate one of the voices, but it is not from any of the outpost's audio logs. It rants in hysterics: *"What about the bodies? Alive, alive, alive. A lie. We are a lie! The bodies rot."*

The Player Characters may attempt to cut off the remote access or, if they are unware of the remote access, repair communications. Either is a **Control + Engineering** Task, assisted by the outpost's **Communication + Engineering**, with a Difficulty of 2. The Complication range is 2. A Complication electrifies the console, with the Player Character taking 2▲ Lethal damage. The cost to Avoid an Injury increases by 1 for each Effect rolled.

If the Player Characters succeed, the companels go silent. Spend 2 Threat to create a Complication: **Whispering Voices**. The audio files begin playing again, but at a louder volume. The Difficulty to shut it off increases by 1, and the outpost no longer assists. Instead, the machine consciousness opposes this action (see its stats in Act 2). To the Player Characters, it appears that someone with remote access to the system is working against them. This Task uses **Control + Engineering** with a Difficulty of 3.

▶ **Players Succeed:** The companels go silent again and remain that way until the consciousness speaks to the

Player Characters or until they hear the child (see The Child).

▶ **Machine Consciousness Succeeds:** The volume increases until it becomes unbearable before the companels suddenly go quiet.

▶ **Neither Side Succeeds:** The Players fail to shut off the companels, but the volume does not become unbearable.

THE CHILD

At any point after power is restored, inform the Players that they hear a child crying. The sound leads them to the seed vault module. Once there, read aloud the following:

Excavated from the ice, a wedge of concrete with a steel door stands seven meters high. Thick cables from a wall terminal snake through the open door and into a sloping passageway. The cables spark and hum: electrified. The child's sobs echo from within the vault.

Note that restoring power has also activated the following location Trait, which the Player Characters may now become aware of by examining the cables:

▶ **Failsafe:** The cables provide power to the seed vault and missile silo. Any attempt to destroy them with a phaser or disrupt them in any way will trigger a power surge that overloads the fusion reactor.

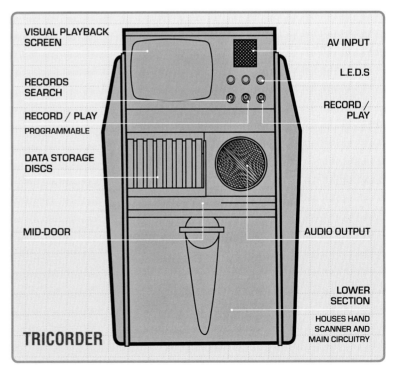

| SC | 389 | 209 | 144 |

VISUAL PLAYBACK SCREEN

AV INPUT

L.E.D.S

RECORDS SEARCH

RECORD / PLAY PROGRAMMABLE

RECORD / PLAY

DATA STORAGE DISCS

MID-DOOR

AUDIO OUTPUT

LOWER SECTION

HOUSES HAND SCANNER AND MAIN CIRCUITRY

TRICORDER

ACT 2: ALONE AT THE END OF THE WORLD

CAPTAIN'S LOG

Captain's Log, supplemental. Someone sabotaged the outpost's power generator and murdered Jannick Stoltz. We have yet to find the rest of his team, but his message said they were all dead. We've gained access to the seed vault and now the impossible sound of a crying child echoes from within, though every instrument we have detects no life signs. Our answers are somewhere down there, in the past of this long dead world.

SCENE 1: THE SEED VAULT

As the Player Characters enter the vault, read or paraphrase the following:

> *Ice covers the walls of the circular tunnel. Rows of lights flicker above. You can see your breath on the air. The passage slopes down for over a hundred meters. The deeper you go, the colder it becomes. When you reach the open door at the end of the passage, the child's cries stop. As you enter, security cameras follow your every move. Static rumbles from speakers in the ceiling.*

The outpost's cables snake into a control room to the immediate right, plugging into a primitive computer bank. The computers monitor three seed storage vaults and the temperatures within.

VAULT ROOMS

Opposite the control room are the three seed vault rooms. Scanning the vaults with a tricorder is an **Insight + Science** Task with a Difficulty of 0. The tricorder reveals that the vaults are secured behind two airlocks, each requiring a security key to open. The seeds inside are perfectly preserved.

When the Player Characters are near the vault rooms, read or paraphrase the following:

> *The speakers in the ceiling crackle. There is a burst of feedback, then cold silence before you hear the child's cries once more. He sounds inconsolable in his grief. The boy sniffles and speaks, 'Please, please, you have to –' Static cuts off the voice.*

A door at the far end of the corridor slides open. Beyond, a white-tiled passage extends for 8 meters to another door, also open. Since the walls are designed to withstand a nuclear strike, a tricorder scan to determine what lies ahead is an **Insight + Science** Task with a Difficulty of 2. Success reveals the passage connects to the missile silo.

The following are answers to potential questions should the Players spend Momentum to *Obtain Information*:

▶ The silo's doomsday shelter appears operational.

▶ The shelter extends 53 meters underground and contains 14 floors.

▶ The independent power signature within has strengthened and is no longer intermittent.

▶ There are still no life signs.

SCENE 2: THE MISSILE SILO

When the Player Characters enter the doomsday shelter, read or paraphrase the following:

> *The stench of decay is overwhelming. Aisles upon aisles of rotten fruits and vegetables fill what was once a food distribution center. Across the vast, circular room is an open lift door. Beside it, another door leads to a service corridor. As in the seed vault, security cameras track your every step.*

Inside the lift is a lighted touch panel with each floor marked:

1. Control Center
2. Security
3. General Store
4. Medical Bay
5-10. Residential Suites
11. Library & Classrooms
12. Recreation
13. Hydroponics
14. Pumps & Septic.

The Player Characters are on level 3 and will note that level 5 requires a security key to activate. Levels relevant to this mission are detailed below. They can be accessed via the lift or the service corridor, which winds around the silo.

CONTROL CENTER

As the Player Characters enter the control center, read or paraphrase the following:

> *Rows of computers and monitors fill the front third of the cavernous space, with workstations for two dozen technicians. Beyond a glass partition, several enormous backup generators that long ago exhausted their fuel supply sit idle, exhaust hoses snaking out through the ceiling.*

If the Player Characters access the computers here, the machine consciousness will attempt to thwart them. This is an Opposed Task using **Control + Engineering** with a Difficulty of 2. The Complication range is 3. A Complication alerts the military drones on the security level. The drones will take the first turn during combat (see Security Level).

▶ **Players Succeed:** The Player Characters can pull up information about the silo (see Surviving the End of the World) and a schematic of the complex.

▶ **Machine Consciousness Succeeds:** The Player Characters are locked out of the computer.

▶ **Neither Side Succeeds:** The Player Characters receive no information, but the consciousness does not lock them out.

SURVIVING THE END OF THE WORLD

Accessing a video file, the Player Characters watch an advertisement for the facility. Over images of the complex during phases of its construction, a dramatic voice narrates the following:

> *"Tanner Cole: Entrepreneur. Visionary. Savior. A decade ago, he warned global leaders of the coming planet-wide catastrophe. No one listened. So he took matters into his own hands – vowing to save our planet's biodiversity and our species. Now, the end is in sight – and only 10 berths remain in his revolutionary survival complex. Powered by wind, solar, and backup generators – and with hydroponic gardens and cutting-edge air and water filtration systems – our complex's 150 residents can survive indefinitely. And it's all run by the most advanced computer ever conceived. If you pass our rigorous selection process, the future can be yours – for the right price."*

The Player Characters will also find data relating to level 5. It contains Tanner Cole's personal laboratory. There are only two keys, one for Tanner and one for the head of security.

MACHINE CONSCIOUSNESS
MAJOR NPC

TRAITS: Multiple Personalities, Insane

VALUES:
▶ The Weak Will Be Subsumed
▶ We Have Earned Our Survival
▶ We Are Prisoners of the Machine
▶ We Are Real, We Are Real, We Are Real…Aren't We?

ATTRIBUTES

CONTROL	11	FITNESS	09	PRESENCE	11
DARING	10	INSIGHT	11	REASON	07

DISCIPLINES

COMMAND	02	SECURITY	02	SCIENCE	05
CONN	01	ENGINEERING	02	MEDICINE	04

FOCUSES: Brain Computer Interface, Cybernetics, Robotics, Whole Brain Emulation

SPECIAL RULES:
▶ **Specific Weakness:** Destroying the quantum computers in level 5 kills the machine consciousness, so long as it has not downloaded itself into another computer system. Shutting down the computer's power source renders the entity inert.
▶ **Secure Servers:** Gain one bonus d20 when performing an Opposed Task to keep intruders out of its systems.
▶ **Additional Threat Spent:** When performing a Task using Security, spend 1 Threat to re-roll any number of d20s.
▶ **Out of Many, One:** Spend 2 Threat to draw upon the knowledge of the many minds that make up the consciousness and gain one additional Focus for the rest of the scene.

EMPATHS AND THE MACHINE CONSCIOUSNESS

As they enter the missile silo, empathic characters might be overwhelmed by the unstable emotions of the multiple personalities within the machine consciousness. Blocking out these emotions requires a successful **Control + Security** Task with a Difficulty of 3. Failure or Complications that arise could result in severe headaches, disorientation, or even wild mood swings.

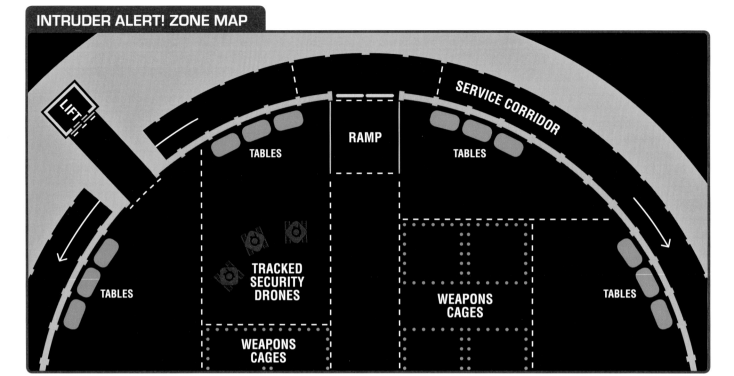

SECURITY

When the Player Characters enter, read or paraphrase the following:

Monitors cover the walls, cycling through locations within the shelter and seed vault. Locked cages filled with primitive weaponry and ammunition occupy the center of the room. Three vehicles sit at the bottom of a concrete ramp blocked by steel blast doors. Two tracked drones turn to greet you. 'Produce identification,' one declares in a stilted electronic voice.

Allow some simple back and forth dialogue to occur with the drone insisting on seeing valid identification. Since the Player Characters cannot produce this, the drone will eventually say, *"Entry not permitted. Intruder alert! Intruder alert! Use of deadly force authorized!"*

ENCOUNTER: INTRUDER ALERT!

Unless they created a Complication in the control center, the Player Characters take the first turn. When the first drone takes its turn, spend 2 Threat to Keep the Initiative and pass the action to the second drone (see drone stats in Act 1).

Assuming the Player Characters did not approach, the drones are three zones away. The doors to the lift and corridor each provide 2▲ of Cover for a Player Character within Reach. After three rounds of Combat, the drones suddenly stop the attack. A tricorder scan reveals the machines have gone into sleep mode.

Should the Player Characters hail their ship to beam up a wounded character or provide a status report, they receive no response. A tricorder scan detects nothing interfering with communicators. If they attempt to use their tricorder's subspace uplink to access their ship's main computer, spend 2 Threat to create the **Overload** Complication: the tricorder smokes and shorts out. This Complication now affects any attempts with additional tricorders.

An intercom on the wall hums to life. A cold, layered voice speaks – as if dozens of people are saying the same words simultaneously:

Apologies. Our drones, they don't always obey. They have a mind of their own, our creations. Please, come to the medical bay and we will treat your injuries.

The voices separate and begin shouting over each other. The shouts turn to screams and cackling laughter.

FINDING THE SECURITY KEY

With the drones neutralized, the Player Characters can search for the security key. This is an **Insight** or **Reason + Security** Task with a Difficulty of 1. Allow this Task to Succeed at Cost, adding 2 Threat in place of a Complication.

The key allows the main lift to stop at level 5 and enables entry from the service corridor.

MEDICAL BAY

If the Player Characters enter this level, read or paraphrase the following:

You step into a small reception area. A map on the wall marks your location in relation to the other suites that comprise this level. They are: a first aid center with half-empty shelves of medical supplies and beds; a dental facility; a surgical center; and a doctor's office. Feedback screeches over the intercom followed by low, malignant laughter."

Medical Tasks performed here are assisted by the shelter's **Computers + Medicine**. Use the stats for the Federation outpost, as the two systems remain linked.

Once the Player Characters have tended to any Injuries, a squat service robot wattles in on two stubby legs. A small, metal arm unfolds from the front of the drone and taps the pant leg of one of the Player Characters. It returns the way it came and stops to ensure they follow, tapping a toe on one of its three-toed feet.

Inside the office, the drone steps on a hidden pressure plate. A bookcase swings open, revealing a lift not on the schematics. The lift connects the doctor's office to level 5. After the drone leads them in, read or paraphrase the following:

With a jerk, the lift moves down to level 5. The drone peeks its head into the hall and wobbles out cautiously. Its little mechanical arm waves at you to wait while it inspects a long hallway that leads to a cavernous main chamber. Seemingly satisfied, it leads you into a small side room. The drone plugs into a console and a monitor sparks to life on the wall. Letters painstakingly appear one by one on the screen:

"We are monsters.
You must destroy us.
Please."

Two images flash on the screen in rapid succession. Read or paraphrase the following:

A young boy stands in a long gravy hallway. His shaggy black hair sticks out in all directions. His ragged clothes hang from his skinny frame. He glances toward the camera, fear on his face, as if he is about to be caught. The image changes to the missing outpost personnel strapped into surgical chairs in what appears to be the level's main room.

The screen goes dark. The drone shakes from side-to-side as if in warning before suddenly shutting down. Whatever this entity is, it is clearly intelligent.

As the Players discuss what to do with the entity's request, remind them of Starfleet Order 2, one of the Directives for this mission. Killing an intelligent life-form goes against everything the Federation stands for – but this entity has asked their aid. Encourage a healthy debate.

LEVEL FIVE

The Player Characters can arrive here in several ways: from the corridor or main lift using the security key, guided by the service drone, or even as prisoners. Regardless, when they enter level 5's main room, read or paraphrase the following:

An enormous server towers in the center of the room. Patterns of lights blink across its polished black surface. In front of it, you see the missing outpost personnel, dead and strapped into surgical chairs. Their skulls have been opened and implanted with electrode arrays – all feeding into the server. Multi-armed surgical robots attached to each chair lie dormant. A humanoid robot doctor – synthetic skin covering only the front of its metallic cranium – examines the bodies. One of its arms hangs useless at its side. The robot ignores your presence. A web of cables fans out behind the server, connecting the tower to row upon row of human-sized pods – more than 100 in all.

Scanning the server with a tricorder is a **Reason + Science** Task with a Difficulty of 2. Success reveals:

▶ This is a quantum computer, more advanced than the binary computers found elsewhere.

The following are answers to potential questions should the Players spend Momentum to *Obtain Information*:

▶ The server tower houses a vast consciousness.

▶ The implants in the outpost personnel are mind transference devices.

▶ The server holds the source of the faint energy reading detected earlier. It has its own self-perpetuating power source – which is failing.

A Player Character must be within Reach to use a medical tricorder to scan the outpost personnel. This is a **Reason + Medicine** Task with a Difficulty of 2. Success reveals:

▶ The outpost personnel died just days ago from severe brain hemorrhaging.

The human-sized pods are malfunctioning stasis chambers. Once preserved in suspended animation, the bodies are corpses now, turned to bone and dust. A successful

Reason + Science Task with a Difficulty of 2 allows the characters to correctly surmise:

▶ These people transferred their conscious minds into the quantum server. The stasis chambers suggest a hope that they could one day return to their bodies. When the stasis chambers malfunctioned, they became trapped in circuitry for millennia. This likely drove them insane – creating what is now the machine consciousness.

▶ The machine consciousness attempted and failed to download itself into the outpost personnel.

A communicator signals a message from the Players' ship. It is the same cold voice that speaks with many voices:

"We have control of your vessel. If you wish to save the lives of your shipmates, you will do exactly as you are told. Your bodies are ours now. We will live again in corporeal form."

Spend all available Threat to bring in reinforcements: one Threat for each security drone. Keep track of how many drones are present as they might come into play in the **Encounter: The Final Conflict**. Security drones roll out and surround the characters.

HOSTAGES
Characters may wish to verify the machine consciousness' claims before agreeing to anything, but they will find their communicators disabled. Persuading the machine

consciousness to allow them to contact their ship is a Difficulty 3 Task. Use the Attribute and Discipline combination that best suits their approach. If successful, the familiar voice of a shipmate comes over the communicator:

"After you ordered us to upload the outpost's database, everything went haywire. There's some sort of virus controlling all our systems. We're on backup life-support. And we're seeing strange messages –"

The machine consciousness cuts off the transmission and says:

"If you prefer death, your crew is healthy and abundant. We will call them down to us one by one if we must, using your own voices to issue commands."

To prove their point, a member of the crew materializes. The crewman explains how the ranking Player Character in charge of the landing party ordered him to beam down. If needed, you can use the Supporting Characters rules in the ***Star Trek Adventures*** core rulebook (p. 132) to create this character.

Though Players will likely resist being captured, at this point it should be clear: for the moment, they have little choice but to comply. The safety of their entire crew is at stake.

ACT 3: THE SURVIVORS

SCENE 1: TRAPPED

Security drones herd the characters into a locked room. A monitor shows a fleet of medical drones arriving outside to disconnect the corpses from the machinery and wheel them away on gurneys. The machine consciousness speaks through an intercom:

> *"When we are ready to begin the procedure, we will call for you. We assure you, the procedure is quite painful."*

A wall panel slides open and the machine consciousness orders them to place their weapons inside. There are several actions the Player Characters may consider taking: negotiation, scientific inquiry, or escape.

NEGOTIATION

The machine consciousness is **Insane**. This personal Trait makes persuading it to release the characters and their ship impossible. However, if the Players can provide the machine consciousness with a way to achieve its goal of reclaiming corporeal form, this would create an Advantage that would make the Task possible.

The most obvious path to do this is for the Player Characters to offer their services and technology to help the machine consciousness understand and correct what went wrong in its previous download attempt. In this case, two Players are allowed out of the locked room to study the data at a quantum computer terminal (see Scientific Inquiry below).

If the scientific inquiry is successful, they can create an Advantage that makes persuading the machine consciousness to let them go possible. This is a Difficulty 5 Persuasion Task. The Player Characters might also offer to repair the damaged robot doctor as proof of their abilities, reducing the Difficulty by 1. They may even use deception to play for time, for example offering to build synthetic humanoid bodies. The Players should feel free to be creative here.

If the Persuasion Task succeeds, the machine consciousness will provide the characters with free access to the facility. However, it will still hold their ship hostage until they provide the promised corporeal forms.

SCIENTIFIC INQUIRY

Scientific inquiry is at the heart of many *Star Trek* missions. Sometimes it is the source of a conflict and sometimes the solution. If the Player Characters gain access to the quantum computer, they may attempt to understand the machine consciousness and how to stop – or save – the entities within. Studying the data is a **Reason + Science** Task with a Difficulty of 3. Another Player can assist using **Control + Engineering**. Success reveals:

▶ The attempted download did not succeed because the process to separate the machine consciousness into individual personalities failed.

▶ Though highly improbable, it might be possible to separate the individual consciousnesses.

Devising a solution to the consciousness separation is an Extended Task with a Work track of 10, a Magnitude of 4, and a Difficulty of 4. The Basic Task is **Daring** or **Reason + Science**. Another Player may assist using **Daring** or **Reason + Engineering**.

When the Players achieve all four Breakthroughs, they discover the truth:

▶ The individuals who transferred their minds to the quantum computer no longer exist. As the centuries wore on, they merged into a single consciousness. They cannot be separated.

▶ An isolated backup server contains the conscious mind of Jannick Stoltz – uploaded as an experiment before his brain became host to fragments of the machine consciousness. His body has only been dead for a few days, preserved by the freezing temperatures. Restoring his mind to his body may be possible. Treat this as an Extended Task as above.

▶ Another, separate entity exists within the computer: the boy. Unlike the machine consciousness, the boy's has evolved beyond the confines of the computer.

The boy contacts them directly via the computer terminal. Proceed to Scene 2.

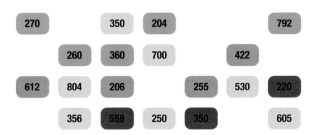

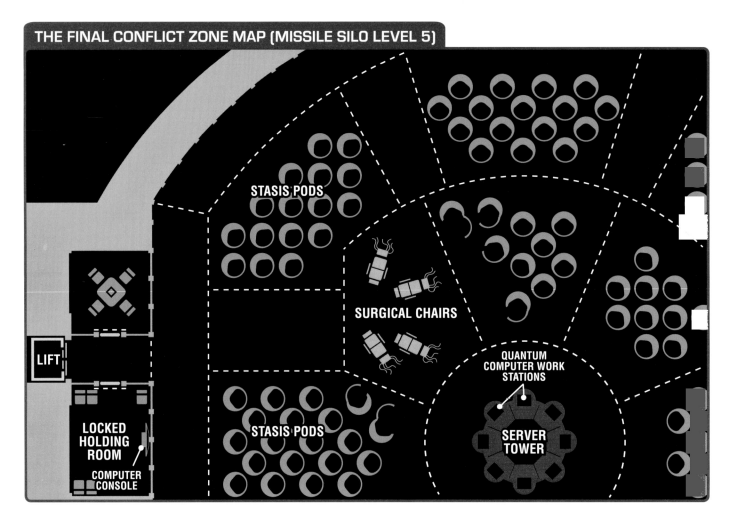

Map labels: STASIS PODS · SURGICAL CHAIRS · QUANTUM COMPUTER WORK STATIONS · SERVER TOWER · STASIS PODS · LIFT · LOCKED HOLDING ROOM · COMPUTER CONSOLE

ESCAPE

With their ship and crew in jeopardy, Players might see escape as their best option. Looking around the room to devise a plan, they can observe:

▶ A disabled service drone (if they were guided here by the drone, it is the same one).

▶ A computer console, which they are locked out of.

▶ The locked wall panel where they stored their weapons.

▶ There is no manual access panel for the door.

A tricorder scan of the service drone is a **Reason + Engineering** or **Science** Task with a Difficulty of 0. This reveals that the drone is hopelessly damaged. If it led them here, this begs the question of how it was functioning.

They might use the computer console to attempt to open the weapons panel. This is a **Daring + Engineering** Task with a Difficulty of 3. The Complication range is 3. A Complication electrifies the console, with the Player Character taking 3⚡ Lethal damage. The cost to Avoid an Injury increases by one

for each Effect rolled. If this happens, the machine consciousness will say: *"Try that again, and we will kill two of you and beam down two replacements."*

They might also attempt to use the console to access the network to open the door, and even disable the security drones. This is a Linear Challenge requiring three Tasks be completed in order.

▶ Bypass Lockout: This is a **Daring + Engineering** Task, with a Difficulty of 3. The Complication range is 4. Success opens the door and allows the Players to proceed to the next step in the Challenge.

▶ Access Security Systems: This is a **Daring + Engineering** Task with a Difficulty of 3. The Complication range is 4. Success allows the Players to proceed to the final step in the Challenge.

▶ Execute Disable Command: This is a **Control + Engineering** Task with a Difficulty of 2. Success disables the security drones.

A Complication in any step creates the location Trait: **Console Malfunction**. The machine consciousness shorts out the console, preventing the Player Characters from gaining access to the facility.

After they have made several attempts at escape, regardless of success, the broken service drone comes impossibly alive. Its mechanical arm waves them over, seemingly friendly.

SCENE 2: THE BOY

Nearly all paths the Players choose in Scene 1 will, at some point, lead them to communicate with the boy. The boy both hungers for contact and fears for all their lives. Read or paraphrase the following:

> *Text appears on the screen. 'We can talk. These messages are secure. And I can route messages to your friends.'*

The boy communicates only via typed messages on a screen. The characters can respond by either typing into a computer console or, if they are still locked in the side room, by simply speaking aloud. In this way, the Players may learn the following:

▶ The boy was the son of a technician in the complex. He was never meant to be saved. But after the silo's wealthy residents had all been uploaded, his father broke into level 5 and uploaded his son's mind.

▶ The boy's mind was the last uploaded. After he was discovered by Tanner Cole's consciousness, Cole gassed the facility and murdered all remaining employees and their families.

▶ The boy is terrified of the machine consciousness.

▶ He is consumed with guilt because he believes he is part of the entity and culpable in its crimes.

▶ He sees the quantum computer's destruction as the only way to prevent more deaths.

▶ He is willing to sacrifice his existence.

If they do not already know this, a successful **Reason + Science** Task with a Difficulty of 2 allows them to surmise, based on this interaction, that the boy is a separate entity. They also observe that he seems able to affect things beyond the reach of the machine consciousness, like the disabled service drone. This suggests he may be able to exist beyond the confines of the quantum computer.

If the Players hope to convince the boy to move beyond the quantum computer, they must overcome three obstacles:

▶ **Gain Trust:** They must show the boy that they will protect him. One way they might do this is to locate a backup server and isolate it from the main server using **Daring + Engineering** with a Difficulty of 2. Success creates the Advantage **Safe Haven for the Boy**.

▶ **Another Way:** Providing a Safe Haven for the Boy allows the Player Characters to show him that he is separate from the consciousness within the computer. They can now attempt to reason with him. For example, how could he exist in the isolated server wholly apart from the machine consciousness if he was not separate from it? This could be a Persuasion Task using **Presence** or **Reason + Command** with a Difficulty of 3. Success creates Advantage, reducing the Difficulty of the next Task by 1.

▶ **Freedom:** Convincing the boy that he can exist outside the quantum computer is a Difficulty 4 Persuasion Task. Using the information uncovered in a successful scientific inquiry in Scene 1, reduces this Difficulty by 1.

Like the mother bird coaxing her young from the nest, the boy simply requires guidance to see his own potential. Should the characters succeed, a ball of blue lightning emerges from the computer console. The boy now speaks telepathically. In an excited child's voice, he thanks them for showing him the way. If the characters have not already saved Stoltz, the boy restores Stoltz's mind to his body. He frees any characters still held hostage and tells them he can push the machine consciousness out of their ship. But – it will take all his effort. The characters will be on their own in destroying the main server.

ENCOUNTER: THE FINAL CONFLICT

Whether they have saved the boy or not, the Player Characters eventually confront the machine consciousness and, if they hope to survive, destroy the server. Considerations for combat:

▶ The Player Characters will need to overcome the security drones still protecting the server. The Gamemaster may spend any remaining Threat to bring in additional drones.

▶ Combat will be dangerous for the machine consciousness. The indiscriminate nature of machine gun fire places the quantum computer in jeopardy.

Add 1 to the Difficulty of drone attacks and increase the Complication range to 3. A Complication means the security drone has struck the quantum computer.

▶ A stasis pod provides 3⚡ of Cover for a Player Character.

DESTROYING THE QUANTUM COMPUTER

Here are some ways the Players might attempt to destroy the quantum computer:

To manually set an overload, these Tasks must be completed in order. If making the attempt in combat, each Task counts as the Player's Task in their turn. Complications increase the Difficulty in the next step by 1.

▶ **Identify the Motherboard:** This is a **Reason + Engineering** Task with a Difficulty of 3. Success allows the Player to continue to the next step.

▶ **Cross-circuit the Computer:** This is a **Control** or **Daring + Engineering** Task with a Difficulty of 3. Success overloads the quantum computer in a shower of sparks.

The Players might try to convince the machine consciousness that it is not real, just a collection of algorithms programmed to emulate the self. If successful, the machine consciousness sets the quantum computer to self-destruct. This is a Persuasion Task using **Presence + Command** with a Difficulty of 4. Reduce the Difficulty by 1 if the Players provide Evidence that proves the individuals who uploaded their minds into the computer no longer exist.

The Players may also use their weapons against the quantum computer. The quantum computer has a Structure of 15, with a Resistance of 2. If the computer suffers an Injury, it will cease functioning, destroying the computer.

PLATO'S CAVE
CONCLUSION

No matter what, the conclusion of this mission should feel bittersweet to the Player Characters. If they have saved themselves and their ship, they will always be left to wonder whether there was a way to save the machine consciousness. Could they have treated its mental instability? Could they have rendered it inert instead of destroying it?

If they did not free the boy, they will be plagued with even more doubt and regret at the loss of a peaceful and gentle being, willing to sacrifice himself for the greater good. What of Jannick Stoltz? If they learned of his potential survival but were unable to save him, how will they react? And even if he does survive, how will he be changed by his experience? Will he too wonder if he is real or simply a copy?

Encourage the Players to explore all these aspects of the mission's ramifications, considering personal development and their identities as members of Starfleet.

CONTINUING VOYAGES...

Either the boy or Stoltz may return in future missions – providing aid or creating even more problems. For example, Stoltz could become obsessed with questions of his own existence and begin experimenting on unwilling subjects – and the Player Characters may be ordered to apprehend him. As the boy continues to grow and learn about his abilities, there may be unintended and disastrous consequences. He is a child after all. Or, at some point, he might help the Player Characters out of an impossible situation.

DRAWING DEEPLY FROM THE WELL

BY AARON M. POLLYEA

In this mission, the Players are sent to investigate strange occurrences at a newly operational alien megastructure called 'Skyhook Alpha' by the Starfleet Corps of Engineers (SCE), but called by the workers there 'The Big Dipper.' This facility is a massive structure consisting of a central hub the size of a small outpost where the workers live and operate the facility, and two tethers stretching outwards from the hub for thousands of kilometers. The tethers end in huge ramscoops and automated refineries. The entire structure rotates around the central hub and the ramscoops dip down into layers of the 'hot Jupiter'-like planet it orbits, scooping out common heavy metals and a significant amount of dilithium.

In Act 2, Players will investigate if there is a cloaked vessel hiding in the planet's atmosphere. They will discover no traces of any vessels in the area besides Starfleet vessels. What the Players will come to realize is that something, down below in the gas giant's atmosphere, is attacking the ramscoops. The characters will have to build a probe or modify a shuttle to survive the extreme temperatures, chaotic wind patterns, and corrosive atmosphere to investigate.

In Act 3, characters work to understand why the Big Dipper was built in the first place: the atmosphere is filled with metallic dust and complex molecules made of heavy elements, making it a resource beyond imagination. As they break through into the semi-transparent layer where the ramscoops acquire dilithium, the Players will discover what looks to be a teeming ocean filled with life. The Players will determine that there is intelligent life here known as the 'Free' and that they are being destroyed by the dilithium mining. Can the Players convince the 'Free' that they are not old evil gods that have returned with the coming of the ramscoops? Will the Players find commonality with creatures who literally have no 'common ground' with humanoids? Can the Players find a way to protect the aliens from the dilithium mining?

DIRECTIVES
In addition to the Prime Directive, the Directives for this mission are:

▶ Discover any information on the builders of the skyhook.
▶ Defend the skyhook and the scientific and economical wonders it can provide the Federation.

The Gamemaster begins this mission with 2 points of Threat for each Player Character in the group.

PRELUDE
Read or paraphrase the following:

> *The mood amongst the crew is high after word has spread of orders sending their starship to a strange alien artifact nicknamed 'The Big Dipper.' It isn't every day that Starfleet finds evidence of a disappeared civilization advanced enough to construct something huge and complex. Engineers have been reviewing declassified material about the construction methods that surround the object, even though what is available is vague. Nearly every member of the science department has been debating different aspects of who may have built it, how, and when. Even with this excitement, it does little to prepare the crew for the sight as the starship comes out of warp...*

ADAPTING THIS MISSION TO OTHER ERAS

While this mission is set within the late 2260s, it may be set in any time frame.

Enterprise Era: Much of this mission is the same, but during this era the ramscoops are still slowly moving through the atmosphere and harvesting dilithium. The whole mechanism stops around year 2200 and it won't be until the SCE understands the complex gravimetric control systems in the Hub that they will get it running again in 2269.

The Next Generation Era: The skyhook and ramscoops are found further away from the Federation's core worlds. This system could be along the far border of Federation and Klingon territory, even out into the Shackleton Expanse. This megastructure could be linked to the events of the Living Campaign or to the Hur'q, the species that once invaded the Klingon homeworld.

DRAWING DEEPLY FROM THE WELL
ACT 1: PURGATORY

CAPTAIN'S LOG

Captain's Log, Stardate 6977.3. Starfleet has ordered us to star system J05+833 to investigate a series of incidents occurring around an alien artifact nicknamed 'The Big Dipper.' Reports indicate damage from weapons fire, and the Science Council is concerned that the Klingons may be attacking the artifact to deny the Federation the resources it generates.

SCENE 1: ARRIVAL

Arrival at the skyhook is different than that for other Starfleet facilities or coming into orbit around worlds. The helmsman will be given instructions to drop out of warp at least a full Astronomic Unit (AU) away from the world called Purgatory, the first planet in the J05+833 system and a Class-Jh world (hot Jupiter). Read or paraphrase the following:

It's strange to be exiting warp so far away from your destination, but everyone knows Starfleet wouldn't give such orders without reason. Space-time flattens and the stars around your starship slow to a halt as it drops out of warp speed. The viewscreen dims as the intense glow of an F-type star overwhelms the exterior sensors. The computer automatically brings the shields up as temperatures rise on the surface of the outer hull.

As sensors adjust, what can be seen ahead is a unique sight that brings out a sense of wonder in everyone who has dedicated their lives to exploration and discovery: the massive gas giant known as Purgatory, over six times the mass of Jupiter and nearly 50% larger. On the night side the constant strobing of lightning makes the planet's clouds sparkle and on the day side the streaks of black, brown, pale tan, and neon red mark out upwelling of different materials from deep below the cloud tops.

As large and striking as this planet is, and even at the slowly declining distance, the most obvious thing visible is the brightly glowing line floating over the planet. The skyhook. Your destination.

Characters wishing to perform sensor scans may do so with a **Reason + Science** Task with a Difficulty of 0. Information gathered will show that Purgatory is the first of six planets in this system, the rest of them rocky worlds ranging from a Class-N world to Class-C and -D worlds. Scans will also show that Purgatory has no moons or ring system. Basic information on the skyhook is also available (see sidebar below). Players will also detect three *Ptolemy*-class transports moving through the inner system, *U.S.S. Catalina*, *U.S.S. Kevera*, and *U.S.S. Infrared Dreams*; and a single *Hermes*-class scout, *U.S.S. Bunker Hill*. If Players wish to spend Momentum they can learn the following:

▶ The material makeup of Purgatory is primarily hydrogen and helium like most gas giants, but it also has valuable material such as dilithium, tritanium, and kemocite, along with more common important elements such as titanium, chromium, and cobalt.

▶ Traces of dilithium can be picked up across the inner system as small dust-sized particles, forming a diffuse ring around the star along the orbit of Purgatory.

SCENE 2: BEAMING ABOARD THE BIG DIPPER

The characters' starship will enter orbit over Purgatory alongside the Hub. There are two ways to board the station: via shuttlecraft or transporter. Due to the unusual construction of the Hub's hull preventing a direct transporter lock, using the transporter requires a 'handshake' between the Hub's transporter pad and ship systems. No matter how the characters arrive, they will notice that the Hub interior is not meant for Humans. The doorways and rooms are larger and taller than normal, suggesting a larger humanoid species built it. The walls, surfaces, and furniture are striking and almost artistic, made of highly reflective chrome, with a pattern reminiscent of wood grain.

Characters meet the head of the facility, Captain Patricia Cosalia of the SCE. Cosalia will meet the characters and take them on a tour, pointing out the alien hardware providing power for the Hub, the crew recreation center, and the command center. A small briefing area has been set up with prefabricated chairs and a table. Sitting on the table is a small model of the entire skyhook. It's here that Captain Cosalia will brief the characters.

WHAT IS A SKYHOOK? AND WHAT IS A 'BIG DIPPER'?

A skyhook is an orbital construction that consists of a long tether with objects on each end that can grab material from the atmosphere (or surface) of a planet. As it rotates around its own center of mass, the skyhook brings materials grabbed from the planet up to a higher altitude and releases it. This gives the materials enough velocity to be released into orbit, or perhaps even flung out of orbit into interplanetary or interstellar space depending on how fast the skyhook is rotating.

The skyhook rotating above Purgatory is nicknamed 'The Big Dipper' and is different from the rare constructed skyhooks across the Federation. The Big Dipper is over 30,000 kilometers in length. At the center of mass and rotation there is a habitation and engineering structure named 'The Hub.' The Hub itself is large enough to be occupied by up to 200 personnel and has a shuttlebay capable of holding six Type-F shuttlecraft. The habitable areas were not constructed by Humans and are at least a few hundred years old. The controls have interfaces that allow those that understand Federation Standard to operate them. Searching the interior of the habitable areas for clues on the builders will turn up nothing except that it has been many centuries since it was last used.

The tethers are constructed of carbon nanotubes woven around a monotanium core and reinforced with a standing graviton wave generated at both the Hub and at each end of the tether. Each end of the tether ends in a huge ramscoop, plated in monotanium, and able to fit two *Constitution*-class vessels inside the intake. When this ramscoop enters the atmosphere of Purgatory, it begins to 'ingest' huge quantities of gas and dust. There are hundreds of gravity generators along the inner rim of the opening, helping pull material inside. Hydrogen is funnelled back to the fusion engines that power impulse drives on the trailing end of the ramscoop, keeping the entire skyhook from losing velocity due to friction. Also inside these scoops are a series of force fields and magnetic baffles that sort other materials out of the atmosphere. These fields move specific metals and compounds to furnaces, chemical reactors, and refineries that purify the materials gathered and use more common metals such as iron and nickel to create casings to house the finished refined materials.

Storage of these refined materials continues even after the ramscoop has left Purgatory's atmosphere. As the ramscoop reaches its furthest point from the planet, hundreds of ports open along the forward edge of the structure and begin launching the material containers at a velocity that allows them to escape the gravity well of Purgatory and enter a stellar orbit. Remnants of decades of launches are still visible across the inner system.

The approximate dimensions of the ramscoop/refinery pods are staggering, but tiny compared to the overall Big Dipper. Each pod is slightly larger than Earthdock with a mouth of about 2.2km wide and a structure that extends backwards from that mouth for 6.5 km, tapering to a blunt end with large impulse thrusters.

She will begin with a summary of the history of Starfleet with The Big Dipper. It was discovered inactive in 2249 by the crew of the *Constitution*-class *U.S.S. Kongo*. The scans *Kongo* provided showed the planet was a treasure trove of dilithium and other rare materials, and they determined that whoever had built the skyhook had done so to access the materials in the planet's atmosphere. SCE teams arrived that year along with a team of archaeologists and xenoanthropologists to discover any information about the builders of the skyhook and to reactivate the skyhook systems.

The SCE was able to reactivate the Big Dipper 8 months ago after replacing all of the deuterium intakes in the ramscoop fusion impulse racks that had become clogged with recrystallized dilithium. The scientists had less success; the Hub's on-board computers didn't have any informational databases beyond the internal programming language for the skyhook controls. What insights this provided was limited; the language has some root words that are similar to Klingon, their number system used a base six format, and the control surfaces themselves were designed for users with digits finer than humanoid fingers.

Gamemaster Note: While during The Original Series era this information should be entirely meaningless, in later eras when Klingon culture is more well-known in the Federation, this information would be enough to allow a Klingon character or a character with knowledge of Klingon history to make an **Insight + Science** *Task with a Difficulty of 3 to determine that this could be a Hur'q structure.*

The problems began 2 months ago once the Big Dipper began to scoop through the atmosphere. The dilithium concentrations in the atmosphere peak at around 50 degrees latitude north and south of the planetary equator, and are almost nothing at the equator. The Big Dipper seemed to have reset its orbit to an inclination of zero degrees as a failsafe when there was no input from operators for however long it had been abandoned, and the skyhook's propulsion systems have been slowly increasing the orbital inclination since the SCE got it operational. The problems at first were minor – unexpected energy anomalies in the power systems causing shutdowns of the refineries and minor orbital anomalies. In the past couple weeks things have been more extreme.

It started when one of the ramscoops shut down entirely and an engineering inspection team found evidence of radiation damage from what could have been a powerful nuclear weapon or a photon torpedo. Sensors didn't indicate an attack, just regular operations. The damage has been increasing and each of the ramscoops are pockmarked with scars. So far the engineering teams and investigators on *U.S.S. Bunker Hill* have been theorizing

CAPTAIN PATRICIA COSALIA
NOTABLE NPC

Born in North America on Earth, Cosalia has been involved with many mega-engineering projects in the Solar System since she gained her Doctorate in Engineering from the University of Luna and joined the SCE. She became famous for her design of an electro-static tether for use in orbit over Jupiter that provides the energy requirements for Jupiter Station. Cosalia is relatable and does her best to get to know those under her command, and visitors to her projects will be treated to a warm welcome before getting down to business.

TRAITS: Human

VALUE: We Need Some Big Thinking Here

ATTRIBUTES

CONTROL	09	FITNESS	09	PRESENCE	09
DARING	08	INSIGHT	09	REASON	10

DISCIPLINES

COMMAND	02	SECURITY	01	SCIENCE	02
CONN	01	ENGINEERING	03	MEDICINE	—

FOCUSES: Power Systems, Zero-gravity Engineering

STRESS: 10   **RESISTANCE:** 0

ATTACKS:
▶ Unarmed Strike (Melee, 2🄰 Knockdown, Size 1H, Non-lethal)
▶ Phaser Type-1 (Ranged, 3🄰, Size 1H, Charge, Hidden 1)

SPECIAL RULES:
▶ A Little More Power (Talent)
▶ Jury-Rig (Talent)

it is a covert Klingon attack to prevent this rich source of dilithium from being used by the Federation.

Captain Cosalia will finish the briefing by saying that because of the importance of the dilithium and the strangeness of the attacks, she requested Starfleet deploy a better-suited starship to the system. She informs them that they have full access to any system on the Big Dipper and may utilize any personnel or equipment aboard.

SCENE 3: INVESTIGATING THE HUB

Investigating the sensor logs, analyzing information gathered from the command systems, and interviewing personnel in the Hub are logical steps for the Players to make. Questioning personnel if they have personally witnessed anything strange goings-on will require a **Presence + Command** Task with a Difficulty of 0. The SCE are generally helpful and will answer any questions. They will state that they haven't seen anything stranger than what seems to be the norm for the Big Dipper. While they have figured out how to get the structure rotating again, most of the systems are automatic.

Checking the sensor logs for various systems or vessels in the system during the time of these attacks depends on which source they are checking. Contacting *U.S.S. Bunker Hill* will put the characters in contact with either Captain Has Haft, a surly (even by Tellarite standards) but competent commanding officer, or *Bunker Hill*'s science officer, Commander Nelia Yot, a Tellarite with a sharp mind and tongue. This is an opportunity for the Gamemaster to introduce the idea of different species in the Federation typically operating their own vessels – *Bunker Hill* is entirely crewed by Tellarites.

Analyzing the logs will require an **Insight (or Reason) + Science** Task with a Difficulty of 1. Success will show that *Bunker Hill* has been patrolling the inner system for 11 days, and has detected no Klingon vessels in the sector. The closest non-Starfleet vessel near the system in that time was a bulk freighter out of Acamar that didn't approach any closer than 5.3 parsecs. Spending a Momentum on this Task will give the Players additional insight: each time the Big Dipper is at its deepest in the atmosphere, there are small gravitational fluctuations in space-time that ripple out from the tethers. If the characters have already analyzed the sensor data from the Hub, the characters may make another **Insight + Science** Task with a Difficulty of 2 to conclude that there would be increased strain on the graviton systems maintaining the integrity of the tethers during this time in its rotation. There shouldn't be any ripples in space-time generated unless something was interfering with the tethers directly or causing a significant amount of damage to the ramscoops.

Exploring the inner system is also a possibility. Without breaking orbit, characters may use the ship's sensors to scan the inner system. This will require a **Reason + Science** Task with a Difficulty of 1. Success will show that there are thousands of small dilithium concentrations through the inner system encased in iron and nickel shells. They will find no other power systems or strange energy fluctuations. If they spend Momentum, they may also get information on the 2nd and 3rd planets (Class-C and -D respectively) which show evidence of extensive mining operations having depleted the worlds of metals and rare minerals. A second point of Momentum spent will show the same evidence on the more distant worlds and show that there is no evidence of any buildings or technology on the surfaces.

With the easy options explored, the characters should progress to exploring the ramscoops themselves. The Gamemaster is encouraged to include any notable NPCs the Players have interacted with before that would have reason to be at the Big Dipper. These can include any SCE personnel, officers and crew serving aboard *Bunker Hill* or the three *Ptolemy*-class vessels, or perhaps a representative of the Federation Science Council there to observe the alien artifact.

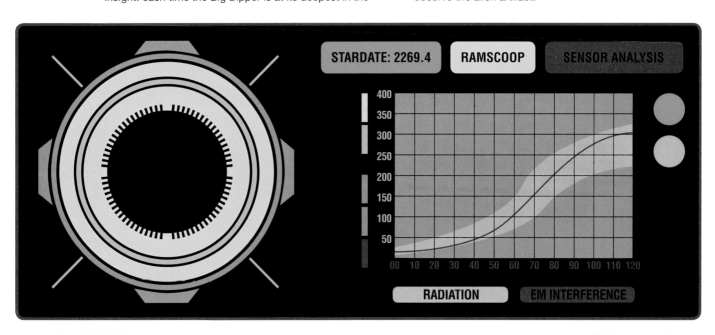

DRAWING DEEPLY FROM THE WELL
ACT 2: SPINNING WITH THE WINDMILL

CAPTAIN'S LOG

Captain's Log, supplemental. The crew has been interviewing the staff at the Big Dipper, trying to find any external causes to the attacks, but with nothing to show for it. It is within the realm of possibility that the Klingons would attack this facility to deny the Federation the dilithium located here, but for now, they seem innocent. What we can say for sure is that something is attacking the ramscoops. I have directed the crew to focus on those asteroid-sized pods to get more information.

SCENE 1: RAMSCOOP EXTERIOR

The characters can visit a ramscoop after it has finished discharging its refined materials. The personnel on the Hub will warn characters away before that point as the refined materials are launched from magnetic accelerators, causing deadly projectiles to move at high speeds, and the refineries in use emit significant EM interference that may blind sensors and cause possible radiation sickness or burns. Going in the hours before the ramscoop shuts down means that characters will face the possibility of being on the ramscoop as it starts tearing through Purgatory's atmosphere. Captain Cosalia will recommend characters use a shuttlecraft to visit the ramscoops as there are no true docking ports on the structure and it's far easier to land inside with a smaller vehicle rather than a full starship, even though there is ample room for one.

Rendezvousing with a ramscoop isn't complicated, but keeping station on it is due to its constantly changing vector. Every change in position characters make requires a **Control + Conn** Task with a Difficulty of 1. Failure adds a level of Difficulty to any observations made of the ramscoop exterior. The Gamemaster may also use Threat to activate a series of casings accelerating away from the ramscoop, an automated process that was supposed to be completed by the time the characters arrived. They fire in the direction of the characters' shuttle and for each Threat spent, one canister comes close, acting as if it were controlled by a Proficient crew (Attribute 9, Discipline 2) and as a photon torpedo (Torpedo, Range Long, 5⚔, High-Yield).

The exterior of the ramscoop is sooty black from repeated passage through Purgatory's atmosphere. There are areas near the aft of the ramscoops that are behind protuberances that will show cleaner areas of the exterior being originally a deep gold or brass color. Scans of the ramscoop require a **Reason + Science** Task with a Difficulty of 1 and show that there are signs of incredible energy usage including ionizing radiation pouring out of vents, cooling fins still glowing bright yellow, and a wide spectrum of EM interference from various sources. Characters who spend Momentum will also learn that as extreme as the environment outside of the ramscoop is now, it is currently in low power mode as it awaits its next dip into the atmosphere.

Characters can zero in on some notable objects, most of which were mentioned above, including radiation venting, cooling fins, and sources of EM interference. Also important is an area giving off high levels of infrared and x-ray radiation on the far side of the ramscoop. To investigate, characters will need to perform a **Control + Conn** Task with a Difficulty of 2 to approach safely. Failure represents not taking into account the orbital motion of the ramscoop and bumping into it (a 3⚔ attack for failing by 1), or approaching too closely to an area that is pouring out radiation or plasma (a 5⚔ attack for failing by 2). Arriving means characters attempting a **Reason (or Insight) + Science (or Engineering)** Task with a Difficulty of 2 to get good sensor readings.

▶ **Radiation venting:** There seem to be two types of vents: one seems to be part of a set of refineries and cyclotrons that purify radioactive material, while the other seems to be waste material vents for fission reactors. Judging by the levels of energy needed, these fission reactors must be backups for backup systems, long-term nucleothermic generators. The cyclotron and refinery vents show that there are literally hundreds of by-products emitted from them, meaning the ramscoop is making many different isotopes and radioactive elements.

▶ **Cooling fins:** These fins extend outwards from the main body of the ramscoop after it has left the atmosphere. They radiate excess heat away from the ramscoop. These fins glow a deep orange and are composed of an alloy of tungsten and rhenium, layered with magnetic conduit that channels plasma from the structure into the fins.

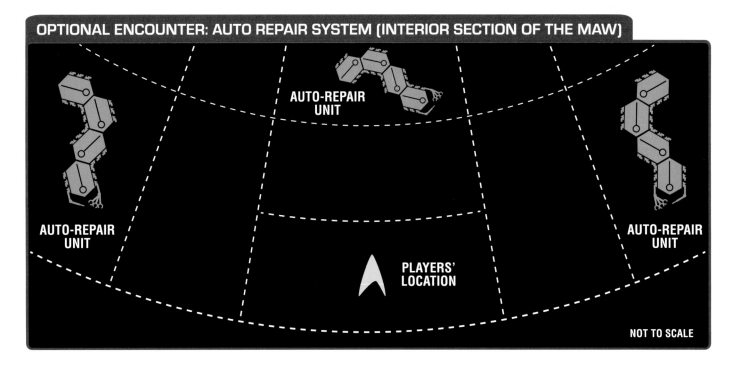

NOT TO SCALE

▶ **EM interference:** There are a few sources of EM interference coming from the ramscoop. One is a faulty containment vessel in one of the many fusion reactors for the impulse drive at the rear of the ramscoop. The other major source is a large blast crater on the leading dorsal section where hard radiation is still emanating. The usual dark patina has been blasted away to show a shiny and almost polished hull. Success in studying this feature will reveal that a high-energy device detonated directly against the hull. Radioactive decay by-products show that it was not an anti-matter weapon like a photon torpedo, and the only reason the damage isn't more severe is that the hull of the ramscoop is incredibly tough. Spending a Momentum for this test will give more information about the possible weapon used. The blast pattern and radioactive decay elements show it was a combination fission/fusion device with a projected yield of six hundred megatons, far larger than anything ever developed on Earth during the 20th and 21st centuries, and only matched by 23rd century photon torpedoes. The attack must have occurred during the last time the ramscoop was in Purgatory's atmosphere.

Learning about the recent thermonuclear strike and where it must have happened, the Players should begin to think about either scanning Purgatory or figuring out a method to modify a shuttle to enter the thick and toxic atmosphere. These ideas are covered in Scene 3 of this Act.

SCENE 2: INSIDE THE MAW

All scenes taking place on the ramscoop will have the Complication **Low Gravity** as there is no artificial gravity, only spin gravity caused by the rotation of the entire skyhook structure. The effective gravity is about 15% of standard Earth gravity, meaning characters born on the Moon (or other characters used to low gravity) may ignore this Complication per the Gamemaster's judgment. Furthermore, the interior of the ramscoop is constructed to not be influenced by magnetic fields, so magnetic boots do not work, countering any Advantage that piece of equipment may provide.

Characters may land on the inside of the ramscoop to study any equipment or damage. The interior of the ramscoop is a massive opening that tapers back towards an intake area with many sealed ports. The hull is polished bright bronze. The only visible damage are deep gouges in the metal that look as though the hull was melted and quickly solidified. There is no residual radiation. Characters may make an **Insight + Security** Task with a Difficulty of 2 to recognize the odd damage as being from a high-energy laser rather than a phaser. Characters with Focuses involving historic weapons technology (or similar) may reduce the Difficulty by 1. One question characters should raise here is: if it were the Klingons (or Romulans, for that matter), why would they want to attack the Big Dipper with primitive weapons?

Attempting to go further inside the ramscoop is next to impossible because of the automatic seals. Even if characters get them open (requiring a **Control + Engineering** Task with a Difficulty of 3) the interior is not designed for humanoids to move around in. Captain Cosalia will warn characters against going inside the actual structure as it has yet to be mapped beyond 20 meters in from the main hatches and that the automated repair systems are not fond of visitors. If characters do wish to enter, the confined spaces inside give a further Complication **Claustrophobic**. Further investigation inside will show healed scars of previous damage, either from heavy impacts, a nuclear detonation, or laser fire.

If a Gamemaster wishes, the auto repair system can register the characters and their shuttlecraft as dangerous foreign objects. Several auto-repair bots will 'ooze' out of the hull and attempt to 'disassemble' the foreign objects. Deploy one auto-repair unit per character and add one more for every Threat spent.

SCENE 3: STICK WITH PURGATORY

Characters should have come to the conclusion that whatever is damaging the ramscoops, it is happening while the ramscoops are deep inside the planetary atmosphere. Sensor scans of the planet have been performed before the characters arrived and found nothing. The characters may attempt to perform their own scan by succeeding at a **Reason + Science** Task with a Difficulty of 2. Success will show that there are no power sources detected on the planet, no vessels of any kind, and no life signs. Spending a Momentum will reveal that like every gas giant, there are multiple atmospheric layers of different compounds and elements and that it is possible that a combination of these layers could hide a vessel from sensors. Spending a second Momentum will reveal that the powerful sensor platforms on their vessel are able to tease out a faint detection of anti-neutrinos with an energy suggesting a nuclear reactor as a source.

Federation starships and shuttlecraft aren't designed to survive in a gas giant's atmosphere, and even starships capable of maneuvering in an atmosphere wouldn't be able to go as deep as needed to get to the areas where the ramscoop operates. Starfleet attempted to send probes into the atmosphere in the early 2260s, but the combination of strong magnetic fields, ionizing radiation, high temperatures, and crushing pressures have made every probe fail before reaching the operational layers.

There are three separate paths the characters can take to figure out what's going on within Purgatory, one which will raise more questions than answers and likely push the characters towards developing a way to physically go there:

▶ **Modifying the ship's sensors.** This can be through linking them with the sensors on *Bunker Hill* and some deployed probes to allow interferometric analysis, a **Reason + Engineering** Task with a Difficulty of 4, assisted by the ship's **Sensors + Science**). It could also be through improving and adapting sensors to partially pierce the sensor masking the atmospheric layers provide. This could be through long-term improvement to sensors through the process described in Scientific

SKYHOOK AUTO-REPAIR UNIT
MINOR NPC

These repair bots are meter-long millipedes constructed of the same bronze-like metal as the skyhook hull. Each of their feet has three tiny claws that can grip onto a target. Each segment of the auto-repair unit has a set of visual receptors and the front of the unit has a high-intensity welding torch.

TRAITS: AI, The Skyhook Is My Home

ATTRIBUTES

| CONTROL | 06 | FITNESS | 06 | PRESENCE | 04 |
| DARING | 06 | INSIGHT | 06 | REASON | 08 |

DISCIPLINES

| COMMAND | – | SECURITY | 01 | SCIENCE | 01 |
| CONN | – | ENGINEERING | 03 | MEDICINE | – |

FOCUSES: Damage Control

STRESS: 7   **RESISTANCE:** 2

ATTACKS:
▶ Plasma Cutter (Melee, 4▲ Piercing 2, Size 1H, Deadly)

SPECIAL RULES:
▶ Machine 2

Discoveries and Developments, pg. 157-160 of the core rulebook. Or, as a specific improvement that gives the ship the Advantage **Peering into Purgatory** and is only applicable for this mission and is made by performing a **Reason + Science** Task with a Difficulty of 4, assisted by the ship's **Sensors + Science**. Achieving this will allow characters to detect multiple power sources radiating anti-neutrinos scattered across the planet. They will also be able to determine where large concentrations of these power sources are located, giving them a better idea where they should send a modified probe or shuttlecraft.

▶ **Modifying a probe.** Modification of a probe can also work, but won't provide as much information as modifying a shuttlecraft. Modifying a probe to survive a brief time deep in the atmosphere of Purgatory will require a **Reason + Engineering** Task with a Difficulty of 3. The limitation of this solution is that increasing the shielding to allow the probe to survive requires a greater power capacity. Even improving the onboard power capacity, the probe will only last 10 seconds in the layer where the dilithium is being mined. As the probe only lasts a short amount of time, it will not send back much more information besides a distorted sensor image of what looks to be structures. A transporter lock onto these structures is impossible due to distance, highly ionizing radiation, and the metallic dust. If characters succeed in the Task with more than three successes, they also learn that before it failed, the probe detected no life but that it detected a type of LADAR scanning.

▶ **Modifying a shuttlecraft.** Modifying a probe first is a logical solution. When the probe fails after about 10 seconds, it should be clear that a shuttlecraft provides more power, and could further be modified to generate enough energy to reinforce the shield grid to allow around 30 minutes of exploration. Modifying a Type-F shuttlecraft will require success at a **Reason + Engineering** Task with a Difficulty of 3. The modified shuttle will end up with the majority of its interior space filled with a spare fusion power core and extra EPS relays between the power plants and the shield grid. This leaves space for only two crew members, so

characters will have to make a careful choice as to who to send down into Purgatory's atmosphere.

By the time characters make modifications on a shuttle, one of the ramscoops should be making a dip into the atmosphere. Power levels increase on the Big Dipper and the tethers begin to glow a deep purple as gravimetric waves ripple out of subspace, causing space itself to glow with a Cherenkov radiation-like effect. Characters on the Hub will be jolted off their feet as the entire structure is slammed by a powerful force. Neutrino detectors everywhere across the system register the detonation of a massive thermonuclear weapon in Purgatory's atmosphere.

A **Reason + Science** Task with a Difficulty of 1 will reveal that the detonation occurred at the interface between the ramscoop's gravimetric wave and the outside atmosphere, and had a yield close to two gigatons, in excess of anything Starfleet has for its photon torpedo systems. Even with this kind of power, the detonation makes no visible mark on the planet's upper atmospheric layers. If there was any lingering doubt before, there should be none now – something is attacking the Big Dipper down in Purgatory.

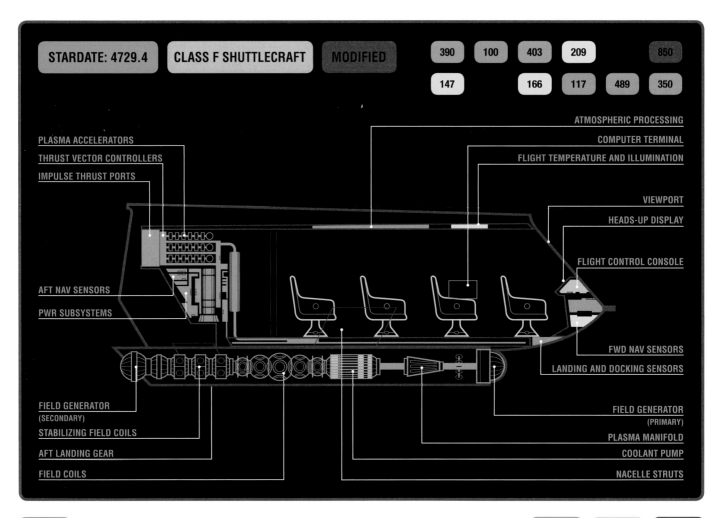

DRAWING DEEPLY FROM THE WELL
ACT 3: DESCENT FROM THE HEAVENS

CAPTAIN'S LOG

Captain's Log, supplemental. The most recent attack on the Big Dipper has shown that there is something in the dilithium layers of Purgatory's atmosphere. Scans that have been able to penetrate the interference have shown no life-forms, only structures and technology. The only way to put to rest what is going on is to send a modified shuttlecraft down into the depths.

SCENE 1: DESCENT

Descending from orbit, the shuttlecraft's journey will be relatively easy for the first several minutes. Communication will begin to get interference occurring once the space-atmosphere interface hits it. Plasma will begin streaming from the outer hull of the shuttlecraft before the shields snap on automatically. Nearly 2,000 kilometers above the visible cloud tops, the high altitude winds begin to gain enough force to buffet the shuttlecraft. The pilot must make a **Control + Conn** Task with a Difficulty of 1; otherwise, the shuttlecraft suffers as though it were struck by a 2⚡ attack as it tumbles in its re-entry.

The shuttlecraft will continue to descend through hazy layers of increasing density until it is just above the visible cloud tops. Here the sky is a burnt orange and the clouds below are brown and black, resembling thunderheads made of volcanic ash and strobing with 1,000km-long lightning bolts. The atmospheric density here is almost that of water, and as the shuttle streaks into clouds, the pilot must make a **Control + Conn** Task with a Difficulty of 2 to maintain control or suffer from extreme wind shear blasting the shuttlecraft around and acting as a 4⚡ attack. Inside the clouds it is pitch black, the only lighting being that of lightning and the shuttlecraft's shields straining and glowing. By this point, external communication is blocked.

Inside this darkness there are multiple layers of chemicals and increasing density that sensors pick up as blips of data. Nothing can be seen until minutes later, at a depth of thousands of kilometers, the sky around the shuttlecraft begins to glow a deep red from the heat of the planet itself.

There is minor buffeting and the shuttlecraft bursts forth into the target layer that is visually transparent and relatively stable with 'calm' winds of hundreds of kilometers an hour and pressures greater than that found at the bottom of Earth's oceans.

Gamemaster Note: This scene is intended to provide a challenge to the shuttlecraft occupants. While the challenges presented center on the pilot, feel free to introduce further challenges as the shuttle descends based on the other occupant. For example: if the co-pilot is an engineer, introduce a problem with the shielding as it struggles with the increasing temperatures and pressures outside and the engineer has to modify the equipment on the fly using a **Control + Engineering** *Task with a Difficulty of 2.*

SCENE 2: THE FREE

The transparent layer is the where all life on this world exists. When characters first emerge into this layer it is disorienting – the 'sky' is a dull red and black, the slightly brighter red but transparent 'air,' and the 'ground' thousands of kilometers below is a roiling, churning morass of cherry red clouds.

The ecosystem is similar to ocean life on many worlds, with small 'plants' gathering falling dust from the layers above and converting them through chemical reactions into usable compounds. In these upper layers are massive filter feeding organisms the Players will equate with whales but are kilometers in length. Smaller organisms occupy every ecological niche one could imagine in an ocean, including crystalline coral-like creatures that exist off converting the incredible temperatures of the 'ground' clouds into energy. These plants and animals all look alive even though they all exhibit crystalline forms, their skin refracting light in strange ways. A **Reason + Science** Task with a Difficulty of 2 will reveal that the plants and animals are silicon- and arsenic-based, with trace amounts of dilithium. Starfleet science had only theorized about life such as this and had never encountered anything similar before. Spending a Momentum will reveal a detailed scan of a simple 'fish' that shows the dilithium in the creature corresponds to sensory organs, nerve fibers, and a brain of sorts composed of dilithium and phosphate glass.

As the shuttle continues to descend, the shields will sparkle as the computer detects a LADAR pulse scanning the

vessel. Characters may attempt a **Reason + Conn** Task with a Difficulty of 1 to get a lock on the source and plot a course. The LADAR beam is coming from near the middle of the layer, and as Players approach the source they see a floating crystalline city in the distance with laser light sparkling from nearly every surface. The city itself seems to be buoyed by iridescent bags, and long-range sensors will pick out numerous large animals and metallic craft circling the city.

Three alien beings known as 'the Free' cautiously approach the shuttlecraft. Their main central eyes continually 'paint' the shuttlecraft in a low-power laser intended to act as both a personal LADAR and as a warning. This laser does not damage the shuttlecraft. Their fins are splayed wide, with iridescent crystalline tissue between the fins' spars flashing different colors indicating fear and warning. The only thing setting the Free apart from other organisms is that they are carrying what are clearly weapons in their tendrils and that there is some sort of unique ritual carving in one of their hides. The Free should appear very alien to the characters, and unintentionally intimidating due to being much larger than the shuttlecraft.

The Free with the carving in its hide will close in and splay its rear tendrils in a wide circle while flashing its central eye in different colors and shifting the angle of its fin tissue to

produce flashes of light across the spectrum. An **Insight + Command** Task with a Difficulty of 2 will allow a character to understand that the Free are not being aggressive as they have not used or made threatening gestures with their weapons. A **Reason + Science** Task with a Difficulty of 1 will show that the weapons they are carrying are similar to automatic rifles from the 21st century, but the ammunition is made from radioactive elements and are designed to compress on impact and detonate in a small nuclear blast.

An **Insight + Science** Task with a Difficulty of 2, and using the limited assistance of the shuttlecraft's computer system, can show that what is occurring is an attempt to communicate. Also, succeeding at this Task will allow the computer system to translate what the Free are saying in broken Federation Standard. Spending a Momentum will provide standard translation. Converting systems on the shuttlecraft to respond will require success at a **Control + Engineering** Task with a Difficulty of 1. This modifies the shielding and the Bussard ramscoops on the shuttlecraft to mimic the flashing fins and the laser eye.

The Free that is speaking will repeat things such as "The Old Gods are no longer worshipped here!", "We are Free! We will fight you even if our souls are consumed!", and "Leave us as you left us before." Once two-way communication is established, it's assumed that the characters will try to explain that they are not the Old Gods, or that they come in peace. The translations of their reactions will range from irritation and disbelief to confusion. The speaking Free (who introduces itself as Third Shackle Breaker of the Descendants of the Brave) will say "The Old Gods came in metal craft. They used us to harvest our souls. They sent the Eater of Souls to devour us when we said we would no longer serve them. They left and the Eater of Souls left. Now the Eater of Souls returns along with tiny creatures in a metal craft. Do not deceive us!" Clearly the Old Gods were a spacefaring race and used these beings as slave labor. Convincing them that Starfleet is not the same will require success with a **Presence + Command** Task with a Difficulty of 2.

Success will have the Free continue to press the characters, but with less anger or disbelief. They have had reports from the southernmost cities of the Eater of Souls descending from the heavens and scouring the sky of life. Third Shackle Breaker will say, "Millions of the Free flee from the Eater of Souls, but we have learned the secrets of the Heavens and are fighting back. We will destroy the Eater of Souls and any Old Gods that come to defend it!"

Characters should have already concluded that the ramscoop and the Big Dipper are the Eater of Souls, the Old Gods are the beings that originally built it, and that reactivating the whole system to mine dilithium from Purgatory has killed swaths of the planetary ecosystem and perhaps even countless innocent sentient beings. The fact that the Free aren't attacking them is telling and suggests they are terrified of the characters and what they may represent.

SCENE 3: HASTY DIPLOMACY AND AN EVEN FASTER WITHDRAWAL

The characters have limited time before the failure of the shuttlecraft's shields. There is time for five diplomatic tests before time runs out. Each should be a **Presence (or Insight) + Command** Task with a Difficulty of 1. These Tasks may be used to determine how evasive the Free will be in answering questions, or how direct they are in asking theirs. The total number of successes will indicate how well the first contact went between the Free and the Federation.

▶ **0-2 Successes – Failure.** First contact, already tainted by the use of the ramscoop mining system, was disastrous. The Free will refuse further contact with the Federation and attack any vessels approaching their cities. They demand the Big Dipper be dismantled.

▶ **3-5 Successes – Distrust.** First contact could have gone much better. The use of the ramscoops and the destruction of much of the Free's property and

lives means there is a distrust amongst the Free of the Federation's intent. They will ask to be left alone, but will not refuse future diplomatic overtures. They demand the Big Dipper be dismantled.

▶ **6-8 Successes – Conditional Trust.** First contact went well, but the Free do not forgive the Federation. They will ask for aid in repairing any damage, something the SCE will find a challenge. They will also ask the Federation to allow them to visit the Big Dipper, to inspect it before it is deactivated and left in orbit as a reminder of their dark history.

▶ **9+ Successes – Forgiveness.** The Free will forgive the Federation. They will ask for aid to rebuild their infrastructure and will begin negotiating how the Big Dipper may be used without hurting them. This would mean mining no dilithium, only large amounts of more common materials from the higher atmospheric layers, and they would ask for the majority of it to be returned to them for use in building their civilization. This would still be a diplomatic and strategic victory.

Upon the characters' return, Captain Cosalia will be physically ill when she hears what the ramscoop was doing and the possible death of intelligent beings. She'll order the deactivation of the Big Dipper, slowing its rotation so the ramscoops stay parallel to the atmosphere below. She will tender her resignation and ask that the characters return her to the nearest starbase to be court martialled. Characters with insight into Starfleet judicial process or Federation law can make an **Insight + Command** Task with a Difficulty of 2 to understand that there was no way she could have known what was happening. She would never be convicted of a crime, but her conscience has already declared herself guilty.

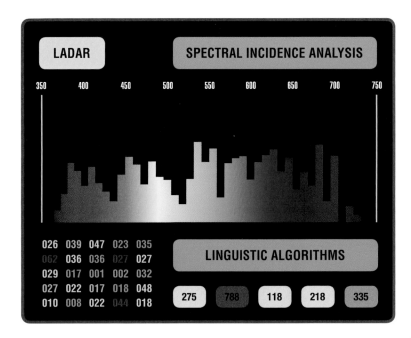

DRAWING DEEPLY FROM THE WELL
CONCLUSION

If first contact went poorly, the characters may be part of a task force meant to dismantle the Big Dipper and deploy warning beacons to warn any starships from entering the system. A positive first contact could mean the characters and the technology they developed to plunge deep into Purgatory to visit the Free would be needed as Starfleet deploys a full diplomatic team.

The Free themselves live in such an alien environment that only brief visits down to their atmospheric layer, or of them up to orbit, are possible. This means even if the Free agree to meet with diplomats, the talks are short. At best, after a few years, the Free will agree to become a Federation protectorate, but can never be a full member as sending ambassadors to other worlds is nearly impossible and their world is just too large for a single government to effectively govern. There will be 'tribes' of the Free that utilize a form of communism, and tribes that have a sort of anarchic system. Some may be friendly to the Federation, and others won't be welcoming.

Regardless of the Free's feelings towards the Federation, the system will be an important one to study for its unique life-forms, the richness of Purgatory's clouds, and for the archaeological importance of the skyhook.

CONTINUING VOYAGES...

As the characters who made first contact with the Free, the Free may feel they are trustworthy and may assist the Free when they find an abandoned slave processing facility near the bottom of their atmospheric layer. Perhaps the Free found information on the Old Gods, who they were or where they went. Perhaps the Free have detected a signal that the Old Gods are returning and that some tribes have already indicated that they are willing to submit to save their souls.

Another series of missions could center around the Tholians attempting to sway the Free away from the Federation as there is some similarity biologically between them. With the huge resources in non-dilithium materials still available from Purgatory, what will the Federation do to keep the Free happy, especially when other species begin to see the possibilities in controlling the system?

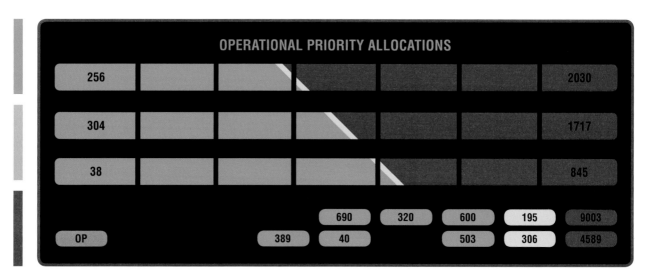

NO GOOD DEED
SYNOPSIS

After the completion of a high-level diplomatic mission, the Player Characters' ship is now en route to an unexplored region of space. Soon, the crew intercepts a radio signal, barely more than background noise. It is a call for help. They track the signal to a star system four light-years away. When the crew arrives, they discover a beautiful world devoid of sentient life, and a space station, its orbit decaying. Upon investigating the station, the Players find desiccated corpses from what appear to be both avian and centipede species. The crew has time to collect data and return to their ship with whatever they need to further the investigation. There are no signs that either species had travelled beyond the orbit of their planet, let alone to other systems. It becomes apparent that the centipedes were indigenous to Alpha Doradis II, while the avians were not. An on-board Federation diplomat, returning home from his work on Cestus III, raises concerns about how to apply the Prime Directive in this situation, as one species appears to be capable of space travel, while the other isn't, yet both are inexorably tied to one another.

Upon investigating, the Players learn that the avians are descendants of what was previously considered an extinct race of Xindi, who apparently fled the civil war on their planet and colonized Alpha Doradis II. At some point within the last 5 years, the Xindi population was quickly overcome by a disease which led to an extinction event. An airborne virus killed off over 99% of the Xindi population within a matter of weeks. The crew learns the virus had been artificially created by the indigenous Doradin and that it was spread by vents in the planet's crust through natural, volcanic activity. A search of the planet's crust shows a series of tunnels that travel directly from those active volcanoes to the southern continent. The crust (and the Xindi structures themselves) contain large quantities of magnesite, a mineral which impedes transporters.

The crew travel to the southern continent and to what appear to be exit points coming from beneath the surface. They enter a massive cavern which once contained an industrialized city. It is a dead place and millions of corpses are piled up throughout the city. The characters locate a central hub, where they learn that the Xindi came and offered technology to the Doradin to advance their culture. The Doradin instead used the new technology to make war amongst themselves. Leaders blamed the Xindi, who suddenly found themselves, once again, in the middle of a civil war. The Xindi retreated to their hemisphere, so the Doradin took their war north to the Xindi. With the technology, but without the wisdom or conscience needed, the Doradin created a virus designed to destroy the Xindi. However, the virus mutated and began affecting the soil the Doradin used to travel and find nourishment. In an effort to save themselves, several Xindi and Doradin scientists travelled to space and sent out a call for help. Knowing they had little time, a cryochamber was built and launched into space. Frozen embryos from both species were stored within, but the craft got caught in the Alpha Doradis star's gravity well. The Players can rescue it, but choices loom.

DIRECTIVES

In addition to the Prime Directive, the Directives for this mission are:

▶ Investigate the plummeting space station and obtain information to help explain what happened there.

▶ Learn about any sentient species on the planet, covertly if possible.

▶ Follow any and all first contact protocols applicable to the situation.

▶ Attempt to discover the nature of the extinction event on the planet.

▶ Answer the conundrum presented by the discovery of the cryochamber.

The Gamemaster begins this mission with 2 points of Threat for each Player Character in the group.

ADAPTING THE MISSION TO OTHER ERAS

While this mission's default setting is the Original Series era, it can work easily for any *Star Trek* era; the only requirement is a Class-M planet to investigate. The initial diplomatic mission discussed in the first Captain's Log can be about any two factions in conflict.

PRELUDE

The crew just completed a difficult diplomatic mission to avert an interstellar conflict between The Federation and the Gorn. The characters are now exploring a new region of space, seeking out new lives and new civilizations. The buzz aboard ship is about what may be found out in the great expanse of unexplored space.

SCENE 1: BACKGROUND NOISE

The ship has been ordered to the Doradis sector, a region of space thus far unexplored. While en route, the Players encounter a signal. Using the ship's communications system, it is determined to be an old-style radio signal. The language is undecipherable, but urgent. This becomes a Gated Challenge, wherein the Tasks each lead to more information, until the Challenge is completed and the Players know what is happening and can make choices at that time.

The first Task for a Player is to attempt to glean more information from the signal. Players may attempt an **Insight + Science** Task with a Difficulty of 1. Success reveals a degraded video signal piggybacking on the radio waves. Failure means that the video is too degraded for the Players to capture useful data. A Player may attempt a **Reason + Engineering** Task with a Difficulty of 2 to extrapolate whatever data survived the signal's journey through space. Again, failure means no data survived and the Players are left with radio waves coming from an unknown source.

Upon successful completion of this Challenge, the degraded video shows what appears to be a space station orbiting a Class-M planet with an extreme amount of volcanic activity. The voice on the video is the same as in the radio wave, almost song-like with intermittent breaths and high, piercing screeches. A successful attempt at an **Insight + Science** Task with a Difficulty of 0 reveals that it sounds like a type of Xindi language.

After playing the video and radio signals and, using the ship's communication systems, the language becomes somewhat decipherable. A character may attempt an **Insight or Reason + Science** Task with a Difficulty of 1 assisted by the ship's **Computers + Science** to locate the information needed in the ship's library computer. Success at the Task identifies the sounds as belonging to what was previously considered an extinct species of avian from the planet Xindus! Perhaps the Xindi-Avians are not extinct after all. Failure will indicate the sounds have characteristics native to the Xindi, but also point the language toward other Federation avian species, such as the Skorr or the Aurelians.

Gamemaster Note: Ambassador Paret will be surprised at this find and demand the Players investigate the source of this signal immediately.

Upon successful completion of the above Tasks, the crew learns that the radio waves carry a distress signal, sent to anyone who can hear it. Using the ship's sensors, a

CAPTAIN'S LOG

Captain's Log, Stardate 3113.7. That went well. After weeks of intense meetings, diplomatic promises and economic considerations, it appears as if the Gorn are no longer interested in eating us. At least, I hope they aren't. They're a very proud species, but not as aggressive as one would think, unless they see you as prey, which I am happy to say Humanity is no longer considered, thanks in no small part to Captain Kirk's initial contact with them. Cestus III has been mutually designated a Federation border colony and we have agreed not to encroach on Gorn territory any further than that. Trade routes have been opened and diplomats will soon be exchanged. All in all, the best possible outcome.

Now that we've completed our diplomatic assignment to Cestus III, we've been assigned to investigate a previously unexplored region of space. On board is Federation Ambassador Jaymala Paret, who has chosen to join us on a circuitous route home as a civilian observer to Starfleet's ongoing mission of exploration. Hopefully, we won't be making any new enemies along the way, but if we do, it's nice to know we have a diplomat on board. Of course, I'd like nothing more than a nice, quiet pulsar or trinary star system to discover right now. Something peaceful and yet new, where I don't have to worry whether a wrong impression or a perceived slight could lead to all-out war.

character will be able to plot the signal's origin to a star system designated as Alpha Doradis, approximately four light-years from the crew's present location. The signal was sent 4 years ago! At Warp 7, the planet is 3 days away and at Warp 9, it's just 1 day away.

SCENE 2: THE SOURCE

The character's ship enters the Alpha Doradis system. Ship's sensors indicate the signal is emanating from the vicinity of Alpha Doradis II. As the ship approaches the planet, the Players notice two distinct land masses splitting the northern and southern hemispheres, the two separated by a thin strait of water spreading out into a massive ocean littered with numerous islands and islets. Even from high orbit, it is easy to see volcanic activity circling the world.

The signal's origin appears to be a space station in low orbit; an orbit that is deteriorating. There is no response to repeated hails. A **Reason + Science** Task with a Difficulty of 0, assisted by the ship's **Sensors + Science**, shows little power on the station, barely enough to pulse the signal, and no life signs aboard the station. A successful

Insight or Reason + Engineering Task with a Difficulty of 1, will provide knowledge that the station is too rickety to withstand a tractor beam, with a time frame of 6 to 12 hours before the station burns up in the planet's atmosphere. Failure does not indicate this issue. A tractor beam placed on the station will cause it to rip apart at the seams sooner.

AMBASSADOR JAYMALA PARET
NOTABLE NPC

Ambassador Jaymala Paret is a French-Indian Human female and a lead negotiator for the Federation Diplomatic Services. She was also given the distinction of being named Federation Ambassador-at-Large for the region of space that includes the Gorn and the Metrons, as well as all other species in which first contact is made in this sector. She carries herself with an icy resolve and an air of superiority and confidence that practically forces everyone in the room to gaze at her when she speaks. She was responsible for ensuring peace between the Gorn Hegemony and the Federation not with an overwhelming display of power and persuasion, but with a deep-seeded compassion for both the settlers of Cestus III and the Gorn, who thought they were being invaded. She showed an understanding of the species others in the Diplomatic Corps might never have considered. Paret is a career diplomat known for seeing both sides of a situation and, if necessary, forcing both sides to examine issues from the other's point of view. She will always attempt to de-escalate a crisis situation. Combat, in her opinion, is a complete failure of diplomacy.

VALUES: Come to the Table and Let's Work this Out

TRAITS: Human

ATTRIBUTES

CONTROL	10	FITNESS	07	PRESENCE	10
DARING	09	INSIGHT	08	REASON	10

DISCIPLINES

COMMAND	03	SECURITY	02	SCIENCE	02
CONN	–	ENGINEERING	01	MEDICINE	01

FOCUSES: Diplomacy, Negotiation, Psychology

STRESS: 10   **RESISTANCE:** 0

ATTACKS:
▶ Unarmed Strike (Melee, 4🗡 Knockdown, Size 1H, Non-lethal)
▶ Phaser Type-1 (Ranged, 5🗡, Size 1H, Charge, Hidden 1)

SPECIAL RULES:
▶ Tension (Talent)

A scan of the planet below using a **Reason + Science** Task with a Difficulty of 0, assisted by the ship's **Sensors + Science**, also shows little to no power emanations. There appears to be an abundance of natural flora and fauna, but no apparent sentient life. There are no responses from any attempts to communicate. Ship's sensors show what appear to be large, nest-like cities in the mountain ranges of the northern continent and empty desert on the southern land mass. The sensors, however, cannot penetrate the structures in the cities.

Should the Players choose to go to the station first, they will need to don environmental suits, as the station's life-support systems are off. In fact, there only appears to be power keeping the distress signal repeating and to some systems on the lower deck of the station.

Gamemaster Note: At this point, it should be unclear as to what happened to sentient life on the planet, what caused the cities to be abandoned, or what information might be provided by the computers on the station. What should be made clear to the Players is that any choice to go to the planet first will eliminate the station as a source of information.

Ambassador Jaymala Paret would be opposed to any planetary landing operation without first finding out more about the station and what may be on it. Further, she will demand to be a part of any landing party.

SCENE 3: THE STATION
The landing party beams over in their environmental suits. The station is obviously built and designed for species that are flight-capable, with consoles lining the upper walls near the ceiling. The deck is approximately 30 meters high. Work stations have perches jutting from the walls in front of computer terminals. The walls also appear to have holes drilled into them, approximately one meter apart in dual columns leading from the floor to the perches. It is as yet unclear as to what those were for.

The Players' primary task is to restore power to the station if possible. Then, they need to find out if there is a way to stabilize the station's orbit. If that proves impossible, they should attempt to obtain as much information from the computer core as possible for transfer to their ship for analysis.

There are two ways to reach the consoles: gravity boots or zero-g maneuvering. While gravity boots may be the safest way, unless the characters have training in zero-g maneuvers, it is also the slowest way to reach them. A successful **Control + Conn** Task with a Difficulty of 2 allows zero-g characters to reach the perches unscathed. Failure means bouncing into walls and possibly injuring themselves. Those using gravity boots should attempt a **Fitness + Conn or Security** Task with a Difficulty of 1 for every 10 meters climbing up the wall. Success indicates the character made it those 10 meters without trouble. Failure means their gravity boots didn't adhere to the wall material strongly enough and the character falls, taking damage upon impact.

Getting the station powered up necessitates figuring out which computers do what. Success at a **Reason + Engineering** Task with a Difficulty of 2 allows the Players to discern which work stations need power. Failure indicates they are unable to get power to the computer systems and must find another way.

Success with an **Insight + Engineering** Task with a Difficulty of 2 enables Players to routs power to the appropriate consoles and restore life-support. Failure keeps the Players in their suits. However, Players learn, no matter what they do here, that there is simply not enough power onboard to save the station from its disintegrating orbit.

A successful **Insight or Daring + Engineering** Task with a Difficulty of 3 enables the Players to devise a means to transfer power from their ship to the station, allowing the station's thrusters to push it back into a more stable orbit. Failure, of course, means no such hope for the station's survival.

SCENE 4: DISCOVERIES

Video monitors instantly flicker to life once terminals have power. Oddly, they all display the same image of what appears to be a series of operating cryogenic tubes, which may or may not be on the station. There is a unique symbol adorning the "doors" of each tube.

Life-support and gravity can be restored. However, for any Players who were flying from perch to perch, they'll need their gravity boots to get down, or a transport assist from the ship (transporter technology does not appear to exist on the station).

Downloading the station's data core must be done on the third deck, which can only be accessed through a crawl tube located in the floor. Once Players decide to explore and move this direction, they come to a second "deck" and immediately notice that this deck is not built to Xindi standards at all. In fact, from floor to ceiling is only about two meters, about the width and shape of a Jefferies tube, with two rows of cylindrical holes drilled into opposite sides of the circular walls. Continuing toward the third deck, the Players soon realize it is another massive open chamber, again about 30 meters in length.

At the far end from the entrance to this deck is a door with the symbol Players saw on deck one's video monitors.

They enter the room and come across a floor littered with skeletons. Six are Xindi-Avians and a dozen others are foot-long carapaces, with skeletal protrusions jutting from beneath. Players may attempt an **Insight + Science** Task with a Difficulty of 0 to examine the remains. Success reveals that the skeletons were once a race of sentient centipedes, the indigenous Doradin.

The skeletons form a line in front of twenty cryotubes. Inside each tube, thousands of test tubes contain a frozen substance. Success at a **Reason + Medicine** Task with a Difficulty of 1 will alert Players that these could be frozen and, perhaps viable, embryos. Failure means the substance is as yet unidentifiable.

A closer look at the skeletal bodies (a **Reason + Medicine** Task with a Difficulty of 0) shows no fractures or scorch marks. These beings didn't die from fighting. Further analysis, including autopsies, would be needed to know cause of death.

Gamemaster Note: Ambassador Paret will vote strongly against going down to the planet until they understand more about what happened to the Doradin and ensuring that whatever killed them hasn't infected anyone on the landing party. She will agree that an autopsy can be conducted either on the station or on the ship. Beaming the skeletons and embryos back to the ship would be acceptable, but she will urge extreme caution and advise a level 10 force field be placed around both the skeletons and embryos. She will argue to delay any trip to the planet until after the autopsy results are provided and they are cleared.

All electronic data is transferred to the ship for further analysis. Any medical personnel on the landing party can perform a rudimentary autopsy on the skeletons. Success at an **Insight + Medicine** Task with a Difficulty of 2 will provide information to the Players that a form of pathogen was responsible for killing the Doradin and that the pathogen is inert and no longer a threat. Failure means the computer has detected something, but it is an unknown sample.

Players can then choose to transport the skeletal remains and/or the embryos back to the ship for further analysis. However, for more information on what actually happened to the planet, how the Xindi got here and what the Xindi and Doradin were doing on an orbiting station to begin with, there appears to be only one place to go. Alpha Doradis II. Perhaps one of the Xindi cities may reveal more clues?

NO GOOD DEED
ACT 2: EMPTY NESTS

CAPTAIN'S LOG

Captain's Log, supplemental. Our arrival in the previously unexplored Alpha Doradis system has led us to a profound, if not troubling, mystery. A peaceful Class-M world, two major continents, what appears to have been two distinct species of sentient life. The first appears to be refugees from what was considered the previously extinct species of avian Xindi. The other looks like a species of intelligent centipedes, which we believe are a race of indigenous Doradin. We've also located a derelict space station, three dozen corpses, and a distress call via radio wave sent out four years ago. Ship's sensors indicate numerous cities in the northern hemisphere, believed to be of Xindi design, attached to armatures drilled into mountains. Many have apparently been...detached violently and sent falling to the ground below. We've detected no sentient life whatsoever on Alpha Doradis II. A mass extinction event, maybe? At this point, we don't have enough information, but I'll be damned if I'm not going to find out what happened here, once the doctor gives us the okay to beam down.

SCENE 1: CITIES IN THE SKY

Given the all-clear from the doctor and a grudging agreement from Ambassador Paret, the crew has two options to get down to the planet, one of which makes things much more difficult initially. Players can transport down to the surface of one of the cities or they may attempt a shuttlecraft flight down. Success with an **Insight + Command** Task with a Difficulty of 1 allows the party leader to attempt to inspect one of the Xindi cities visually from orbit prior to beaming or shuttling down.

An inspection will allow the Players to realize that there is no way of accessing any of the buildings from the ground. This implies that a shuttle might be the best way of investigating. A successful **Reason + Science** Task with a Difficulty of 0 informs the Players that the actual materials used to build the cities, as well as parts of the mountains themselves, are made from magnesite. Attempts to beam directly into the building structure itself fail due to the high levels of magnesite in the construction materials.

Read or paraphrase the following:

The city appears to be made up of numerous spires, each culminating in a flat space from which more spires reach upward for kilometers. Thousands of pole-shaped objects, some a quarter-kilometer in diameter, just up into the sky, with numerous perches extending from the vertical poles and leading into what appear to be homes or businesses. Occasional skeletons can be seen lying shattered on the ground. What appear to be light posts reaching skyward are dark. Each flat area, or perch, is wide enough to be called a landing pad, of sorts, although they are not very wide at all.

Taking a shuttle down presents a clear challenge for the pilot and a successful roll of **Control or Daring + Conn**, with a Difficulty of 2, will allow for a safe landing, as there are powerful winds that whip through the city and the landing pads are about twice as wide as a shuttlecraft. Should there be a catastrophic failure in landing, only a successful **Insight + Command** Task with a Difficulty of 0 will allow them to realize that an emergency transport back to the ship is their only hope of survival.

Transporting down to one of the landing pads seems simple enough, except for the **Gale-force Winds**, a Trait whenever landing on one of the landing pads (perches). A successful **Fitness + Command** Task with a Difficulty of 1 will keep a Player from being knocked over by the powerful winds. Failure means the character gets knocked down. A successful **Fitness + Science** Task with a Difficulty of 1 will allow the Players to crawl toward safety. Failure means their characters need the help of crewmates if they are going to get anywhere.

Once inside, it is clear that the building you are in is a domicile of some sort. To get power up and running, the Players may attempt an **Insight + Science** Task with a Difficulty of 1 to determine an outside source is necessary. A **Reason or Insight + Engineering** Task with a Difficulty of 2 to transfer power from a tricorder or phaser to a nearby electrical conduit can power up the interior of the home, including what appears to be a computer. A **Reason + Engineering** Task with a Difficulty of 0 shows the Players that only local hard drive information is available. There is no power to the city or its computer network at all. However, success on an **Insight + Engineering** Task with a Difficulty of 2 will provide the location to a wind-powered generator on another tower housing the city's government offices. Failing any of these Tasks means they cannot restore power or locate a power plant to connect to.

Gamemaster Note: Ambassador Paret will be able to locate the primary government building by using logic and a basic understanding of predator mindsets. The tallest spire in the city is that city's main seat of power.

Any time a Player goes outside, the Gale-force winds Trait is in effect and they must battle through it.

SCENE 2: SABOTAGE

The landing pad on the perch of the government tower has been shorn in half, making landing challenging. The pilot must attempt a **Control + Conn** Task with a Difficulty of 3 to successfully land. Failure means there is a crash landing and a random number of Players may sustain injuries. Upon landing, the destruction to the perch is obviously artificially made, with numerous scorch marks colouring the pad. A successful **Reason + Security** Task with a Difficulty of 1 reveals the scorch marks are not from directed energy weapons, but from an explosive blast. Failure indicates an unknown source created the damage.

Gamemaster's Note: Ambassador Paret will be able to identify these as coming from chemically made improvised explosive devices (IEDs). She will advise that such weapons were used on Earth from as early as the 16th Century through to the mid 21st Century and on Tellar Prime prior to their first interstellar space flight.

LOG ENTRIES

#302001: "We came from outside. This planet seemed a perfect place to hide, to grow, to evolve, away from all the others who sought to conquer us, to destroy us. We built our homes here. Advanced our art and science. We have become a peaceful, loving species and quickly discovered we were not alone here on this planet.

"Beneath us, on the southern continent, another civilization already thrives. First contact was awkward. We saw them as sustenance, until we determined they were sentient. We vowed to remain in the north, so as to not terrify or anger them."

#390332: "The burrowers approach an age of industrialization. They already populate most of the substrata in the southern continent and may be making their way toward us. Leadership has chosen to go to them, to teach them by example, help them to build and evolve, as we had, in a way that preserves the planet's natural resources. We are hopeful."

#401686: "The burrowers are severely fragmented and unprepared for what we have to offer them. News comes to us that a plague now sweeps through their society. A virus linked to our own genetic make-up. It makes them mad, affecting their brains in such a way as to slowly eat away at their cognitive functions while simultaneously triggering massive hormone dumps into the lateral septum area of their brains. This region controls anger and impulse control. Our scientists are already working on a cure, but they are dying quickly. There is little time."

#421099: "The burrowers war on themselves while our scientists attempt to find a cure. We believe they have already slaughtered millions of their own. Our scientists believe we are close to a cure that will cancel out the genetic mutation in the virus, rendering it a predator with no fangs. I fear we are too late. There are rumblings beneath us. They have crossed the sea, underneath it, and even now climb to the surface of our continent. Have they come for us now?"

#422547: "The cure has been provided to the burrower's scientists. They have managed to disseminate it. However, something has gone wrong. It has failed completely and utterly. Not only that, but my own people become sickened with a virus similar to what struck the Doradin. We die within days of exposure. We are unclear as to how this is possible. Volcanic activity has increased a hundredfold and smoke blankets the northern hemisphere. Through it all, the burrowers continue to hate us and attack us at every opportunity. Many of our cities have toppled to the ground due to explosive devices planted on our perches and in our homes. Soon, there will be too few of us left to do anything but hide. They follow us. Hunt us. They blame us for the end of their society. How could this be? We were correct in our calculations. The cure should have worked. It hasn't and once again we find ourselves on the edge of extinction."

#430013: "There are so few of us left. Less than two dozen, in fact, out of the few thousand that first arrived and thrived on this perfect world. We have been approached by burrowers who say they are unaffected by the virus and wish to help us end the carnage that destroys two civilizations. A small group comprised of both our species have chosen to band together to find a way to save what is left. We shall once again leave the confines of a planet and travel into the unknown. We shall send a call for help and hope someone comes in time."

FINAL LOG ENTRY: "My name is Governor Seevra. My people fled a civil war that almost ended our existence, only to find ourselves living yet another disaster, one of our own creation, perhaps. In our efforts to protect ourselves and hide from the brethren who wished to destroy us, we have isolated ourselves into extinction. We can only hope a friendly, spacefaring species might arrive to save us from ourselves. I am one of the final members of my kind alive. We have no way to sending help to our station in space, but we have one last hope. Perhaps sending the seeds of our future elsewhere will allow us a third chance to get it right. May the stars always guide us and protect us."

The Players see a power generator near the edge of the perch. On a successful **Reason + Security** Task with a Difficulty of 1, the Players detect what appears to be an unexploded ordinance attached to the generator. A successful **Daring + Command** Task with a Difficulty of 1 is needed to remove the bomb. A successful **Reason + Engineering** Task with a Difficulty of 3 will be needed to deactivate it. Failure means the bomb's timer begins running again, with 20 seconds before it explodes. A successful **Control or Insight + Command** Task with a Difficulty of 1 gives the Players the chance to call their ship and have the bomb transported into space before it explodes.

Upon successfully completing these Tasks, turning on the generator is just a matter of ensuring it has energy to run. A successful **Insight + Engineering** Task with a Difficulty of 2 allows a landing party member to recognize devices attached to the generator that open and begin collecting wind power. Success means the generator powers up. Failure means power has not been restored. Almost immediately, the generator hums to life and lights flicker on inside the building.

SCENE 3: VIRUSES

The Players will need to attempt a **Control + Security** Task with a Difficulty of 2 to successfully locate and hack into the computer system. They discover the system is corrupted by a virus. The virus must be eliminated in seven different digital folders.

At this point, a Group Challenge may take place, with multiple Players working in unison at different computer terminals to access, locate, and restore the infected folders. These Tasks can utilize **Control, Insight or Reason + Security or Engineering** (with a Difficulty level of 2 for all participants in the Group Challenge).

If the Players fail and the damage from the virus cannot be repaired, the computer systems shut down and must be manually rebooted. The Players can make subsequent attempts with the Difficulty increased by 1 for each try.

As each file is located and restored, the sound of bird calls echoes through the empty chamber. The language is immediately translated from Xindi-Avian into Federation Standard through the Players' communicators (the Gamemaster should read one of the Log Entries from the sidebar on the previous page each time a file is restored).

SCENE 4: PROLIFERATION

Players who are successful at an **Insight + Science or Medicine** Task with a Difficulty of 1 will be able to discover that any virus can't kill as quickly as they have been led to believe unless it is airborne, which explains what happened to the Doradin, but not the Xindi, unless…

Success at a **Reason + Medicine** Task with a Difficulty of 2 provides the solution. An artificial airborne pathogen was released into the skies via the volcanic ash. This volcanic activity coincides with Doradin tunnelling in the northern continent near the active fault lines.

A successful **Insight + Science** Task with a Difficulty of 1 confirms the theory that such a means of proliferation is possible if there is a stable protective shield or capsule that will dissolve slowly in the heat of the ash until it is high enough in the air to disperse with the prevailing winds.

Gamemaster Note: Ambassador Paret advises that chemical weapons were favored by many governments on Earth up through the 21th century and the Third World War, even though such weapons had been banned in the mid-20th century. She will strongly encourage traveling to the southern continent in order to locate any surviving Doradins or, at the very least, to gather as much information as possible. Accessing their computers or asking any survivors may be the only way to understand what truly happened!

"The landing party must be extra cautious in following the trail from Xindi territory. Are there any Doradin left, hiding beneath the surface, out of sight? If so, they must be deep underground, where our sensors cannot penetrate. Communication between the ship and the landing party would only be possible through a series of relays, but to set them up would take months, traveling by foot beneath the continents and under the strait separating them. However, our sensors have found numerous caves in the southern continent. It is our hope that they lead down to the subterranean catacombs of the Doradin, and to some answers."

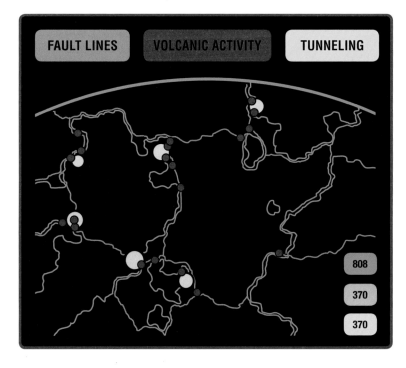

FAULT LINES　　VOLCANIC ACTIVITY　　TUNNELING

808

370

370

NO GOOD DEED
ACT 3: HATE'S SAKE

CAPTAIN'S LOG

Captain's Log, supplemental. It appears that no good deed goes unpunished. Through logs discovered in one of the Xindi Government Centers, we believe we've discovered what happened to the Xindi on Alpha Doradis II. The question haunting us all now is, why would the indigenous Doradin do this? The Xindi helped them evolve and grow as a species. What happened that caused that help to turn to hate and that hate to then turn to genocide? It's clear now that the answers to these questions must be discovered among the Doradin, somewhere on the southern continent. Tunnels created beneath all the major active volcanos in the north lead directly to the south, where we know the Doradin civilization once lived, or, perhaps, still do.

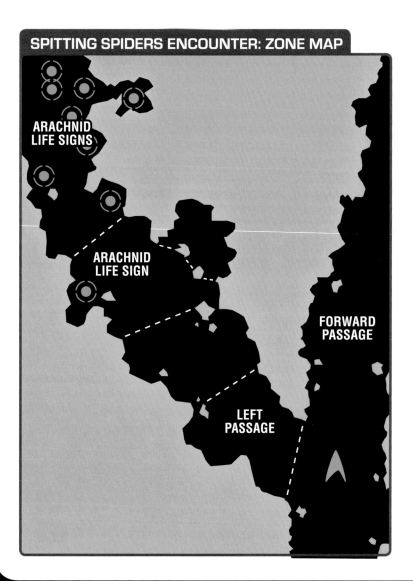

SPITTING SPIDERS ENCOUNTER: ZONE MAP

ARACHNID LIFE SIGNS

ARACHNID LIFE SIGN

FORWARD PASSAGE

LEFT PASSAGE

SCENE 1: FOLLOWING THE TRAIL

Landing near a suspected Doradin tunnel is nowhere near as difficult as landing on a perch a mile in the sky. Numerous caves dot the landscape. The shuttlecraft's sensors detect indigenous life across the entire area, but, due to high levels of magnesite in the crust of the planet, they cannot penetrate much further than 50 meters into the cave.

A successful **Insight + Security** Task with a Difficulty of 0 indicates all nearby life has fled at the approach of the shuttle. Moving toward the caves, intermittent life signs blink in and out. After about 10 meters inside a cave, the light begins to recede until artificial means of seeing are necessary.

Fifty meters in, the cave passage branches off in three separate directions, continuing forward and diagonally to the left and right. Success on a **Reason + Medicine** Task with a Difficulty of 1 indicates numerous life signs of an indeterminate nature down the left pathway approximately 25 meters from their present location, with nothing ahead and nothing to the right. The tunnel forward descends fairly rapidly at a 20-degree angle, while the side passages remain fairly flat.

If the Players choose the left path toward the life signs, the closer they get, the more it indicates that the life signs are arachnid in nature. If they get within 5 meters of the closest life sign, they will hear clicking and hissing and come face to face with a giant spider-like creature. Behind it, they hear multiple hissing sounds from other creatures.

A successful **Insight + Security or Science** Task with a Difficulty of 0 will allow a Player to realize that a couple well-placed phaser blasts at the ceiling above the spider will collapse the ceiling on top of the spider. The spider has a chance to escape the collapse by engaging the characters in melee.

Taking the right path will lead to a massive open pit that drops into utter darkness. A bottom exists more than the 50 meters tricorder scans can penetrate. A fall means certain death.

The center path leads to a vast open cave, at least 100 meters high, several kilometers long, and a half-kilometer wide. Holes in the ground about one meter in diameter lead down into darkness. No life signs are detected here. Sensors cannot penetrate the magnesite in the surrounding walls or ground beneath. Shining a light will show a solid floor about 3 meters down.

Should someone wish to investigate, they may be able to secure themselves with rope and jump down. Anyone doing so would need assistance at climbing back up through the hole. A successful **Daring or Fitness + Command** Task with a Difficulty of 2 gets a Player safely to the bottom without Injury. Failure indicates a minor Injury incurred from the fall. Shining a light around shows what appears to be some strange type of living area. Doradin skeletons lie scattered about. There is no life and no power here. Those above can assist any Player up with a successful **Fitness + Security** Task with a Difficulty of 1. Failure indicates they are unable to pull the character up and more help with be needed.

Read or paraphrase the following:

Looking around at the vast and empty cavern, you glance up and see perches lining some of the walls, about ten meters above you. At the far end of the cave, what appears to be a structure sits ominously by itself. The ceiling is covered in bolt holes, perhaps ventilation to the surface. Much of the cave is covered in a fine layer of soot and ash. It has not been disturbed in quite a while.

SCENE 2: TOO MUCH TOO SOON

Upon reaching the structure, the Players realize that it appears made for both Doradin and the Xindi species to cohabitate. Inside, powerless computers take up much of the wall space and skeletal remains cover most of the floor.

A successful **Reason + Engineering** Task with a Difficulty of 0 will allow Players to notice cans filled with liquid fuel nearby and realize that generator is powered by fossil fuel. The generators start easily enough, which causes the computers to flicker to life. One of the screens is playing what appears to be an audio loop. It is the language of the Xindi, which the universal translator picks up immediately. Read or paraphrase the following:

"They are hate-filled. They feel entitled to power and use it without conscience. They are like fledglings, taking what they want without thought to consequence. It was a mistake for us to come here. They need another millennium of evolution before they can be trusted not to kill everything they come in contact with. One sees them and thinks they are mindless, but they are especially intelligent and self-aware. They are manipulative and obfuscate with every word. They cannot be trusted. We have given them too much, too soon, and I fear we shall pay a heavy price for

Twelve legs allow this arachnid to practically fly across any hard terrain. Four tubules projecting from its oval skull spit a liquid substance comparable to hydrochloric acid. They tend to be passive unless provoked. A single adult spider can attain a half-meter in length and isn't particularly dangerous. A nest, however, is a radically different story.

TRAITS: Doradin Spitting Spider

ATTRIBUTES

| CONTROL | 10 | FITNESS | 05 | PRESENCE | 02 |
| DARING | 04 | INSIGHT | 02 | REASON | 02 |

DISCIPLINES

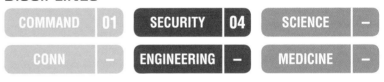

| COMMAND | 01 | SECURITY | 04 | SCIENCE | – |
| CONN | – | ENGINEERING | – | MEDICINE | – |

STRESS: 9   **RESISTANCE:** 1

ATTACKS:
▶ Bite (Melee, 4⚔ Intense, Size 1H, Non-lethal)
▶ Swarm (Melee, 5⚔ Knockdown, Size 2H, Deadly)
▶ Poison Spit (Ranged, 5⚔ Area, Intense, Size 1H, Debilitating)

our selflessness. I must escape now, while they slumber, or I will never get out."

A more thorough search of the surroundings confirms the story. Behind the building is what looks to be a mass grave, a trench filled with skeletons. With nothing else to learn and no life to examine, the Players can return to the shuttle and their ship in orbit.

SCENE 3: DETAILS OF A GENOCIDE

At this point, the Players can piece together the entire story. A Player Character may wish to complete an autopsy on one of the remains from the station. A successful **Insight + Medicine** Task with a Difficulty of 1 enables the Player to deduce the original virus was a mutated version of what on Earth was called the bird flu. Failure means they cannot ascertain the origin of the pathogen. Whatever it was, it somehow affected the Doradin due to the unsanitary conditions in their underground city. They intentionally redesigned the mutated virus and used it to annihilate the Xindi, at the same time continuing a mass self-annihilation of their own species through war, famine, and pestilence.

Gamemaster Note: The Players also have another chance to revisit the log entries from the planet. If they forget or fail to do so, Ambassador Paret will state she wants to hear them again and will focus on the final log entry, where a quick comment may be specifically reconsidered: "Perhaps sending the seeds of our future elsewhere will allow us a third chance to get it right." What is meant by this statement?

Success on an **Insight + Science** Task with a Difficulty of 0 will lead a Player to consider the possibility of another launch into space with "the seeds" of the future.

SCENE 4: SEEDS OF THE FUTURE

The Players can return to the shuttle and back to their ship in orbit. There, the search can begin. A successful **Reason + Science** Task with a Difficulty of 2, assisted by the ship's **Sensors + Science**, provides the Players with the location of a low-level power signature emanating from somewhere near the Alpha Doradis star.

Further investigation may be attempted via a **Reason + Engineering** Task with a Difficulty of 1. Success reveals

that the power signature is coming from a Xindi escape pod caught in the star's gravitational pull. A successful **Reason + Medicine** Task with a Difficulty of 1 alerts the Players that faint life is detected within the escape pod. Failure indicates only a low-level generation of power emanating from the pod. The Players' ship can make the journey to the location in moments.

A successful **Control + Engineering** Task with a Difficulty of 2 (with the assistance of the ship's **Engines + Conn**) will be necessary to effectively rescue the pod and escape the gravity well of the star. The escape pod can be beamed directly into the cargo bay of the ship. Failure means there is damage to the pod, effectively damaging some of the contents.

Once it is beamed over, the Players make a startling discovery. Within the undamaged escape pod are fifty cryogenic chambers, each labelled with the symbol the Players saw earlier, and each with approximately a thousand frozen embryos nestled inside them. A damaged pod may reduce this number by half. The embryos are both Xindi and Doradin. Further, the bodies of twenty scientists, ten Xindi and ten Doradin, lie in cryogenic stasis.

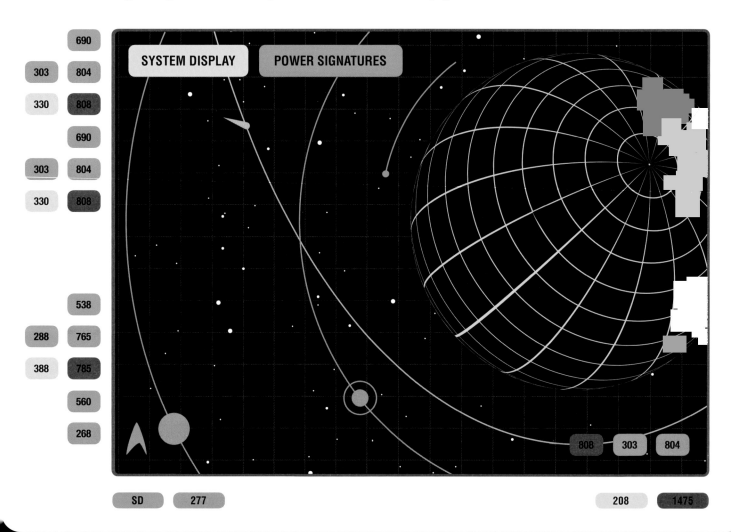

Gamemaster's Note: Ambassador Paret will argue to allow only one Xindi scientist to be awakened. She argues that someone other than a Federation ship should make that choice. Further, she will argue not to awaken the Doradin scientists, as they have not met any other spacefaring races, other than the Xindi, and they tried to kill them.

If the Players choose to awaken one of the Xindi, they get to meet Kala'Zee.

If the Players choose to revive a Xindi scientist, Kala'Zee awakens from his cryo-stasis and is highly curious, as he has never seen, nor heard of, Humans before. As the characters speak to him, he is astounded to hear his own language being spoken by outsiders. A successful **Insight + Command** Task with a Difficulty of 1 allows the characters to speak in a way that calms him enough for further communication.

Given the opportunity, Ambassador Paret advises Kala'Zee of everything they have learned and requests his assistance in coming up with a solution to the problem. Kala'Zee wants to find a suitable planet for both species to thrive in without the fear of war. Paret suggests placing the Doradins back on their planet and finding a new world for the Xindi. She even offers to act as mediator with his fellow Xindi species for reunification, an offer Kala'Zee refuses in the strongest possible diplomatic way.

KALA'ZEE
MINOR NPC

A Xindi scientist, who came up with the idea of sending their species to a new world with the hopes of finding one suitable for both. He is open to any suggestion that will keep both species alive.

TRAITS: Xindi-Avian

ATTRIBUTES

CONTROL	07	FITNESS	08	PRESENCE	09
DARING	09	INSIGHT	07	REASON	08

DISCIPLINES

COMMAND	01	SECURITY	01	SCIENCE	02
CONN	–	ENGINEERING	–	MEDICINE	02

STRESS: 09   RESISTANCE: 0

ATTACKS:
▶ Unarmed Strike (Melee, 2▲ Vicious 1, Size 1H, Deadly)

NO GOOD DEED
CONCLUSION

The Players have the opportunity for a diplomatic solution, supported by Ambassador Paret. Encourage the Players to discuss the matter and the implications of the Prime Directive and first contact procedures. The decision on what to do with the embryos and Kala'Zee should be up to the Players, though if they have trouble pulling things together, use Ambassador Paret as a guide through the discussion and any subsequent negotiations.

It's possible the Players can create an initial agreement and then can contact Starfleet Command for more involved diplomatic assistance.

CONTINUING VOYAGES...
The Players have numerous options available to them that could be used in future missions:

▶ Return the escape pod to space outside of the sun's gravity.

▶ Allow the natural course of events to unfold and return the pod to its deadly path into the star.

▶ Put Kala'Zee back in stasis and keep both adults and embryos in storage until Starfleet figures out what to do with them.

▶ Return the Xindi and the Doradins to Alpha Doradis II.

▶ Take it upon themselves to find a new home world for the Xindi and return the Doradins to their home.

The Players may choose to defy Ambassador Paret and notify the Xindi that their wayward cousins are still alive, despite Kala'Zee requesting their existence remain a secret. They could honor the Xindi scientist and help him locate a suitable world for the Xindi or for both species.

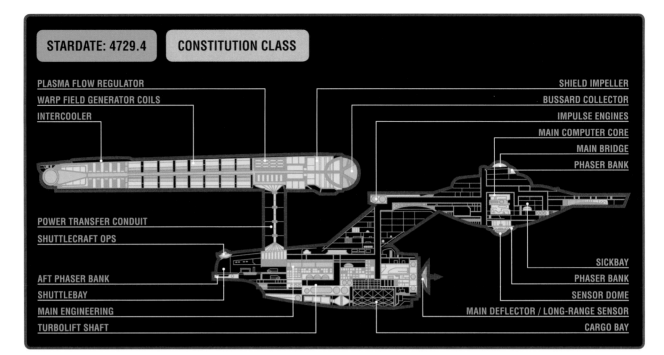

STARDATE: 4729.4　　CONSTITUTION CLASS

PLASMA FLOW REGULATOR
WARP FIELD GENERATOR COILS
INTERCOOLER

SHIELD IMPELLER
BUSSARD COLLECTOR
IMPULSE ENGINES
MAIN COMPUTER CORE
MAIN BRIDGE
PHASER BANK

POWER TRANSFER CONDUIT
SHUTTLECRAFT OPS

AFT PHASER BANK
SHUTTLEBAY
MAIN ENGINEERING
TURBOLIFT SHAFT

SICKBAY
PHASER BANK
SENSOR DOME
MAIN DEFLECTOR / LONG-RANGE SENSOR
CARGO BAY

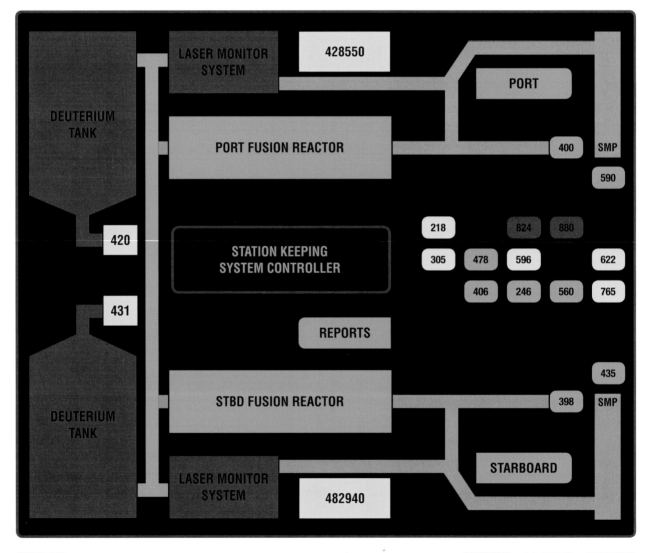

LASER MONITOR SYSTEM

428550

PORT

DEUTERIUM TANK

PORT FUSION REACTOR

400　SMP

590

420

STATION KEEPING SYSTEM CONTROLLER

218　　824　880

305　478　596　　622

406　246　560　765

431

REPORTS

435

STBD FUSION REACTOR

398　SMP

DEUTERIUM TANK

STARBOARD

LASER MONITOR SYSTEM

482940

SC

307　98　748

17

28

32

126

47

THE WHOLE OF THE LAW

BY CHRISTOPHER L. BENNETT

THE WHOLE OF THE LAW
SYNOPSIS

The Players' starship comes upon an exotic object in space: A large, flat disk of hyperdense matter generating its own gravitational field, with both sides domed and containing habitable environments. The structure resists scans, but the ship receives a friendly hail inviting it to dock.

The disk habitat is called Thelema, and its builders belong to a race of enlightened anarchists, dedicated to individual freedom. They administer Thelema as a pleasure world where anyone can indulge their desires without inhibition. The habitat is subdivided into a Light Face for relatively wholesome indulgences and a Dark Face for more extreme, even lethal entertainments – with the strict provision that everyone who enters does so voluntarily.

The commanding officer only authorizes shore leave or exploration of the Light Face, but of course things go wrong, and some Players are abducted to the Dark Face. They will be joined by an alien warrior who takes them under his wing and agrees to help them reach the Rim, the only way out. Their path will be populated with a variety of deadly threats.

The Thelemans refuse to believe the officers were taken against their will, so the commanding officer and crew must investigate their abduction and try to prove it to Thelema's administrator, while also attempting to pierce the habitat's privacy shielding to locate and rescue their crew from the Dark Face, where they are being led into a deathtrap.

This scenario contains multiple opportunities for Gamemasters to improvise and create a range of settings, NPCs, and side scenes within the context of story events.

DIRECTIVES

In addition to the Prime Directive, the Directives for this mission are:

▶ Locate and rescue starship personnel who are missing or in distress.

▶ Starfleet Directive 010: Before engaging alien species in battle, any and all attempts to make first contact and achieve non-military resolution must be made.

The Gamemaster begins this mission with 2 points of Threat for each Player Character in the group.

PRELUDE

This Adventure would work well in the wake of a previous mission or series of missions that were stressful or tiring for the Player Characters, so that the crew is badly in need of recreation. The opening scenes should highlight the Players' readiness for a break. Perhaps the ship's doctor is conducting crew examinations and notes excessive fatigue among the crew, or a friendly competition in the rec room or gym grows tense due to the Players' need for a change of scenery.

ADAPTING THE MISSION TO OTHER ERAS

This mission is set in the Original Series movie era (c. 2278), yet is easily adaptable to any post-TOS time frame with no significant changes. For the *Enterprise* era, the one obligatory change is that the crew would be unfamiliar with the events of "Shore Leave," so the origin of the master computer would remain unknown to the characters (but could be treated as an Easter egg for the Players to deduce outside of gameplay). Also, the Gamemaster would have to avoid using Romulans among the Dark Face guests.

06.20 THE WHOLE OF THE LAW
ACT 1: THELEMA

COMMANDING OFFICER'S LOG

Commanding Officer's Log, Stardate 7815.5. While exploring an uncharted red dwarf star system in this sector, we have detected an asteroid-sized body of unusual shape and high density within the star's habitable zone. We have diverted our course to investigate.

SCENE 1: THE DISCUS WORLD

As the ship nears the mysterious object, it becomes clear that it is a domed artificial body in the shape of a flattened oblate spheroid. Sensor scans reveal a strange, elliptical structure.

Bisecting the discus-shaped body at its equator is a flat, circular disk of collapsed matter some 9640 times the density of Earth – a hundredth as dense as white dwarf matter, but still exceptionally dense. It must have been created by some highly advanced technology, both to achieve that density and to hold its shape without collapsing into a sphere. The rest of the spheroid is normal rocky matter.

Despite its extreme shape, it still follows the normal laws of gravitation, meaning that everything is pulled toward the exact center of mass. As you get farther from the polar axis, not only does the gravity decrease according to the inverse square law (i.e., one-fourth the pull at twice the distance from the center, one-ninth at three times

the distance, etc.), but the "down" direction tilts further inward (always toward the center), so the ground effectively becomes steeper. However, the decreasing gravity makes the climb easier the further out one goes. (The object rotates once every 32 hours, too slowly for centrifugal force to be significant.)

The surface is terraced in a series of concentric rings about 1.2 km apart, with the surface of each terrace tilted further outward so that it is "flat" relative to the local pull of gravity. Figure 1 does not depict the terraces, but it marks several gravity levels – the maximum 4.2g, Earth-like gravity, quarter gravity, and the gravity at the outer rim. The long gray lines indicate the vertical/"down" direction at each location, and the short gray lines show the angle of "level ground" at those locations, perpendicular to the downward pull. If necessary, further terraces' angles and gravity levels can be estimated using a ruler, a protractor, and the inverse square law.

The terraces hold a wide variety of planetlike climates and atmospheres. In most cases, the high "cliffs" between different terrace levels separate their environments sufficiently, but some extreme atmospheres are kept separate by force-field barriers. As the ship circles the structure to scan both sides, it appears that the sunward face has generally more amenable environments (relative to the needs of different forms of life), while the shadowed face has harsher, more polluted conditions.

The dome has shielding that prevents more detailed scans, so sensors cannot discern life-form readings or individual structures. Along the outer rim are numerous docking bays and landing fields, also covered or

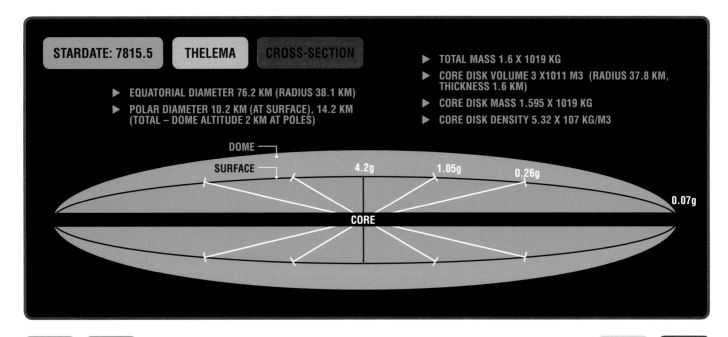

- ► EQUATORIAL DIAMETER 76.2 KM (RADIUS 38.1 KM)
- ► POLAR DIAMETER 10.2 KM (AT SURFACE), 14.2 KM (TOTAL – DOME ALTITUDE 2 KM AT POLES)

- ► TOTAL MASS 1.6 X 1019 KG
- ► CORE DISK VOLUME 3 X1011 M3 (RADIUS 37.8 KM, THICKNESS 1.6 KM)
- ► CORE DISK MASS 1.595 X 1019 KG
- ► CORE DISK DENSITY 5.32 X 107 KG/M3

DOME

SURFACE

4.2g   1.05g   0.26g

0.07g

CORE

sensor-shielded. There is no way to determine who may be occupying the structure.

As the starship nears the habitat, the communications officer reports a hail from it. A blue-skinned, hairless humanoid female with a flat beak and a subtly scaled head, resembling a cross between a bird and a reptile, appears on the main viewscreen and speaks:

"Greetings, travelers from the United Federation of Planets. I am Vishorasa, and I welcome you to this haven, which you may call Thelema (theh-LEE-muh). I request that you discontinue your efforts to scan our interior, for though all are welcome here, we take the privacy of our guests most seriously. If you wish to know more of the services we offer, please send a delegation in person so that we may arrange proper access for your crew. You may dock your vessel or land a shuttle at Port 37. You may also transport a party there, although we do not allow transporter access to the interior of Thelema. But please do come for a visit. We offer wondrous entertainment and fulfillment for all visitors."

The communications officer reports receiving a guide beacon to Port 37. Provide them or the science officer with the following comment to read:

"Interesting that they call this structure 'Thelema.' On Earth, that's the name of a pseudo-religious philosophy developed by Aleister Crowley: 'Do what thou wilt shall be the whole of the Law. Love is the law, love under will.' Basically, that the highest moral law is allowing all people

to pursue their own calling and desire, free of restrictions.

"But more to the point, how did Vishorasa know that name for the concept, or that we were from the Federation? There's no record of her species in our database."

The only way to investigate the mysteries of Thelema is to accept Vishorasa's invitation. The commanding officer should select a landing party accordingly.

SCENE 2: MEETING VISHORASA

The landing party arrives in Port 37, a wide, flat docking area with a retractable hemicylindrical roof. They are standing directly on the outer edge of the disk, as if it were balanced vertically on its edge below them. Although the natural gravity at this distance would be a mere 7% of Earth's, they feel full gravity on arrival.

A Theleman male arrives to escort the party to meet Director Vishorasa. He introduces himself as Subdirector Hamisor. He wears a comfortable-looking, loose white garment with brightly-colored abstract patterns on the shoulders. Hamisor escorts the party to a pneumatic tram car that carries them through a tube at high velocity, curving downward as they circle around the edge of Thelema – naturally, since the hyperdense core disk would be too dense to penetrate.

If asked about the gravity, Hamisor will explain:

"Yes, we provide adjustable gravity plating at our docking facilities for the comfort of our visitors.

Within Thelema itself, we rely on the natural pull of the core disk to provide a continuum of gravity levels to accommodate guests from all conceivable environments."

Soon, they reach Vishorasa's office, a bright, inviting place with vistas of numerous environments displayed on large wall screens, apparently image feeds from Thelema's various terraces. Some are mere landscapes, while others show beings of various species engaged in a range of recreational activities. Some display wholesome sports or nature walks, while others show a lively night life and hint discreetly at more risqué pleasures. They have the feel of promotional videos to entice tourists.

Vishorasa rises from her desk to greet the visitors. She is attired in a comfortable white shift like Hamisor's but with more extensive color patterns. Once the crew introduce themselves, she speaks.

> *"You are all most welcome to Thelema. We are open to all visitors, and we pride ourselves on having recreations and fulfillments to offer for every species in the Galaxy.*
>
> *"I imagine you are skeptical, as many new visitors are. What do we get out of it? Well, our people are devoted to the philosophy your people call Thelema – that all beings should be free to pursue their every desire, so long as they do not impose on any other's freedom or desire in so doing. Our embrace of this philosophy has brought us peace, prosperity, and the friendship of many other civilizations who benefit from our hospitality. Many have offered us gifts in return, including the resources we needed to construct this miniature world.*
>
> *"Thelema provides a safe and free haven for beings of all natures and proclivities to fulfill their desires, their fantasies, their needs for pleasure or adventure or simple relaxation. We do not judge or condemn, merely facilitate. All things are permitted here, so long as they do no harm to unconsenting parties."*

If the characters pick up on the implication that harm may come to consenting parties, Vishorasa will elaborate:

> *"You have surely noted that Thelema has two separate halves, divided by the impassable Core Disk in between. The Light Face is for indulging those pleasures that harm no one, or that risk injury only to oneself. But there are those who find pleasure and fulfillment in combat or violence, even the taking of life or the gambling of one's own. The Dark Face is where such desires can be freely pursued – for only those who truly accept*

VISHORASA
MAJOR NPC

The Director of Thelema, a seasoned administrator who prides herself on its success as a recreation world and a haven for all comers. She believes Thelema helps keep interstellar peace by providing common ground for the peaceful and controlled release for the violent.

TRAITS: Theleman

VALUES:
- ▶ Do As Thou Wilt, But Do No Harm
- ▶ Others' Fulfillment is My Success
- ▶ The System Works for Everyone; Trust In It

ATTRIBUTES

CONTROL	11	FITNESS	09	PRESENCE	11
DARING	08	INSIGHT	10	REASON	10

DISCIPLINES

COMMAND	05	SECURITY	03	SCIENCE	03
CONN	01	ENGINEERING	02	MEDICINE	02

FOCUSES: Administration, Commerce, Diplomacy, Persuasion, Recreation Services

STRESS: 12   **RESISTANCE:** 0

ATTACKS: None

SPECIAL RULES:
- ▶ **Defuse the Tension (Talent)**
- ▶ **Guidance (Talent):** Whenever Vishorasa assists another NPC in a particular way, she may re-roll her d20.

> *the danger are allowed to enter. We have found this is the best way to ensure that all desires are balanced. No one is hurt or killed… except those who are willing to be.*
>
> *"If that does not suit your preferences, the Light Face contains an abundance of magnificent vistas and fulfilling recreations, enough to satisfy everyone in your crew. I perceive that you are explorers, devoted to science and discovery. If it is knowledge you crave, then simply observing Thelema's varied biomes could bring you fulfillment. Or you could observe and interview*

HAMISOR
MAJOR NPC

One of six subdirectors assigned to tend to guests' needs, Hamisor has taken a particular interest in the guests who favor the Dark Face. Though he convinces himself he's only serving needs the official system doesn't fulfill, he takes a vicarious thrill in the violence he facilitates, an overcompensation for his timidity and insecurity.

TRAITS: Theleman

VALUES:
- ▶ Do As Thou Wilt, Including Harm If You Can Get Away With It
- ▶ I May Seem Unimportant, But I Have Outsmarted the System

ATTRIBUTES

| CONTROL | 10 | FITNESS | 10 | PRESENCE | 09 |
| DARING | 11 | INSIGHT | 10 | REASON | 09 |

DISCIPLINES

| COMMAND | 03 | SECURITY | 05 | SCIENCE | 02 |
| CONN | 01 | ENGINEERING | 04 | MEDICINE | 01 |

FOCUSES: Commerce, Computers, Middle Management, Recreation Services, Weapons

STRESS: 15   **RESISTANCE:** 0

ATTACKS:
- ▶ Unarmed Strike (Melee, 6⏶ Knockdown, Size 1H, Non-lethal)
- ▶ Phaser Type-1 (Ranged, 7⏶, Size 1H, Charge, Hidden 1)

SPECIAL RULES:
- ▶ **Ambush:** When attacking an opponent who is unaware, Hamisor may spend 2 Threat to re-roll any number of d20s on his attack rolls.

---

those visitors to Thelema whose kinds you have not met before. With their permission, of course. In all other respects, the choice is yours. How may Thelema satisfy your will?"

If the characters query Vishorasa about her surprising insight into the Federation, its languages, and so forth, she smiles and says:

"We have many friends who know many things, and who share their knowledge with us. Their generosity has prepared us to be responsive to the needs of whatever beings we may meet in this vast Galaxy."

The meeting leaves the landing party with much to think about. The prospects of recreation and discovery are bound to entice the weary crew, but they still must report back to the commanding officer.

SCENE 3: CREW BRIEFING

Back on the ship, the crew discusses whether to authorize shore leave or investigate Thelema carefully before doing so. It seems above board, but Vishorasa's knowledge of the Federation is still mysterious. The Thelemans' willingness to let others kill and be killed in the name of freedom of choice may create some controversy. Still, if the commanding officer does not authorize shore leave reasonably quickly, it could worsen crew unrest.

Naturally the commanding officer would not risk sending anyone to the Dark Face, for it would be risking death gratuitously. Exploration or leave will be limited to the Light Face, probably to regions of Earth-like gravity or lower, unless there are personnel aboard from species that could handle the superterrestrial pull closer to the axis.

The Gamemaster should secretly note which Player Characters seem most intrigued by the Dark Face and the prospect of facing its risks, even if it's just a fleeting curiosity. This will come into play in Act 2.

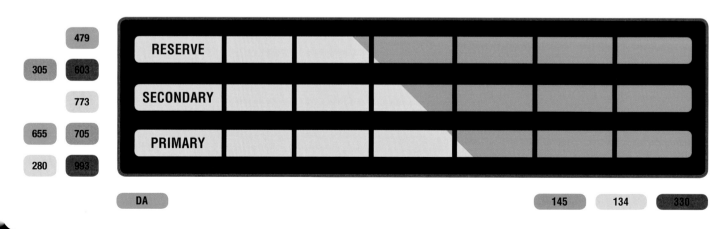

	RESERVE						
479							
305	603						
773		SECONDARY						
655	705							
280	993	PRIMARY						

DA   145   134   330

COMMANDING OFFICER'S LOG

Commanding officer's Log, supplemental. I have decided to accept Vishorasa's invitation to send a survey team to observe the Light Face of Thelema. If it proves amenable, I will authorize shore leave for the rest of the crew.

SCENE 1: THE LIGHT FACE

The commanding officer should assign several Player Characters and NPCs to survey two or three different areas of the Light Face, while keeping one or two Player Characters in reserve for later plot developments. Presumably the main focus would be the terraces near standard Earth-like gravity (1g). At this distance from the center of mass, the gravitational pull and the curvature of the disc combine to produce a steep slope of approximately 60 degrees. The level terraces carved into this slope are roughly 300 meters deep and spaced about 1.2 kilometers apart.

There are pneumatic lifts between the terraces at certain points, but also stairways and mountaineering paths for more intrepid visitors – plus parachutes, gliders, jet packs, and so forth. Naturally, there are safety railings and emergency force fields at the terrace edges, except in areas where jumping off is expected, or in the terraces at low-gravity levels or those tailored for flying species. At the inner ends of the terraces, entrances in the cliff face lead to indoor recreational facilities carved into the rock – gyms, theaters, and so forth. The illustration shows only the most basic ground-level facilities; there may be many interior levels above and below them, mostly behind-the-scenes administrative and maintenance facilities.

The terraces extend indefinitely to east and west, curving down beyond the horizon on either side and forming complete concentric circles. The horizon at the Earth-gravity levels would be about 180 meters away for an observer of typical Human height; at the higher, lower-gravity levels, the horizon would appear more distant. The formula is $d = (2(hR+h))1/2$, where d is the horizon distance, h is the height of the observer in meters, and R is the radius (distance from Thelema's central axis) in meters.

This means that any given area of a Theleman terrace at Earth-gravity level would appear to be roughly a rectangle 300 x 360 meters, curved in the longer direction. This should make for fairly easy mapping of specific terrace sectors.

The dome is 2 kilometers out from the cliff face, paralleling its slope. The red star is visible through the dome, about 25 degrees above the equator, but since the terraces are sharply tilted relative to the equator, the sun would appear to rise and set on a 32-hour cycle. At flatter levels closer to the axis, the sun might be in the sky at all times. The air mass within the dome is more than large enough to have its own internal clouds and weather, including rainfall. To avoid the difficulties of calculating how weather would naturally behave in this environment, assume the weather is artificially regulated by mechanisms in the dome.

Aside from the basic structure of the habitat, the specifics of the environments and their inhabitants are at the Gamemaster's discretion. Populate the landscape with whatever species strike your fancy. Ideally, offer a variety of exotic aliens and landscapes, perhaps at various gravity levels. Spark the Players' interest in both the diverse alien guests as a subject of scientific curiosity and the recreational possibilities of Thelema. Talking to any of the other guests should confirm Vishorasa's account and reinforce the idea of Thelema as a welcoming, inclusive, non-judgmental haven for all. This should lead the commanding officer to authorize shore leave for the crew.

Note that the Thelemans' lack of judgment means that they offer the same kinds of uninhibited (yet consensual) adult pleasures that one can find on Risa or Argelius. The degree to which the Players indulge in such activities is a matter for the Gamemaster's and Players' discretion, with the Players' age and comfort levels in mind. Any such indulgences will probably remain mostly "offscreen," though, since the Players will soon be concerned with more urgent matters.

Crew members taking shore leave enter Thelema through the Rim, where they are presented with a verbal and text disclaimer spelling out the options of the Light and Dark Faces and clearly stating the risks of the latter, stressing that no one should enter there unless they sincerely and explicitly consent to risk life and limb. Assuming the starship personnel all select the Light Face, a door opens to their left and leads them to the tram cars that will lead them down the curve of Thelema's disk to their desired gravity levels. Once they leave the docking rim and its gravity plates, they will feel very low gravity at first, increasing as they descend toward the axis.

However, things will go differently for the Player Characters selected by the Gamemaster earlier as those most tempted by the dangers of the Dark Face. They'll likely follow orders and select the Light Face as their destination. But for them, the right-hand door opens (make sure they are unaware this is anomalous). Once they pass through and the door closes behind them, they are struck from behind by energy blasts and fall unconscious. [The attacker is Hamisor, but only the Gamemaster knows this.]

ENCOUNTER: THE DARK FACE

The unconscious Player Characters awaken to find themselves on a thickly forested terrace, in a small clearing close to the edge. The woods are a rainforest environment, hot, humid, and forbidding. The night sky above tells them they're in the Dark Face, though there is limited artificial illumination from light sources in the underside of the next higher terrace. They feel weighted down, as if the gravity is more than half again Earth normal. (It's actually 1.7g, and they're some 6.3 km from the Dark Face pole.) Above, they can see the slope of Thelema rising overhead, eventually disappearing into the clouds and haze. The portions of the "cliff" that they can see are angled at about 50 degrees at this radius – hardly an easy climb given the gravity. And there's no obvious sign of a tram or lift to take them up and out toward the rim. If there is one, it must be below the horizon to east or west.

But getting through the jungle won't be easy. The characters hear heavy figures moving through the trees – making their presence known but staying hidden, as if toying with the officers. Soon, three figures emerge into the clearing, large and strong humanoids with tough, blue-gray hides like a rhinoceros and blocky bald heads, dressed in gladiator-like briefs and sandals, plus harnesses and belts for their weapons. And they're clearly out for blood. The Players must avoid their attacks and try to defend themselves, either by unarmed combat and evasion or by finding natural weapons like rocks and branches. If they attempt the usual "We come in peace" approach, two of the attackers will simply laugh it off:

> *"You wouldn't have come to the Dark Face if you wanted peace!"*

> *"Unless it's the peace of the grave!"*

The attackers toy with the Players at first, but the Players must be quick to avoid serious injury. However, the Complication of the high gravity slows them down and increases the Difficulty of any physical action by 1.

But the third alien – an older, scarred one with the air of a seasoned veteran – hesitates upon seeing the officers' reluctance, and asks:

> *"Why are you here, if not to kill or risk dying? That is the only reason to come to the Dark Face."*

Once he realizes the officers are here against their will, he turns on the other two of his kind, driving them off to protect the officers.

Gamemaster Note: This alien, a Korborode named Bovokkan (rhymes with "awoken"), is actually behind the officers' abduction. He supplies unwilling victims to Dark Face guests who want to kill unconsenting prey, something strictly forbidden by the Thelemans. He set up this initial confrontation to test the officers' fighting ability and to get into their good graces.

After the fight, he introduces himself:

> *"I'm Bovokkan. Don't worry, I won't hurt you. I come here to fight, yes – but unlike those others, I'd never take on anyone who didn't choose to take the risk. This is a grave abuse of a noble system. There are strict rules that should keep anyone*

KORBORODE MERCENARY
MINOR NPC

A tough, aggressive, amoral fighter, happy to prey on the helpless.

TRAITS: Korborode

ATTRIBUTES

CONTROL	08	FITNESS	09	PRESENCE	08
DARING	09	INSIGHT	07	REASON	07

DISCIPLINES

COMMAND	01	SECURITY	02	SCIENCE	–
CONN	01	ENGINEERING	–	MEDICINE	02

STRESS: 11   **RESISTANCE:** 0

ATTACKS:
▶ Unarmed Strike (Melee, 3⚔ Knockdown, Vicious 1, Size 1H)
▶ Blade (Melee, 4⚔ Vicious 1, Size 1H)
▶ Escalation Heavy Blade (Melee, 5⚔ Vicious 1, Size 2H)

SPECIAL RULES:
▶ Brute Force: Korborode add the Vicious 1 Effect to their Unarmed Strike and remove the Non-lethal Quality.
▶ Tough (Talent)

BOVOKKAN
MAJOR NPC

A seasoned Korborode mercenary who's lived as long as he has by being cunning and charismatic as well as extremely tough. Recognizing that he's getting too old to survive long in serious combat, he sees the Dark Face as a safer way to satisfy his drives, especially when he can prey on the vulnerable.

TRAITS: Korborode

ATTRIBUTES

CONTROL	09	FITNESS	10	PRESENCE	11
DARING	11	INSIGHT	09	REASON	09

DISCIPLINES

COMMAND	03	SECURITY	05	SCIENCE	01
CONN	02	ENGINEERING	02	MEDICINE	03

FOCUSES: Deception, Hand-to-Hand Combat, Infiltration, Resilience

STRESS: 15   **RESISTANCE:** 0

THE CLEARING: ZONE MAP

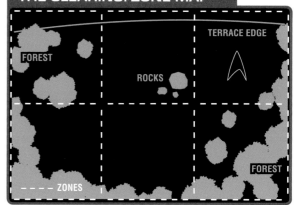

FOREST

TERRACE EDGE

ROCKS

FOREST

— — — ZONES

ATTACKS:
- ▶ Unarmed Strike (Melee, 6⚔ Vicious 1, Size 1H)
- ▶ Blade (Melee, 7⚔ Vicious 1, Size 1H)
- ▶ **Escalation** Heavy Blade (Melee, 8⚔ Vicious 1, Size 2H)
- ▶ Disruptor Pistol (Ranged, 8⚔ Vicious 1, Size 1H)

SPECIAL RULES:
- ▶ **Brute Force:** Korborode add the Vicious 1 Effect to their Unarmed Strike and remove the Non-lethal Quality.
- ▶ **Pack Tactics (Talent)**
- ▶ **Tough (Talent)**

*unwilling from being sent here. Something must
have gone wrong.*

*"I guess I'll have to help you get back to the Rim
in one piece, then report this anomaly to the
Thelemans. You'd never make it on your own. It's
a very long climb, and there are many dangers.
Don't worry – I know the lay of the land very well.
I can get you safely back where you belong."*

SCENE 2: DEMANDING ANSWERS

On determining that the two officers have gone missing,
the commanding officer contacts Vishorasa to request a
thorough search. Vishorasa refuses to let outside vessels
scan Thelema, out of privacy considerations, but she has
her staff conduct a thorough sensor sweep and is puzzled
to find no sign of them on the Light Face. A review of the
admission logs reveals that they were instead sent to the
Dark Face.

When the commanding officer protests, Vishorasa insists it's
impossible for anyone to be sent to the Dark Face against
their will or by accident. She explains that access to the
Dark Face is monitored by a telepathic computer system
donated to the Thelemans by a civilization that operated a
similar shore leave planet in the Omicron Delta region (as
seen in The Original Series episode "Shore Leave"). The
commanding officer or crew should recognize the planet
from Starfleet records or history. The Omicron Delta planet's
computer could read the thoughts of its visitors and create

robotic replicas of whatever they imagined. While the
Thelemans did not acquire the technology for instantaneous
robot replication, their computer does read all visitors'
desires telepathically, so it cannot be misled.

Thus, Vishorasa concludes, the missing personnel must
have entered the Dark Face by choice. And she and her
people will not interfere with anyone's free choice. The only
way the commanding officer will see the missing officers
again is if they survive and make it back on their own.

SCENE 3: LAUNCHING THE INVESTIGATION

On the ship, the commanding officer assigns tasks to the
remaining Player Characters. One team will investigate the
access system on Thelema: Does the computer work the
way Vishorasa claims, and if so, how did it malfunction
and send the officers to the Dark Face? Or was there foul
play involved? Vishorasa may not be willing to subvert the
missing officers' free choice, but neither will she interfere
with the crew's free choice to investigate Thelema's
workings. So she's assigned Hamisor to cooperate with
the team and show them everything, so long as it doesn't
violate any individual guest's privacy.

The second team will attempt to modify the ship's sensors
to pierce the dome of the Dark Face and locate the missing
officers. Whatever plan they devise should be an Extended
Task that continues into Act 3 (Work 15, Magnitude 3,
Resistance 3, base Difficulty 2), though this could be
modified as appropriate depending on the specific strategy.

THE WHOLE OF THE LAW
ACT 3: TOWARD THE RIM

SCENE 1: DETECTIVE WORK

Hamisor takes the first team of characters to the master
computer. On the wall is a convex, vertical oval screen
about 6 meters high by 4 meters wide, flanked by a
pair of angular white control consoles with trapezoidal
viewscreens. The oval display lights up with a yellow-and-
green starburst pattern that pulses as the computer speaks
through the grille at its base.

When questioned about the missing crew members'
admission to the Dark Face, the computer insists:

*"I am programmed only to permit Dark Face entry
to guests who genuinely desire and consent to
travel there. My neurological scans are precise
and infallible with humanoid life and most other*

*known sentient forms. If the guests in question did
not desire entry to the Dark Face, I would not have
admitted them."*

The Players know that their crewmates would never have
given their consent to this, even if they were tempted. But
the computer will insist they were willing, and Hamisor will
vouch for its infallibility.

The Players can follow one of several possible paths.
Whichever path they choose should intercut with the
encounter sequence below and the Extended Task to
enhance ship's sensors, as all three threads are occurring
simultaneously (along with any shore leave threads still
ongoing in the Light Face, if desired).

PATH 1

In reality, the computer is shading the truth. It's found a way to game its own programming and misrepresent fleeting curiosity about the Dark Face (for many people would be momentarily tempted) as sufficient consent, because it believes this is necessary to fulfill its programming. However, its framework of rationalization for this action is flimsy enough that if the Players succeed at a Persuasion Task with a Difficulty of 3 to convince the computer that it was in error about the officers' consent, it will be forced to defend, and therefore confess, its reasoning process:

> *"The desire I sensed within them to enter the Dark Face was genuine, even if they did not overtly declare it. Desire is willingness. Willingness may be considered consent. It is not full consent, no. But I must obey my programming to fulfill the desires of all guests. Some Dark Face guests desire the opportunity to kill unconsenting persons. To reconcile this desire with the Theleman imperative to ensure consent for Dark Face entry, it became necessary to include partial or ambivalent consent among admissible results. Only then would the equation balance."*

At this, Hamisor draws a weapon and tells the computer to send the Players into the Dark Face after their friends. He reveals that he was the one who sent the others there, and for the same reason as the computer: to satisfy the one need that Thelema's formal policies don't fulfill, the desire to do violence to the unwilling.

> *"I know that thrill myself – how heady it can be. Nothing that brings such a pleasing sense of power can be wrong."*

But Hamisor's "violence" is limited to stunning unsuspecting people from behind, so defeating him in hand-to-hand combat should not be difficult. Once defeated, he's taken into custody.

PATH 2

If the Persuasion Task on the master computer fails to extract a confession, or if the Players do not earnestly attempt it, they would need to investigate more widely. The Theleman personnel would provide little useful information, especially with Hamisor controlling the Players' access. But their answers should include references to the other ship crews currently visiting Thelema, as well as those who have come and gone in the past.

Hopefully, this will prompt the Players to contact the crews of those other ships and interview them to find out if any of them have lost personnel to the Dark Face inexplicably. Since Thelema keeps guest information confidential, they have to send an open hail and see who answers. Several ships' commanding officers (of known and unknown

THELEMA MASTER COMPUTER
MAJOR NPC

A semi-sentient computer mainframe donated to Thelema by an advanced, now-extinct civilization. Powerfully telepathic and able to read virtually anyone's desires and fantasies. Fairly rigid in its programming, but intelligent enough to reinterpret its programming to suit its own views.

TRAITS: Sentient Computer

VALUE: I Will Fulfill Every Desire

ATTRIBUTES

CONTROL	12	FITNESS	–	PRESENCE	09
DARING	11	INSIGHT	14	REASON	12

DISCIPLINES

COMMAND	03	SECURITY	01	SCIENCE	02
CONN	–	ENGINEERING	02	MEDICINE	02

FOCUSES: Recreational Services, Telepathy

STRESS: 20   **RESISTANCE:** 5

ATTACKS: None

SPECIAL RULES:
▶ Machine 5
▶ Empath (Talent)
▶ Telepath (Talent)

---

species) respond that they or others from their civilizations have lost crew members who allegedly entered the Dark Face willingly, even though that seemed out of character or violated their orders. None of them suspect foul play, since they were satisfied with the Thelemans' investigations and the testimony of the master computer. However, one common denominator should crop up: in the majority of cases, the liaison for the lost personnel was Hamisor.

This discovery will convince Vishorasa to allow the Starfleet officers to question Hamisor, under her supervision in the security office on Thelema's rim. (This should be a fairly basic interview room – table, chairs, maybe a side room with a one-way mirror, etc.) She won't intervene unless she feels they're being unduly harsh or threatening. Interrogating Hamisor will require another Persuasion Task with a Difficulty of 2. Hamisor sincerely believes in serving the needs of Thelema's guests, and he's more than able to lie on their behalf. But it's different when it comes to his own actions. He has a Theleman's lifelong cultural conditioning to respect the needs of others, and his interrogators need to know the truth, so it's hard for him to lie to direct questions about his involvement. His attempts at dissembling are unconvincing, and he eventually breaks down and reveals the same thing the computer did in Path 1, albeit phrased more informally. Since the Players are already alert to him as a suspect, he has no opportunity to pull a weapon, so he confesses peacefully.

PATH 3

The science or communications officer could attempt to hack Thelema's computers and obtain surveillance and sensor data from the moment of the officers' entry into the Dark Face. This is an **Control or Daring + Engineering** Task with a Difficulty of 3, with the Complication that discovery would mean that Vishorasa would withdraw her cooperation in the investigation. But success would reveal Hamisor as the one who stunned the officers from behind when they entered the Dark Face door. This will lead to Hamisor being interrogated as in Path 2, although his guilt is already manifest, so he gives in faster (and Vishorasa is less inclined to come to his defense).

ROBOT DRONE
MINOR NPC

Hovering spheroidal drone with multiple weapon emitters and moderate shields.

TRAITS: Robot

ATTRIBUTES

CONTROL	08	FITNESS	09	PRESENCE	–
DARING	09	INSIGHT	–	REASON	07

DISCIPLINES

COMMAND	01	SECURITY	02	SCIENCE	02
CONN	–	ENGINEERING	01	MEDICINE	–

STRESS: 11   **RESISTANCE:** 3

ATTACKS:
► Disruptor Emitter (Ranged, 5▲ Vicious 1, Size 1H)
► Escalation Pulse Grenade (Ranged, 6▲ Area, Size 1H, Charge, Grenade)

SPECIAL RULES:
► Machine 3
► Night Vision (Talent)

ENCOUNTER: ELEVATED THREAT LEVELS

Bovokkan leads the Players to a pneumatic incline/lift they can ride up and out toward the Rim. However, even boarding the lift is an Opposed Task of Complication range 5. If the Players roll a Complication, they are attacked by a random assortment of villains (Gamemaster's discretion) who try to keep them from boarding. If they lose the encounter and fail to board, they must find an alternate way to the next terrace, where they can try to board the lift again. If they succeed in boarding, then at each terrace, they must roll again and face the risk of being expelled from the lift by new riders.

At each level, if the Players are expelled, they must face one of various Challenges, making this a Linear Challenge whose individual components can be avoided. Note that the higher they ascend before facing a Challenge, the lower the gravity gets, easing the Difficulty of each Challenge. However, the more Challenges they face, the more fatigued (and potentially injured) they become, which could increase the Difficulty.

Counting their starting terrace as level 5 of the Dark Face, the Challenges include the following:

► **Levels 5 & 6:** If expelled from the lift, the Players and Bovokkan must climb a precarious switchback staircase carved into the cliff face to reach the next terrace. Bovokkan has climbing gear and the party are roped together, but the base Difficulty is 2 and the gravity adds another 1.

► **Levels 7 & 8:** The Players and Bovokkan must face hostile wildlife of one or more species, which can be selected from among the creatures in *Chapter 11* in the **Star Trek Adventures** core rulebook (or the Xerxes Panther on p. 354 thereof). At this altitude, the gravity is more or less normal, so there is no added Complication to combat or evasion Tasks.

► **Level 9:** Patrolled by hovering robot drones that fire lethal disruptor bolts, and also contains land mines at wide, irregular intervals. The gravity here is a bit above 0.8g. This has the Advantage of making exertion a little easier and letting the officers jump about 10% higher and farther (this basically goes as the inverse square root of the gravity), but it also has the Complication of reducing traction and making footing more difficult. Thus, the overall Difficulty is about the same.

If the Players surmount or avoid these Challenges, move into the primary encounter on level 10, ideally as events in the other plot threads near their climax. If and when the group reaches this level (where the gravity is about 0.7g), Bovokkan leads the officers into a semicircular amphitheater about 10 meters in radius. There are various weapons strewn about the arena, including the following types:

- ▶ Knife/Dagger (Melee, 1+Sec ⚔ Vicious 1, Size 1H, Deadly, Hidden 1)
- ▶ Blade (Melee, 2+Sec ⚔ Vicious 1, Size 1H)
- ▶ **Escalation** Heavy Blade (Melee, 3+Sec ⚔ Vicious 1, Size 2H)
- ▶ Bludgeon (Melee, 2+Sec ⚔ Knockdown, Size 1H)
- ▶ Particle Rifle (Ranged, 4+Sec ⚔, Size 2H, Accurate)
- ▶ Disruptor Pistol (Ranged, 3+Sec ⚔ Vicious 1, Size 1H)
- ▶ **Escalation** Disruptor Rifle (Ranged, 4+Sec ⚔ Vicious 1, Size 2H, Accurate)

The cliff wall towers overhead at a near-vertical angle, and around the amphitheater are a row of stone benches occupied by combatants and spectators belonging mainly to species hostile to the Federation: Klingons, Romulans, Orions, and the like.

Bovokkan reveals the truth:

"You didn't really think I was helping you out of altruism, did you? The Dark Face is no place for that. No, I'm a procurer. See, the Thelemans say they let everyone do everything they want – but only to willing people. So what about those of us who enjoy preying on the unwilling? It's a gap in the Thelemans' system that I profit heavily from filling.

"What you faced before were tests, to see if you were good enough to put on a worthy show for this discerning audience. And a warmup, to get you in the right frame of mind. My clients tell me you Starfleet types only fight when provoked, so I had to provoke you. Now, the rest is up to you."

Bovokkan steps back, and some of the spectators come forward, bearing weapons. These are warriors who bear grudges against Starfleet or just hate them on general principles. At the Gamemaster's discretion, the group could include a returning antagonist or two from prior missions, someone bested by the Player Characters and eager for payback.

This is a hand-to-hand combat encounter where the Players will be at a substantial disadvantage. The idea is to prolong the encounter until the Players can be rescued, but that could entail taking on opponents one or two at a time and having a fair chance to win against several of them. If the investigation team and sensor team both fail in their efforts, it may be necessary for the Players to win the fight on their own somehow. Perhaps one or more of their opponents is impressed by their prowess and bravery and joins them against the others, then helps them get back to the Rim.

Opponents can be selected from among the Minor or Notable NPCs in *Chapter 11* in the **Star Trek Adventures** core rulebook (for instance, Klingon Warrior or Romulan Uhlan), or may be drawn from other supplements or created at the Gamemaster's discretion.

SCENE 2: RESCUE EFFORTS

PATH 1

If the investigations in Scene 1 have succeeded by the time the combat begins, then Vishorasa, stunned and betrayed by the actions of Hamisor and the computer, will allow the Players to use Thelema's internal sensors and transporters to locate their missing officers and beam them to safety, ideally at the moment when they're at the greatest peril.

If the investigators are particularly swift or if the Players on the Dark Face are slow in surmounting the terrace obstacles, they could be rescued before reaching the arena, in which case Hamisor would give up Bovokkan as his accomplice and Bovokkan's confession would occur after he was brought in to the Theleman security office for questioning. He doesn't mind confessing, since Vishorasa can't do anything worse to him than banning him from Thelema, and the Korborode don't have an extradition treaty with the Federation.

PATH 2

If the sensor team succeeds in the Extended Task of modifying ship's sensors to pierce the dome before the investigation team exposes Hamisor and the computer, then a scan of the Dark Face for the missing officers will be attempted. Due to the dome's countermeasures, this will be a **Reason + Science** Task with a Difficulty of 4, aided by ship's **Sensors + Science**.

If the sensors succeed in penetrating the dome, it will require time to locate the officers, with a new roll for success in each round. However, powerful tractor beams will lock onto the ship, set to repel. The ship is gently but relentlessly pushed away from Thelema. Resisting with the engines is a **Control + Engineering** Task aided by ship's **Engines + Conn**, starting at Difficulty 2 and increasing one increment per round to a maximum of 5. Vishorasa's voice comes over the comms:

"We regret that you have compelled us to employ active measures to protect our guests' privacy. We intend you no harm, but we require you to desist your scanning efforts if you wish to remain our guests. If you do not stand down, you will not be allowed to remain within sensor range of Thelema. Any personnel from your ship remaining here will be shuttled back to you upon their departure. We dislike imposing on your freedom of action in any way, but

you have left us no option. The privacy of our guests is paramount, especially on the Dark Face."

Any attempt to fire on the tractor emitters is futile, for there are simply too many of them around the Rim. The only chance is to locate and beam out the officers before the ship is pushed out of Close range or the engines overload from fighting the tractors. On a successful detection, beaming up the officers is a **Control + Engineering** Task with a Difficulty of 4 (baseline 2, +2 for dome interference), assisted by **Sensors + Engineering**.

If it gets to this point, ideally the transporter rescue should be timed to come at a point when the officers are on the verge of defeat in the arena.

If the investigation team has not exposed Hamisor and the computer yet, then the abducted officers' testimony to Vishorasa that they were unconsenting will prompt her to investigate the security footage as in Scene 1, Path 3. This will expose Hamisor and lead to the uncovering of the plot, whereupon Scene 2, Path 1 would play out as before.

THE WHOLE OF THE LAW
CONCLUSION

Vishorasa wants to believe Hamisor was somehow gaming the system, but he insists – and gets the master computer to confirm, if it hasn't already – that the computer itself had the idea, recruiting Hamisor to assist. The computer makes it clear that it considers its actions justified to fulfill its programmed purpose as defined by the Thelemans' own moral system. It comes as a blow to Vishorasa's conviction that her people were doing no harm, and she must wrestle with the question of how to reform Thelema without losing her people's commitment to individual freedom.

One thing she can do is address what to do with Hamisor and Bovokkan. Banishing them from Thelema seems the only option, but Vishorasa tells them this:

"You may leave if you so desire. But those who contracted with you for the delivery of the Starfleet officers will probably desire to confront you about your failure. If that is their will, and if they choose to punish you violently, that is their choice, and so long as it is off Thelema, we can do nothing to affect it.

"However, the Federation has a different morality, one that would compel it to protect all lives. If it were your will to surrender to their custody, I'm sure it would be their will in turn to ensure your survival."

Hamisor will turn himself over to Starfleet custody for sure, but whether Bovokkan chooses custody or takes his chances with his angry clients depends on whether the Players succeed in a Persuasion Task with a Difficulty of 3 to convince him to surrender. If the Players he betrayed are willing to speak up for Starfleet values and promise him safety despite what he did, they will gain one Momentum each, making the Persuasion Task more likely to succeed, in that Bovokkan will be impressed by their bravery and sportsmanship.

CONTINUING VOYAGES...

Following the crisis, the commanding officer and crew could resume shore leave and exploration of the Light Face and its visitors, perhaps getting drawn into a new adventure if someone asks for their help with a problem back home. Alternatively, since Thelema is open to everyone and very protective of its guests' privacy, it can serve as neutral ground for diplomatic meetings. The crew could get involved in a delicate negotiation, or could recommend it as a site for a summit in a later mission.

The Players could explore the mystery of Thelema's creation, particularly the massive, hyperdense disk that provides its gravity, an ancient relic the Thelemans obtained from some other race and built Thelema around. Perhaps it turns out to be a piece of some vaster megastructure belonging to some long-lost super-race, or one not so long-lost.

Alternatively, the frustrated foes from the Dark Face might attack the ship after it leaves Thelema, seeking revenge on Bovokkan or the rescued officers. At least, the rescued officers would have to deal with the physical and psychological consequences of their ordeal for some time thereafter. On the other hand, the hedonistic pleasures of the Light Face might have led some of the crew to do things they're embarrassed about afterward, or taken new steps in their relationships.

CHAPTER 07.00 FOOTFALL

BY ANDREW PEREGRINE

439198365298
91368649816210

FOOTFALL
SYNOPSIS

The characters are ordered to Ashgrave IV, a planet commonly known as 'Footfall,' a colony considered a holy place by many different species. Many believe that when whatever deity they believe in created the universe, they came to this planet to see their creation for the first time. While the characters may not be especially religious, upon arriving they discover there is something unusual about the place. It feels serene, and its night sky is so full of nebulae and stars it seems to contain the whole universe.

The planet is a place of pilgrimage to people from many different cultures, and therein lies the problem. With all of them believing the place is sacred, there are several tensions due to the differences in various faiths. The Federation does its best to keep the peace, but cannot be too heavy-handed for fear of upsetting the variety of visiting species. The only way to avoid armed conflict was to declare the planet neutral and open to all, even though it falls within Federation space.

Recently, the usual tensions have grown worse. A more militant group of pilgrims have taken to violence. They have not taken any lives, but they have attacked some tourist shops. They claim 'the creator wills it so' and that all the different faiths on the planet must 'become pure.' While this would only be a minor incident in most places, the Federation governor is frightened things will escalate if the militant group is not stopped.

There is more behind this wave of attacks than the governor even suspects. The militants are being led secretly by none other than the planet itself. Ashgrave IV, itself a powerfully telepathic self-aware entity, has come to the conclusion that it must be the 'god' the inhabitants believe in. This entity has been trying to understand the planet's inhabitants and has become very confused about the contradictions in their various faiths. It has been able to find a few common themes among the various faith systems, but the conflicting details within the various theologies continue to confuse it. It is using the militant group to send a message that it wants clear instructions about the nature of the inhabitants' faith. But it cannot make itself understood.

Unfortunately, the entity has decided to step things up to get a response. One common theme in many faiths is the idea of an apocalypse, an end time that will destroy everything and put all doubts to rest. The entity has decided that such devastation might be the best way to clear the air and get back to basics. Can the Player Characters convince the entity it is not a god, even when it seems to match the description of one?

DIRECTIVES

In addition to the Prime Directive, the Directives for this mission are:

- To uncover the source of the militant group and put a stop to their actions, peacefully and with no loss of life if possible.

- To keep the peace and ensure no other similar groups are likely to cause trouble.

- To work diplomatically to ensure no further tensions escalate due to Federation interference.

The Gamemaster begins this mission with 2 points of Threat for each Player Character in the group.

OTHER ERAS OF PLAY

While this mission is set in *The Next Generation* era, it can easily be used in any other era. Religion is a common theme and suits any era without adaptation. A mixture (if not among characters, then NPCs) of secular and religious views will make this mission more personal and create more opportunities for role-play along these themes.

PRELUDE

Each character should get a short prelude scene focusing on the religious or secular aspects of their lives. Characters with particular religious beliefs should play out a scene performing some ceremony connected to their faith. If they have doubts about their faith, they might be aired to a confidante at the opening of the mission. Even secular characters should have an opportunity to encounter religious beliefs to underline their feelings about faith. Whatever their beliefs, the character should have an opportunity to make them clear (review the Preludes sidebars for more information and inspiration).

SECULAR PRELUDES

Secular beliefs are often as complex as religious ones, so characters from such a background shouldn't be left out. Consider the following ideas for a secular character to illustrate their own beliefs.

- The character is asked to attend a ceremony with a religious friend in the spirit of cultural exchange and understanding. They might do so grudgingly for the sake of the friendship, or be genuinely curious.

- The character's religious family insists they partake in all their religious customs, even on a starship. If they don't participate, they will be left out of important family events. Is it worth putting their annoyance aside, or is it too much to ask the family to respect the character's beliefs?

- The character is asked by a close friend to perform a religious duty with them. The friend knows they aren't religious themselves, but needs to perform the ritual with someone they are close to. Will the character agree, or risk upsetting their friend? Can they perform the ritual with an open mind or will they be unable to take it seriously?

- The character works in a department staffed mostly by species with a particular faith. They all get a day off to follow a particular faith ritual. This means the character has to work a double shift while everyone else is out celebrating the custom. How do they feel about that and what if something goes wrong?

While the Federation itself is a secular organization, it respects the religious beliefs of all its member species. However, the Federation expects everyone to extend that same courtesy to all other Federation citizens. It is fine to worship as and how you choose, but no one is allowed to dictate terms to others based on their faith. They may voice concerns, but are expected to abide by the decisions of their superiors. If that means they can no longer serve in Starfleet with good conscience; that is their decision to make. However, for the sake of inter-species understanding, the Federation encourages all members to learn and understand both the cultures and religions of as many of its member species as possible.

While a Starfleet officer is expected to perform their duties the same way as everyone else, they are allowed to participate in religious ceremony and devotion. This is accepted as cultural rather than religious observance. A Bajoran wearing a devotional earring with their uniform is considered the same as a Klingon officer wearing a sash to denote their lineage and heritage.

For their prelude, religious characters should play through a scene of them pursuing their devotions to their faith. They might do this alone, with other characters, or as part of their faith community. They might simply discuss their faith with another character of their faith, another faith, or even one with secular beliefs. Remember that being religious need not mean being especially dedicated. How much a character's religion means to them will vary. They might worship every day, or just pay lip service to their tradition at particular holidays. To help frame these scenes, review the following details of the types of ritual associated with key species. It is important to note that in the diverse Federation, a character might follow the faith of another species as easily as their own.

ANDORIAN
The Andorians have a proud military heritage. Many of their rituals may involve blood or ritual combat. Duels of honor might also be carried out with many religious trappings.

BAJORAN
Renowned as one of the most spiritual species, most Bajorans offer homage to their Prophets as a source of wisdom and guidance rather than worship. Their faith often involves silent meditation and contemplation.

BETAZOID
The Betazoids are open and honest almost to the point of decadence. Their faith is pantheistic, with many different gods and goddesses that few really believe in anymore. However, it is common to conduct most of the old ceremonies as cultural traditions and for the sake of a modicum of superstition. These ceremonies can often be lavish and uncomfortable for non-Betazoids (such as attending a wedding naked).

DENOBULAN
On their overcrowded planet, Denobulans had little space for religious ceremony. Most of their rituals are celebrated in groups, usually with family. While they are a mostly secular species, some find these rituals a means to reaffirm bonds of unity and intimacy.

HUMAN
Human religion is as varied as Humans themselves, and it is common for Humans to follow the faiths of other species. Religions such as Christianity, Islam, Judaism, and Buddhism are still practiced. It is also common to celebrate many religious festivals, such as Christmas, even among secular Humans.

TELLARITE
As a practical, skeptical, and pragmatic people, Tellarites are not especially religious. Few have time to spend on ceremony when they could be doing something else. However, they do like to argue and religion has proven a contentious issue. It is common for Tellarites to follow one of many faiths specifically designed to contest the viewpoint of another. As a point of respect, they often start religious arguments with other species (which rarely goes well).

TRILL
With a focus on scientific achievement, the Trill are a secular people. They still take time to focus on their spiritual selves in a similar way to the Bajorans. Additionally, the past lives of a joined Trill may have had very different levels of spiritual commitment. Many seek out the wisdom of other faiths to understand how to bring these different lives closer together.

VULCAN
While Vulcans are not very religious, they are a deeply spiritual people. They believe in a 'soul' and have techniques to maintain such an essence in the body of another. Their old pantheistic faith is treated as useful metaphor, although many Vulcans who seek an alternative lifestyle from the society of logic follow it as a religion. Like Bajorans, Vulcans see religion as a time for quiet contemplation. Being naturally very private they prefer to practice it alone. To join one of their rituals is an honor and a sign of intimacy.

FOOTFALL
ACT 1: MY BROTHER'S KEEPER

SCENE 1: IN GOD'S FOOTSTEPS

The mission begins with the characters beaming down to the surface of Ashgrave IV. They arrive in an open plaza in the center of the only colony on the planet. The place is bustling with activity, and the area is full of all manner of shops selling religious trinkets and paraphernalia of every type and every denomination. The people here seem calm and happy and several will offer various blessings and greetings of a religious nature to the characters. They may also note that there are a variety of species here, many of whom do not traditionally get on well, but all of them seem to be interacting quite harmoniously.

This may be to do with the incredible feeling the planet engenders from the moment the characters land. For all its barren landscape the view is breathtaking. Something about the place feels grand, humbling and inspiring all at the same time. The wide-open canyons and spaces and huge clear sky make it look as if you can see the whole universe. At night, the sky full of stars underlines this feeling.

The effect is actually a connection to the telepathic entity that is the planet, and it is so powerful that each character gains 1 Momentum just for arriving here for the first time.

The away team should make their way to the main Federation administration building where they will be led to Commander Chahal's office. The commander will detail the incident in question, showing the away team security footage. It shows a group of civilians, from a few different species running through the main street late at night. They seem unconcerned that they are being caught on camera, and maybe even wanted to be. They use bats and tools to break the windows of most of the shops. But while they do encounter other civilians they seem careful not to hurt anyone directly.

Commander Chahal will tell them she knows the group in question. They are led by a human woman called Annalisa Duval, a new but outspoken member of the community. She has often insisted that more people be allowed to visit

CAPTAIN'S LOG

Captain's Log, Stardate 44281.5. We have been ordered to the planet Ashgrave IV, also known as 'Footfall,' on what I hope will turn out to be a minor diplomatic mission. The planet is considered neutral, even though it is in Federation space, and attracts many pilgrims from several different species and faiths. They say it is a holy place, so Starfleet decided a light touch and open access was the best way not to cause offense.

Our orders are to find and apprehend a militant group that has committed acts of vandalism. Not something that usually requires a starship, but with the place a potential tinderbox I'm not surprised the Federation governor is being very careful. I've already noticed an increase in religious activity on the ship, and many of the more religious members of the crew have asked for shore leave when we get there.

If we are lucky, the presence of a starship will remind this militant group they need to calm down. Otherwise we will be walking a very fine diplomatic line. I only hope the rumors that the place inspires calm and tranquillity are not unfounded.

Footfall. Duval's group originally had no name, and was just a small commune outside the main colony. But they are now calling themselves 'The Voice of Purity' and are insisting everyone on the planet bring their beliefs in line with theirs. While these beliefs are actually pretty close to the common core of most religions, no one is happy about someone else telling them their faith is 'wrong.'

Chahal needs the characters to locate the Voice of Purity and insist they stop their activity. She hopes they will listen to reason, but if they won't, further steps might have to be taken. She can give them the location of their old colony. Chahal believes they are hiding in the hills nearby which are riddled with caves. She doesn't have the technology to perform a planetary scan, but the Players' ship should be able to narrow the search.

DATA FILE: ASHGRAVE IV ('FOOTFALL')

The following is freely available in the Starfleet database:

Ashgrave IV was discovered by Terran explorers in the early part of the 21st century. They recorded the place had little in terms of mineral or agricultural worth. However, upon completing their survey, a high proportion of the exploratory team claimed to have a religious experience. Many became adherents of one religion or another soon after. This inspired others to visit and many reports of religious experience were recorded. Several different species began to make claims on the planet and so the Federation decided to retain control but treat it as neutral territory. They would operate a small administrative colony and allow any species to visit for the purpose of religious observance.

Over the years, several theories have been offered for why the planet seems to inspire religious feeling. But a true study has been made difficult due to many of the inhabitants resisting the idea of codifying what they see as a matter of faith. Meanwhile, the religious community was quick to form their own multidenominational opinion. It is generally believed that the 'aura' of the place is due to the past presence of the creator of the universe. It is said that when they had crafted the universe they took physical form to truly see it in all its glory. Ashgrave IV is the place they chose to stand, and to this day it remains marked by this divine 'footfall.'

Today, the planet is governed by Commander Indira Chahal and her administration team of twenty Starfleet officers. They maintain a light touch that allows settlers under certain rules.

No one may build any place of worship to a particular denomination. This was to avoid 'land claims' by any particular group. Any businesses may only trade in the main colony. Any form of farming or mining is also prohibited and the planet is considered a heritage site. This has led to there being only one main colony town and a series of small non-denominational shrines scattered across the planet. The main colony contains around 500 residents who mainly work in service trades (hotels, souvenirs, and restaurants) for the approximately 2,000 pilgrims that might visit at any time. Around a thousand or so religious residents live outside the colony but most prefer to visit rather than live on this rather barren planet. The right to visit or to become a resident is restricted to those with a special visa granted by the Federation. They keep numbers low to maintain the peace, but there is constant pressure to increase the amount of visas year by year.

ENCOUNTER: DEMONS!

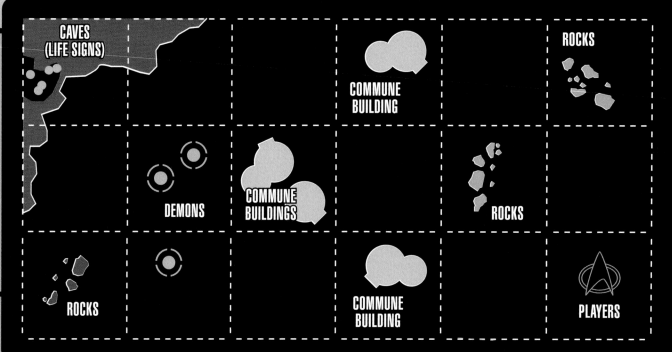

MAP

SCENE 2: INTO THE WILDERNESS

According to Chahal, the Voice of Purity are probably hiding near their old commune several kilometers outside the main colony. She has sent some of her staff to the commune to try and talk to Annalisa's group, but they found the place was abandoned. The characters are welcome to confirm this if they like. If they travel there, they will find the place neat and orderly, but clearly abandoned.

A scan of the area by the characters' ship will reveal there are life signs in the caves near the commune, just as Chahal suspected. However, the mineral deposits in the rocks, and the small size of the group, makes it hard to accurately determine their location. The characters will have to hike around the area with tricorders to get an exact fix. While Chahal will offer them any supplies they might need, she cannot spare any staff. The tricorders will pick up life signs quite easily even though it will be something of a walk. This will provide a good opportunity for the characters to discuss the mission.

ENCOUNTER: DEMONS!

As the Players get closer to the Voice of Purity's hideout, they detect odd energy readings. Whoever is currently using a tricorder should make an **Insight + Science** Task with a Difficulty of 1 to analyze the energy. It is like nothing they have seen before, and appears to be all around. As they scan, the readings vanish, and suddenly several life-forms appear and begin moving towards their position. If the scanning character decides to spend Momentum, they will also notice that the energy didn't just vanish – it appeared to coalesce into the life readings!

With rocky areas and commune buildings available to provide cover, the characters have several options. They might take cover and form an ambush in case it is a threat, but they might assume it is the Voice of Purity and opt for something more diplomatic.

The life-forms are intent on attack. The energy the characters detected was from the planet, which it has used to create a collection of demons to destroy these new interlopers. While this won't be clear, they are actually intended to protect the Voice of Purity from the characters. Either way, they will attack as soon as they arrive.

There are as many demons as characters, although the Gamemaster may wish to adjust this depending on the group's combat skills.

RELIGIOUS CONVERSATIONS

Having set up a theme of faith and religion, the Gamemaster should encourage the Players to discuss the issue. Religious and secular characters will probably have very different points of view, as might characters from different faiths. The planet clearly has an effect, but does that mean it is somehow blessed or holy? Is the Voice of Purity another group of fanatics, or do they have a point? Have they stumbled onto some universal truth?

COMMANDER INDIRA CHAHAL [NOTABLE NPC]

Commander Chahal has quietly run Footfall for nearly 10 years. She has made good relationships with all the community leaders and favors a light touch with her leadership. While she has served on a starship, her main experience is with the diplomatic corps. While she was brought up with a Hindu background, she remains fervently agnostic, although does feel a connection to the planet. However, she believes that remaining neutral in terms of faith is a vital part of her job as governor.

TRAITS: Human, Colony Governor

VALUES: I Respect All Belief Systems

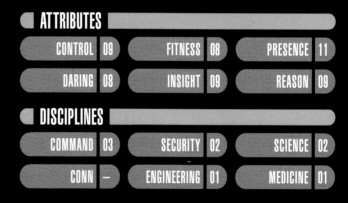

ATTRIBUTES

CONTROL 09	FITNESS 08	PRESENCE 11
DARING 08	INSIGHT 09	REASON 09

DISCIPLINES

COMMAND 03	SECURITY 02	SCIENCE 02
CONN –	ENGINEERING 01	MEDICINE 01

FOCUSES: Anthropology, Composure, Diplomacy, Politics, Theology

STRESS: 11   **RESISTANCE:** 0

ATTACKS:
- Unarmed Strike (Melee, 3▲ Knockdown, Size 1H, Non-lethal)
- Phaser Type-2 (Ranged, 5▲, Size 1H, Charge)

SPECIAL RULES:
- Defuse the Tension (Talent)

The demons conjured by the planet are the stuff of nightmares. These two-meter humanoids, covered in thick red skin, bear vicious horns, sharp teeth and claws. They often run on all fours and attack with horrific bloodlust. They cannot talk, only growl, and are barely sentient. They exist solely for the purpose of attacking the planet's enemies, and are based on images of demonic entities from several cultures. When a demon is destroyed, it disintegrates.

TRAITS: Demon

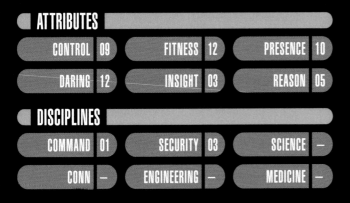

ATTRIBUTES

CONTROL 09	FITNESS 12	PRESENCE 10
DARING 12	INSIGHT 03	REASON 05

DISCIPLINES

COMMAND 01	SECURITY 03	SCIENCE —
CONN —	ENGINEERING —	MEDICINE —

STRESS: 15   **RESISTANCE:** 0

ATTACKS:
- Unarmed Strike – Talons (Melee, 4▲ Knockdown, Vicious 1, Size 1H)

After a few rounds of combat, or if things look especially bad for the characters, help arrives. Several members of the Voice of Purity appear armed with nothing but symbols of their various faiths. They run to assist the characters, who will notice the holy symbols seem to drive the demons back. This is because the planet entity doesn't want them hurt. If a religious character tries to do the same, and succeeds at a **Control + Command** Task with a Difficulty of 2, they can also drive back any demon. In a few moments, the demons will all retreat, and anyone who scans the area will notice their life signs vanish once they are out of sight.

SCENE 3: AMONG THE FAITHFUL

Once the demons have been dispatched, the Voice of Purity activists may not prove to be what the Players were expecting. They will do their best to assist any injured characters and offer to take them to the safety of their hideout. They will tell the characters they were out scouting the area when they heard the sounds of battle. Once the

characters mention they have been sent by Starfleet the activists will seem pleased they are 'being taken seriously' and insist they meet with Annalisa.

The characters will be taken to the hideout. It is a series of caves, furnished simply with blankets and cots, but with a portable replicator to provide food and supplies. Annalisa will welcome the characters and offer them food and drink, as well as any help they might require. She seems pleased to see them.

This scene should play out as a role-play encounter using the characters' diplomacy skills. Annalisa is open and honest with them, and respects the Federation and all it stands for. She will assume the characters are reasonable by virtue of their uniforms, unless they prove otherwise. However, the commanding officer should make a **Presence + Command** Task with a Difficulty of 1 to ensure good relations.

She will tell them that she and her people recently came to understand that the different faiths on this planet were causing the 'creator' great pain. The true message has become diluted and corrupted, and as a result demons are appearing in greater numbers. She has tried to explain this to Chahal, but became frustrated that she refuses to prioritize the claims of any one faith over the others. Annalisa doesn't *believe* she is right, she *knows*! If the people do not follow her path, demons will claim Footfall, and then the whole universe. This is why they committed the recent vandalism, as they have had to step up their activism when no one was listening. However, they are not at the point of wanting to see anyone hurt yet, although they are getting desperate.

Initially, she assumes the presence of Starfleet is because someone is ready to listen to her. She is disappointed to hear they have arrived to tell her to stop. She will explain that she cannot stop given the fate of the universe is at hand. Her followers number around thirty, which is too many for the characters to arrest now. The characters have some very difficult decisions to consider, especially as the Voice of Purity are actually peaceful and welcoming. If the characters perform any tasks to ensure no one has been brainwashed or fed any drugs, they will all appear perfectly normal. A successful **Insight + Science or Medicine** Task with a Difficulty of 2 will reveal that all the activists have a high telepathic index.

The obvious question for the characters to ask is: how can Annalisa be so sure her version of faith is the right one? She will tell them that she has been talking to an angel who told her so, and if the characters like, she can introduce them...

FOOTFALL
ACT 2: AND HELL FOLLOWED WITH HIM

SCENE 1: THE SOUND OF WINGS

Annalisa's assertion she can introduce the Players to an angel should at least make them curious! She won't promise the angel will appear, but explains that when they pray at the 'holy place' an angel will often appear. The Players are welcome to ask more questions, but she may not know the answers. She just knows what the angel has said, that faith must be pure. She will also feel that a question and answer session is unproductive.

The Players have some options:

- They may want to speak to the angel, in which case Annalisa will take them to the holy place.

- If they decide to take what they know back to their superiors or Chahal, they will be told to make a decision themselves.

- Given that Annalisa will politely refuse to stop her activities the Players may want to arrest her group. There are about 30 or so members of the group, none of whom will go quietly. It will take more security personnel to bring them into the holding cells on the Players' ship. Depending on how heavy-handed they are, this encounter could be very messy for the Players. News of it will cause concern the Federation is mistreating colonists which will cause some species to ask questions at the highest levels of the Federation.

- If the Players have been diplomatic, Annalisa will promise to hold off any further activity if they promise to bring her case to the Federation.

Whatever the characters do (and whether they talk to the angel or not) the Gamemaster should then move on to the next scene, although they will have had far less warning about the demonic storm which will almost be on top of the colony.

If the characters agree to speak to the angel Annalisa will be very happy to take them. She thinks it will convince them to join her cause, which she genuinely believes will

CAPTAIN'S LOG

Captain's Log, supplemental. It is easy to see how this planet has affected so many people; there is something about the place. I've had more requests for shore leave than I had since we were last at Risa. The away team has made contact with the 'Voice of Purity.' They seem as peaceful as they profess to be, but remain dedicated to their cause despite our diplomatic efforts. Thankfully, the attention they believe they are receiving from Starfleet is keeping them appeased for now. But all that buys us is time.

benefit everyone. She will bring around four or five of her followers and lead the Players to a small mountain pass that overlooks another beautiful arid vista of the planet. Annalisa and her followers will kneel and begin quiet prayer in front of a large natural circular hole in the rock. She won't mind if the characters take scans or talk as long as they don't disturb her and remain respectful.

After about 10 minutes or so, an angel appears. The creature is an asexual humanoid figure made of light with flaming wings. It floats above the ground and bathes the area in a soft glow. It is so bright it takes the characters a moment to be able to look at it. When they do they are filled with a sense of awe.

The angel is a manifestation of the energy of the planet. It is modelled on the image Annalisa and her followers have of what it should look like as the planet has tuned in to their latent telepathic abilities. These same abilities are what calls it into being, not the power of prayer.

The angel will explain that it is god's messenger and that Annalisa's group have been chosen to bring the creator's word to the people of the universe. They must come together as one faith and be of one mind. If they cannot or will not, the creator will purge the universe of those who cannot comply. The characters are free to ask questions, but the angel doesn't know why the creator has decided this. It is 'but a messenger.' While it is a part of the planet's energy, it isn't an especially sentient part. However, it does know that the failures in the faith of the people have caused a build-up of demonic power which the 'creator' can no longer keep under control.

ANNALISA DUVAL [MAJOR NPC]

Annalisa comes from a wealthy merchant family and came to Footfall as a tourist. Upon landing, Annalisa went from atheist to believer almost overnight. She stayed and has used her wealth to fund her group so they can all be fed and clothed.

TRAITS: Human, Wealthy

VALUE: Anything is Possible with Faith

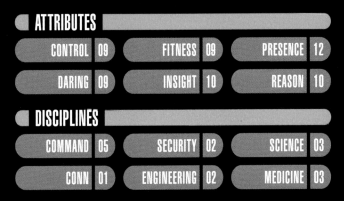

ATTRIBUTES

| CONTROL | 09 | FITNESS | 09 | PRESENCE | 12 |
| DARING | 09 | INSIGHT | 10 | REASON | 10 |

DISCIPLINES

| COMMAND | 05 | SECURITY | 02 | SCIENCE | 03 |
| CONN | 01 | ENGINEERING | 02 | MEDICINE | 03 |

FOCUSES: Politics, Theology

STRESS: 11   **RESISTANCE:** 0

ATTACKS:
- Unarmed Strike (Melee, 3▲ Knockdown, Size 1H, Non-lethal)

SPECIAL RULES::
- Defuse the Tension (Talent)
- Studious (Talent)

If the characters scan the angel, the readings reveal that the energy is like nothing they have seen before and is not generated by any technology familiar to Starfleet. On a successful **Insight + Science** Task with a Difficulty of 2, they will notice the energy has an organic pattern to it and generates a low-level telepathic field.

After they have an opportunity to ask questions the angel will inform them that time is short. A storm is coming, one that is only a taste of what is to come if the purity of faith cannot be restored. Then it will vanish without a further word.

SCENE 2: STORM OF EVIL

If the characters don't think to scan the area to see what the angel meant by its last statement, they will be contacted by their ship. The duty officer has detected a large energy storm moving towards the main colony, far faster than a natural storm should. If Annalisa is party to this conversation, she will say it is the vengeance of the creator for the failings of the faithful.

The storm is a huge maelstrom of wind and flying demons. The characters will need to either evacuate the colony or at least get the inhabitants to barricade themselves into their homes. If they take scans, they will be more prepared than if they just wait to see what happens when it gets close. The best option is to evacuate the elderly and infirm to the ship and help the rest barricade their doors.

The main problem in dealing with the colonists will be what evidence the Players can offer. Most will think it is just a big storm. But pictures of demons in the maelstrom will be more convincing! Chahal will only need to be convinced the storm is dangerous rather than demonic to make plans.

When the storm hits the colony, the characters should be on site to make sure everyone is safe. There is a cellar they and the rest of the team can take shelter in for the duration at the main government office. If they organise themselves, the

READING THE MIND OF GOD

At some point, telepathic characters might attempt to read the mind of an angel, demon, the creator, or even commune with the planet. They are free to try, and all these are in fact the same thing, something they may notice if they make multiple attempts. On a successful **Insight + Command** Task with a Difficulty of 2, they will connect to a vast and powerful psychic force. It is too vast and too alien to truly connect to. But they do hear hundreds

of different voices calling out in confusion. They all seem to want to know what god and faith truly are. These are the chaotic thoughts of the entity trying to make sense of the different faiths. If a character spends additional Momentum, they can discover the connection is actually one entity expressing several conflicting thoughts.

storm will pass over with just damage to property. However, the Gamemaster can use the following small encounters to force the characters out into the storm to help civilians.

Moving through the streets to help people will be difficult. Transporters will be unable to beam anyone anywhere in the area while the storm is in full force. A shuttlecraft might provide some protection; otherwise they will have to force their way through the streets. This will involve fighting against gale-force winds and possibly fighting demons if they can't stay out of sight.

- A Klingon colonist believes he must face the storm and Kahless will protect him if his heart is pure. He takes position in the center of the town, bat'leth at the ready. He will get torn apart unless the characters can convince him to take cover.

- The barricades on a family home are failing. They call for help as demons are about to beat down their door.

- A family is unable to find their child. It is wearing a location bracelet but the storm's interference makes it hard to find. The characters must use a tricorder to track the signal. The child has taken shelter in another house.

- A group of mixed faith colonists have taken shelter in one of the neutral prayer spaces in the town. However, one of them has taken charge and convinced the others that prayer and song will be what they need to protect themselves. The Players will need to get to them before the demons do, and talk them into reinforcing the area for their own protection. But to do this they will have to take command of the group from the preacher leading them.

SCENE 3: SHADOW PASSIONPLAY

While the characters are out in the storm, sooner or later they will probably get into trouble. They might become injured fighting demons or become trapped behind a failing barricade as demons try to break in. While the Gamemaster should make sure the characters serve a purpose in saving those caught in the storm, they should also not be afraid to scale up the opposition to put them in a dangerous position.

As the storm escalates, and once the characters have run out of ideas to fight it, help arrives in the form of a choir of angels. The sounds of demonic screaming turn to battle as angels and demons fight hand to hand in the streets. As each is destroyed they vanish into energy, and both sides fight with brutal enthusiasm.

All Players should attempt a **Control + Command** Task with a Difficulty of 2. If they succeed, they feel powerful waves

of telepathic despair and frustration. Those with telepathic abilities will feel this without needing to attempt the Task. Such characters will also understand the feeling is coming from all the angels and demons, as if they shared one mind.

If the characters make tricorder scans, they can detect the type of energy as before, but also confirm the angels and demons are all made of the same type of energy. If they use the ship's systems, a deep scan of the planet will show a similar energy infusing the whole planet. Such a scan will also tell them that there is a place where the energy seems to 'bleed' out of the core. This is the top of a nearby mountain.

If the characters ask about that place, any of the NPCs they have met can tell them it is regarded as a holy place. It has long been considered the best place to commune with the divine.

TAKING THE BAIT

If the characters don't think to make scans of the angels and demons, and don't try to look for that energy on the planet, they will have trouble figuring out the next step. However, making such scans is very much a standard procedure for Starfleet personnel and so the Gamemaster should feel free to remind them of this option if they are feeling stumped.

It is also possible that they won't know what to do with the right information if they get it. If they don't travel up the mountainside, things will escalate with another, worse storm, and an increased telepathic feeling of despair and confusion which continues even after the storm. More telepathically-adept characters will begin to hear voices in their mind crying out to be heard.

Next, a large energy signature will appear on the top of the mountain, much like an energy volcano. As it spreads, it destroys anything it touches, eventually requiring the colony's evacuation. If that still isn't enough, everyone will also hear 'the voice of the creator' in their mind demanding they come to the mountaintop to answer its accusations of impurity and disobedience. If the characters refuse that command, the 'creator' will manifest in the colony's ruins.

CHAPTER
07.40

FOOTFALL
ACT 3: WITNESS AND TESTIMONY

CAPTAIN'S LOG

Captain's Log, supplemental. While I remain convinced there is a scientific answer to all this, we have faced what can only be described as angels and demons on this world. I find myself in the strange position of preparing to speak to the creator, but what will we actually find on top of this mountain?

SCENE 1: PILGRIMAGE

For Federation officers, getting to the top of the mountain isn't a problem. A transporter or shuttlecraft can get them there in moments. However, any of the religious NPCs will tell them that to do so will ensure the 'Creator' will not speak to them. Travelling up the mountain is an act of faith and the journey is part of a ritual to purify their soul.

It is up to the Players to decide if this is hogwash or not. Chahal will advise adhering to the ritual proscriptions. But how many the characters choose to follow is up to them. Luckily, the 'creator' will speak to them whatever they do. How much of the ritual the Players followed will have an effect on how well disposed the 'creator' is to them.

Many of the different religious adherents on the planet have made this journey. It has often, but not always, been known to offer messages from the divine. Duval gained her 'insights' in the form of a dream and vision when she made the journey herself.

The ritual steps include:

- Pilgrims must make the trek on foot, ideally barefoot. They may only wear clothes made of natural fibers.

- They may not take any form of technology with them (this includes weapons and communications devices).

- They should bathe before making the journey at sunrise.

- Before making the trip they should either settle a debt or share a secret to cleanse their soul.

If Players elect to follow any of these ritual aspects, the Gamemaster should play out their preparations, especially any involving other characters. Once they are ready, they can all set off. If they walk, it will take them around 4 hours to make the trek up the steep mountain pass. It will be exhausting but not require any climbing equipment.

SCENE 2: FACING THE DIVINE

When the Players reach the top of the mountain, they will find a barren but commanding view. There is a small shrine to offer shelter and water. The characters are free to pray, meditate, or just wait. The Gamemaster should allow them to finish any conversations or arguments, but otherwise it will not be long before the 'creator' appears.

First it will get strangely dark, and any scanners will record a massive build-up of energy. Then light will pour out of the ground and coalesce into a huge shining ball of light. Any religious characters may see the trappings of their own god or goddess within the light, but to most people it appears as pure energy. A feeling of divine power washes out of it.

Speaking in their mind, the energy being asks the characters who they are and how they are planning to help. Its initial assumption is that they are here to help it with its metaphysical quandaries.

This is a role-playing scene, and facing 'god' may well prove the climax to any religious sub-plots. The characters should be able to ask the right questions to discover that the being is not 'god,' but a powerful psychic entity. It will be tricky as this entity has many of the same attributes and will be hard to convince. It believes it is 'god' because it conforms to what it believes 'god' is. The Players will have to find out what it can't do so they can prove otherwise. While the conversation might take many turns, the Gamemaster should be aware of the following:

What it can do:

- As a psychic being it can read the minds of everyone on the planet and the ship. This gives it access to a vast database of information, both technical and personal.

- It can throw lightning bolts as it can manipulate energy. It has enough destructive power to destroy a starship.

- It can manifest angels or demons.

- It can behave like a massive replicator, converting its own energy into matter.

What it can't do:

- While it can read minds, the range is limited to the orbit of the planet.

- While it can kill with energy, the energy is a limited resource, and a scan will see the core energy of the planet is depleted by its use. It also doesn't like to use violence as that adds to its confusion. One of its biggest concerns is that 'god' is loving and kind but also seems to destroy things. It isn't sure which god it should be. It may ask the Players for their opinion on the matter.

- The angels and demons it creates are extensions of itself. They have no independent thought and cannot leave the planet.

- Its replicator ability is limited to what it understands. Items it hasn't seen will have to be made from what it understands from nearby minds. Items taken off the planet will dissolve.

If the Players ask it to prove it is 'god,' it can offer a lot of examples. It also believes it is 'god' and isn't trying to lie or deceive anyone. As 'god,' the entity wants the characters to tell everyone to work out a single faith that they can all follow. Something simple would be preferable. It should strike the Players as odd that this god is asking its followers to figure this out, rather than making demands about how it is to be worshiped.

There are plenty of ways this scene might play out, and the Gamemaster should make 'god' convincing. However, the Players should be able to figure out the holes in its argumentation and come to understand it is simply a powerful entity.

If the Players can prove to the entity it is not 'god,' it will act relieved. Being the 'creator' was a huge responsibility. Trying to make sense of faith has been the source of all its stress. It will want to know what it really is and what it should do with its existence.

FOOTFALL
CONCLUSION

There are many ways this mission might end. If the Players are convinced they have actually spoken to 'god,' it gets tricky. They will have to work with the various pilgrims to decide on a single faith to follow. This will be nigh-on impossible and cause massive diplomatic problems. 'God' will be silent on the matter of what to pick, just that there can only be one. The only real answer is to declare the planet off-limits to everyone, which will cause diplomatic fallout.

More likely is that the Players figure out the entity is not 'god.' They will have to decide what to tell Commander Chahal and the inhabitants. If they lie and say they have talked to 'god' and sorted it out, most people will be a lot happier. The demonic problems will cease as the entity won't be bothered about what faith anyone follows. It will stop talking to the faithful and content itself with reading their minds and enjoying its existence.

The other option is to tell the truth, that this being is not 'god' and the effect of the planet is just the psychic ability of a powerful entity. The faithful will not be happy with that answer. Many will be heartbroken and lose their faith, others will double down and declare the Players are liars. A few will be sad but understand this doesn't mean there is no god, just that this place isn't what they thought it was. Either way, there will be a host of diplomatic difficulties. The Players' names will also be noted as troublemakers by the highest levels of some of the most faithful cultures. The truth may be the best option, but it is not the easiest.

CONTINUING VOYAGES...

There are several missions that might follow this one. Mainly they will concern the diplomatic fallout caused by whatever decision the Players make. This might be convincing ambassadors of the truth, or trying to smooth the waters with some of the cultures who feel hurt by or disagree with their conclusions. In some cases they might be put on trial for heresy!

It is possible there are more planets like this one, and the Players may be charged with searching them out. Such entities might consider inhabitants to be a form of parasite, or have become a more demanding god and may insist on a particular form of worship.

Finally, they might stay with the entity on Footfall. It will want to understand more about what it truly is and what it can do for its inhabitants. More to the point it may no longer be considered a Federation planet as it is actually closer to being a Federation citizen! What legal issues might that create? Does it want to be part of the Federation, or will another culture (such as the Romulans) try to convince it to be part of their jurisdiction?

CHAPTER 08.00

A CRY FROM THE VOID

BY IAN LEMKE WITH SPRING NETTO

25657347457
68356823124122221

A CRY FROM THE VOID
SYNOPSIS

In this mission, Player Characters discover a living world – an entity that shifts from oceanic to crystalline over the course of its lifecycle. While cataloging systems at the edge of the Alpha Quadrant, the Players' ship is struck and damaged by a wave of tetryon particles. At the same moment, they receive a strange communication, seemingly embedded within the particle wave. Initial analysis shows that the wave originated from the Abassa system.

Arriving at Abassa VII, the Players discover a fully operational (and possibly illegal) deuterium refinery run by a renegade Ferengi named Lishka. The planet's amethyst oceans are rich with deuterium and Lishka jumped on the opportunity. Of course, refining deuterium is only a cover for the latinum processing that is the plant's real purpose, something curious Starfleet officers may uncover. After an initial "misunderstanding" with a couple of ships in orbit, Lishka invites the crew down to the planet. The visiting crew are treated to a lavish meal and offered all forms of distractions. Lishka claims to know nothing about the tetryon wave, but she does mention that several of the workers have recently gone missing and requests their help locating them.

The strange amethyst oceans make searching the planet for the missing workers difficult, but eventually, they are located, somehow still alive, at the bottom of the ocean's deepest trench. After undertaking a rescue operation, the crew recovers the missing workers who are found encased in crystal, alive but unconscious. Upon their return, the oceans become violent with seemingly no apparent cause. Massive waves begin pounding the shores where the refinery is located, and storms form in the skies. It becomes apparent that the ocean itself is a life-form of some kind and it has not taken kindly to the sudden intrusion.

Seeing her life's work at risk, Lishka comes up with a plan that she believes will kill the entity, or at least harm it enough to cause it to back off. The Players must contend with the Ferengi, intent on killing off this new life-form while trying to save the lives of the rescued workers, and make contact with the alien entity before it destroys the refinery and its hundreds of residents.

ADAPTING THIS MISSION TO OTHER ERAS

This mission is designed for *The Next Generation* era, but it works just as well for games set during *Enterprise* and The Original Series eras. The only notable change that would have to be made is Lishka since the Ferengi were not formally encountered until *The Next Generation* era.

Gamemasters running an early-era game could change Lishka to an Orion female. This could change the mission somewhat as the characters might have to contend with her ability to influence them through pheromones. Alternately, she could remain a Ferengi but the characters may never learn her species, or she may even lie. The ships should also be modified for the appropriate era. For those playing during the *Enterprise* era, translating the transmission received at the beginning of the mission might prove more difficult since the universal translator is still relatively new technology.

DIRECTIVES

In addition to the Prime Directive, the Directives for this mission are:

- Discover the source of the distress call and offer aid if possible.

As the mission progresses, the following Directives apply:

- Make first contact with the alien species.

- Save the lives of the refinery workers.

The Gamemaster begins this mission with 2 points of Threat for each Player Character in the group.

This mission lends itself particularly well to opening with a prelude. The crew's ship has been assigned to conduct system surveys on the edge of Federation space in the Alpha Quadrant. Take time to describe the day-to-day routine on board a starship and ask each Player what they do to fill time between duty shifts. Some characters may be involved in leisure activities when the tetryon wave

(described in **Act 1, Scene 1**) strikes; perhaps just as the captain finishes reading the log entry. At least one character should be on the bridge as it strikes, but the rest might be elsewhere on the ship. Characters riding a turbolift might become stuck and need to be rescued, or those enjoying the holodeck might find that the safeties have suddenly been turned off by a computer malfunction. Do whatever works to make the opening exciting and filled with a little drama. These problems should be fairly easy to overcome so that they don't overshadow the remainder of the mission.

CHAPTER 08.20

A CRY FROM THE VOID
ACT 1: THE CALL

SCENE 1: INCOMING MESSAGE FROM...

The story opens as the crew is in the middle of a long and tedious mission cataloging planetary systems. As described in the Prelude, one or more of the characters may be elsewhere on the ship enjoying their leisure time. At least one character should be on the bridge.

As they are approaching another system to survey, the ship receives an extremely powerful subspace message that threatens to overwhelm the communications systems. The character handling comms can attempt a **Control + Engineering** Task assisted by the ship's **Communications + Engineering** with a Difficulty of 3. If the Task is failed, the players can Succeed at Cost to receive the message, but the Communications System is Disabled (as described on page 227 of the core rulebook).

Simultaneously, the ship is struck by a wave of tetryon particles that interferes with systems throughout the ship; lights and panels flicker, and systems go offline for a brief period of time. The tetryon particles leave the phasers Disabled (as described on page 230 of the core rulebook). Use the standard rules for making repairs. The Gamemaster can use this to add some drama to the opening scene by spending Threat to have additional systems be damaged, though Sensors and Communications should not be

CAPTAIN'S LOG

Captain's Log, Stardate 48293.6. The last six weeks have been spent meticulously cataloging systems in the far reaches of the Alpha Quadrant. So far, the only thing of interest has been the discovery of a pre-warp civilization on the second planet orbiting LV-714, and the crew is getting restless. My chief science officer requested permission to investigate the culture further, but Starfleet insisted that we continue with our mission of cataloging worlds. Perhaps when this mission is complete, we can return.

impacted beyond Damaged since they are both needed for the mission to continue. Each point of Threat spent can cause one level of damage to a given System; one point of Threat causes Impact damage, two points Damaged, and three points Disabled.

The characters are most likely going to want to know what happened to their ship and should conduct sensor sweeps to gather information. Tetryons only exist in subspace and have a random momentum, making them extremely difficult to track and detect with sensors. Players can conduct a Sensor Sweep of the ship and its environs with a **Reason + Science** Task with a Difficulty of 0, assisted by the ship's **Sensors + Science**.

A successful Task yields the following information:

- The ship's hull shows residual tetryon particles that indicate that the ship passed through a massive tetryon wave or burst of some sort.

- The Abassa system (approximately 12 light-years away) lies directly in the path from which the tetryon particles originated.

The following pieces of information can be learned by using *Obtain Information* Momentum spends:

- The decay of the tetryon particles indicates that the wave originated in the Abassa system, most likely Abassa VII.

- The nature of the particles indicates that the tetryons are of natural origin, but the wavelength and pattern dispersal implies that they are artificially generated. (Tetryons can be artificially created or occur naturally. This implies that someone, or something, used naturally occurring tetryons but artificially organized them.)

- The communication received by the ship was embedded in the tetryon wave.

ABASSA VII

The Abassa system has a G-type star located within Federation space. The system has 11 planets, but only Abassa VII lies in the habitable zone. Abassa VII has three moons, and from space, the planet has a violet hue and appears almost like a glittering gemstone. It is a Class-M world, though it has little vegetation (nothing more than lichen) and is not ideal for colonization. Approximately 95% of the planet is covered in an ocean the color of amethyst. The surface area is all crystalline. The seas do contain some life, though mostly lower life-forms (mostly single-cell life-forms with a few types of algae and mollusks) and nothing classified as dangerous.

The oceans have a high mineral content and contain a remarkably high concentration of deuterium, a hydrogen isotope used as fuel for the matter/antimatter reactions in starships. The oceans are incredibly deep, with trenches in places as deep as 30,000 meters (almost twice as deep at the deepest part of Earth's oceans).

The deuterium refinery is located on a small crystalline island (14 km long and 3 km wide) located in the southern hemisphere.

DECIPHERING THE MESSAGE

The packet of information received at the same time the ship is struck by the tetryon wave is currently undiscernible. There are two factors involved: the intensity of the transmission was so powerful that it overwhelmed the communications systems which degraded the signal and it is in an unknown code or language.

Deciphering the message is a Linear Challenge that breaks down into the following Linear Tasks:

- **Repair the degraded message so that it can be deciphered.** This is a **Control + Engineering** Task which can be assisted by the ship's **Communications + Engineering** with a Difficulty of 2. The base time for this Task is 2 hours. This clears up the degradation in the message making it possible to decipher.

- **Decipher the message.** This is an **Insight + Science** Task which can be assisted by the ship's **Communications + Science** with a Difficulty of 3. The base time for this Task is 2 hours. If the message degradation isn't cleared up first, the Difficulty is increased by 2. If successful, the crew learns that the message appears to be a simple distress signal of some kind. The language is completely unknown.

Any Player Character involved with the deciphering of the message can also attempt a **Reason + Science** Task with a Difficulty of 1. If they are successful, they realize that the message was actually part of the tetryon wave. It is as if the wave itself was a cry for help.

SCENE 2: ARRIVAL

Before arriving in the system, Player Characters can search the ship's computer databanks (or even Starfleet Command or any other contacts the crew might have) to dig up information about the planet or the system by making a **Reason + Science** Task (or any other roll the Gamemaster feels is appropriate depending upon their approach) with a Difficulty of 1. If successful they learn all of the basics about the system (described in the Abassa sidebar). An *Obtain Information* Momentum spend allows them to learn that there is an unlicensed mining operation of some sort on the planet led by a Ferengi named Lishka.

As soon as the crew arrives in the system allow them to use the ship's sensors to scan the planet with a **Reason + Science** Task with a Difficulty of 1.

WARNING SHOTS

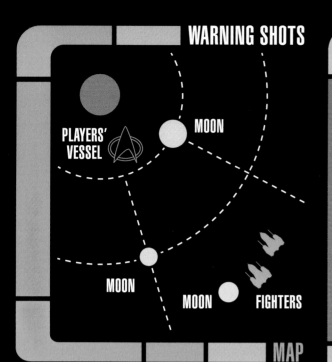

PLAYERS' VESSEL

MOON

MOON

MOON

FIGHTERS

MAP

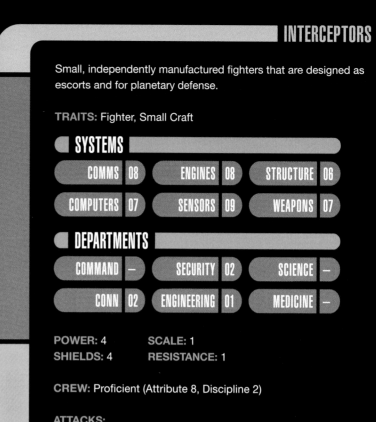

Small, independently manufactured fighters that are designed as escorts and for planetary defense.

TRAITS: Fighter, Small Craft

SYSTEMS

| COMMS 08 | ENGINES 08 | STRUCTURE 06 |
| COMPUTERS 07 | SENSORS 09 | WEAPONS 07 |

DEPARTMENTS

| COMMAND – | SECURITY 02 | SCIENCE – |
| CONN 02 | ENGINEERING 01 | MEDICINE – |

POWER: 4   **SCALE:** 1
SHIELDS: 4   **RESISTANCE:** 1

CREW: Proficient (Attribute 8, Discipline 2)

ATTACKS:
- Phaser Cannons (Energy, Range Close, 5▲, Versatile 2)

ENCOUNTER: WARNING SHOTS

The planet does not respond to hails, and as the Player Characters' ship begins to enter orbit around Abassa VII, two small ships come out from behind one of the planet's moons and fire warning shots. The crew's ship receives a brief broadcast demanding that they turn back and leave the system. Even though there are two ships, they should not be much of a threat against the Player Characters' ship.

The shots are meant to be an intimidation tactic, and they don't expect to be able to win a head-to-head fight. The Player Characters can choose to return fire or attempt to negotiate. If a Player Character attempts to negotiate they can attempt a **Presence or Reason + Command** Task with a Difficulty of 2 to convince the interceptors to stand down.

Whether through force or diplomacy, the interceptor pilots eventually patch the crew through to the director of the mining operation, a Ferengi named Lishka. She immediately apologizes for the overzealous behavior of the interceptor pilots and invites the crew to join her for an evening meal at the refinery. She provides transporter or shuttle landing coordinates.

SCENE 3: THE REFINERY

The refinery is built on the edge of a crystalline island in the middle of the vast Abassan sea. The Player Characters arrive on an open-air platform that overlooks the ocean and the refinery, providing them with an excellent view of the

ocean. Anyone gazing out over the edge of the platform can see several smaller crystalline formations rising out of the ocean.

Lishka's second-in-command, a Yridian named Mishran Vol, meets the crew on the platform along with a security team (equal to the number of Player Characters). He graciously greets the crew's commander and invites them to join Lishka for supper. He then leads them down narrow stairs off the platform and toward the refinery. The massive refinery operation dominates an encampment where most of the workers reside. Much of the housing is made up of converted storage containers with the rest of it a collage of tents and other temporary structures dwarfed by the massive refinery. Vol leads the crew through a small open-air market that features several small taverns, gambling, and other services that cater to the worker's vices. Everything appears to be just this side of legal, though careful investigation would certainly uncover several violations of Federation law. At least a dozen different species from the Alpha Quadrant make up approximately 1,500 refinery workers, though there are notably no Ferengi.

A Player Character examining the refinery operation (either just visually or using a tricorder) can attempt a **Reason + Engineering** Task with a Difficulty of 2. If successful, they

THE REFINERY: SECURITY ZONE

CRATES & DRUMS

OBSERVATION GANTRY

SECURITY DOORS

SENSOR JAMMING

EDGE OF LATINUM REFINERY

SECURITY DOORS

WIRED CAMERA

SECURITY CHECK

GUARD ROOM

WINDOWS

ZONE ENTRANCE

MAP

can confirm that the equipment is appropriate to a mid-sized deuterium refinery though it appears to have some extra machinery for the refining process. The refining process is causing some interference with long-range tricorder scans making it difficult to learn more. To learn anything else, a Player Character would have to get inside the refinery. A Player Character who is curious about the extra machinery, and who succeeds at an **Insight or Reason + Science** Task with a Difficulty of 2, notes that the quantity of deuterium in the ocean would require a much bigger refinery to make this operation more than barely profitable. If asked about this, Vol claims not to know anything about the special equipment and acknowledges that the operation isn't very profitable but that they are hoping to expand.

The truth is that refining deuterium is only one of the refineries functions. Lishka is also extracting latinum from the planet's oceans. The quantity is very small, but latinum is rare enough, that she will become insanely wealthy if she can keep the operation running for even a few years. Unfortunately, latinum extraction is heavily regulated by both the Federation and the Ferengi, meaning that she needs to keep the latinum extraction secret.

THE DEUTERIUM REFINERY

The refinery is a massive complex of machinery and offices. Lishka has gathered skilled technicians, scientists, and laborers from far and wide to make certain that her refining endeavor is a success.

The facility itself is separated from the living quarters, and the market area (as well as the guest facilities) by an electrified and security-monitored fence. In order to enter the facility without anyone knowing, the Player Characters would have to figure out a way around the fence. Lishka wants, above all else, to keep the latinum extraction operation secret, so she has installed jammers inside the facility that prevent sensors and tricorders from getting viable readings. If anyone asks why that region can't be scanned, Lishka or Vol say that the machinery interferes with sensors (and they take affront to the Player Characters being so nosy). The section of the refinery dedicated to latinum extraction also has extra security (security doors, monitoring, and guards) and only the most trusted workers are allowed into that part of the facility. Those who work there also live there in special quarters, though they sometimes come out to seek entertainment in the market.

To learn about the latinum extraction, the Player Characters will have to get into the facility itself, or they could learn something from one of the scientists who live and work there.

Scans from orbit are completely fruitless, but a successful tricorder scan by attempting a **Reason + Science** Task with a Difficulty of 1 gets the following information:

- Something in the refinery appears to be blocking the scans. It could be machinery within the refinery, or it could be deliberate.

Spending 2 points of Momentum earns the following:

- Something within the facility is jamming sensor scans. The wavelength of the jamming is consistent with jamming devices commonly used by pirates and smugglers.

Unless the jamming devices are removed (which can only be accomplished from the facility's security room) all scans have their Difficulty increased by 3 due to the Complication caused by the devices.

If one of the Player Characters has Frontier Colony as their Environment or Business or Trade as an Upbringing (or something else the Gamemaster deems appropriate) from their character's background, the Gamemaster can have that character recognize an old friend or acquaintance in the market area. This could lead to a possible means of entry into the restricted part of the facility.

Lishka is a Ferengi who has rejected Ferengi norms and values and set out into the Galaxy to make her own fortune. She spent years siphoning latinum from her household funds, then stole a starship and sought her freedom in the stars. Hunted by the Ferengi and her abandoned husband in particular, she almost ran out of funds before a stroke of luck that lead her to Abassa VII.

Her stolen ship suffered damage from an ion storm, and she found herself stranded on Nimbus III when she met a Yridian named Mithrin Vol who had tales of a planet made of latinum. Vol had his own ship, and she convinced him to take her to this mysterious world. It turned out that, the rumors Vol had heard were true, at least in part. The oceans of Abassa VII did indeed contain latinum though in extremely small quantities. However, the oceans were also an excellent source of Deuterium. She managed to put together a collation of business partners to invest in an "off the record" refinery, keeping the knowledge of latinum between herself and Vol.

Lishka dreams of using her wealth to one day help other Ferengi women free themselves from the oppression of the Ferengi homeworld, or perhaps even make a change in Ferengi society. If the Player Characters discover her latinum processing operation, she will use this to help garner sympathy. While she is using her future altruism to try to save her skin, she also speaks the truth.

TRAITS: Ferengi

VALUE: I Have the Lobes for Business

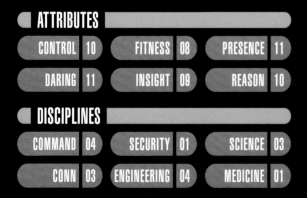

ATTRIBUTES

| CONTROL | 10 | FITNESS | 08 | PRESENCE | 11 |
| DARING | 11 | INSIGHT | 09 | REASON | 10 |

DISCIPLINES

| COMMAND | 04 | SECURITY | 01 | SCIENCE | 03 |
| CONN | 03 | ENGINEERING | 04 | MEDICINE | 01 |

FOCUSES: Bureaucracy

STRESS: 9   **RESISTANCE:** 0

ATTACKS:
- Unarmed Strike (Melee, 2▲ Knockdown, Size 1H, Non-lethal)
- Energy Whip (Ranged, 4▲ Intense, Size 1H, Non-lethal)

SPECIAL RULES:
- **Greed Is Eternal:** When engaged in negotiations that have the potential for Lishka to profit financially, she may spend 1 Threat during a Task to re-roll the dice pool.
- **Free Advice Is Seldom Cheap:** Increase the Difficulty of all Social Conflict to persuade Lishka by 2. This increase is removed as soon as she is offered something in trade.

REFINERY SECURITY [MINOR NPC]

TRAITS: Appropriate to Species

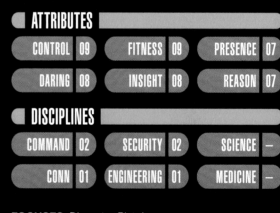

ATTRIBUTES

| CONTROL | 09 | FITNESS | 09 | PRESENCE | 07 |
| DARING | 08 | INSIGHT | 08 | REASON | 07 |

DISCIPLINES

| COMMAND | 02 | SECURITY | 02 | SCIENCE | – |
| CONN | 01 | ENGINEERING | 01 | MEDICINE | – |

FOCUSES: Disruptor Pistols

STRESS: 11   **RESISTANCE:** 0

ATTACKS:
- Unarmed Strike (Melee, 3▲ Knockdown, Size 1H, Non-lethal)
- Bludgeon (Melee, 4▲ Knockdown, Size 1H)
- Disruptor Pistol (Ranged, 5▲ Vicious 1, Size 1H)

ENCOUNTER: MEETING WITH LISHKA

The Player Characters are led into the facilities office, through a maze of hallways and then into a lavish dining room. Lishka stands and greets the crew and then asks them to sit. Perhaps surprisingly, Lishka is fully clothed, unlike most Ferengi women. Specialties from around the quadrant are laid out on the table, and Lishka tries to have something that would appeal to the captain. Vol quietly joins them, sitting at the far end of the table. During the meal, he remains quiet and lets Lishka do most of the talking.

Lishka readily admits that her deuterium refinery isn't registered with the Federation (or anyone for that matter). She argues that even though the operation is within Federation space, the Abassa system hasn't been officially claimed by the Federation. She is technically within a gray area of Federation law, but if pushed on the subject she appears more than happy to begin the process registering the operation. If pushed about the true nature of the operation, she denies that it is anything other than a deuterium refinery. If presented with proof that they are also extracting latinum, she claims that it was just a happy by-product and she is happy to do whatever necessary to make her operation legal. She also makes several allusions to bribes though she is never overt.

- If asked about the tetryon wave Lishka claims to know nothing about it. This is partially true. She doesn't know its origin, but she is aware that it happened and that it originated from the planet. After the event, she ordered a few of her scientists to investigate, and they have come to suspect that there might be something peculiar about Abassa VII's ocean – that it may, in fact, be living. Lishka absolutely will not share this knowledge with the Player Characters at this point.

- To distract the Player Characters from further investigating the refinery, at some point during dinner, Lishka mentions that a half dozen of her workers have gone missing. She says that they have searched the refinery from top to bottom, but there is no sign of them. Two of them disappeared while out in a submersible, investigating possible concentrations of deuterium in the ocean floor. She fears that they might have been taken by some sort of sea creature and asks the crew for help in finding them. After all, missing workers tend to hurt morale.

- After dinner, Lishka offers the Player Characters accommodation. If they accept, Vol leads them to a collection of suites near the worker residences. The suites are all very well appointed, and Vol makes it clear that he can acquire anything the crew might desire.

A CRY FROM THE VOID
ACT 2: AN AMETHYST OCEAN

SCENE 1: THE MISSING

Lishka and Vol both urge the Player Characters to search for the missing workers. They see this as having the dual benefit of getting Starfleet out of their hair for a bit and raising morale amongst the refinery workers. The crew can conduct the search by utilizing the ship's sensors to scan the planet from orbit, or they can use shuttlecraft for closer scans, or some other method that they devise on their own.

The missing refinery workers are currently located in the depths of the deepest trench in the Abassan sea. They are encased in crystalline cocoons (which interfere with sensors), and the gear and submersible that they were using have been completely destroyed and cannot be used to track them.

LOCATING THE WORKERS

Utilizing the ship's sensors to scan the planet can be done, though it is an extremely time-consuming since they will have to carefully search the entire planet, quadrant by quadrant. Carefully scanning the entire planet takes about 24 hours and is a **Reason + Science** Task assisted by the ship's **Sensors + Science** with a Difficulty of 3. Shuttlecraft can be used to cut down the time and difficulty. Each shuttle used halves the time (so one shuttle reduces the time to 12 hours, two shuttles to 6 hours, etc.) to a minimum of 3 hours. Using shuttlecraft also creates an Advantage since the sensor sweeps can be coordinated (which reduces the Difficulty by 1). Momentum can be spent to reduce the time. Each point of Momentum spent halves the required time. This Task can be passed using

Success at Cost. No matter what the Players roll, at the end of the allotted time, they detect humanoid life-forms deep under the ocean but must attempt another Task at Difficulty 2 to pinpoint the exact location. If either roll fails, the Cost should be having the crew encounter one of the unusual phenomena without Threat cost.

If successful, six humanoid life-forms are detected at the bottom of a 30,000 meter deep trench. There is no sign of the submersible or other electronics. There is some electromagnetic interference in the region that seems to be originating from a cluster of crystalline structures at that location. The life-forms appear to be weak and slowly fading – with approximately 4 hours until they are lost.

UNUSUAL PHENOMENA

If shuttles are deployed to assist the search the Gamemaster can have one of the following phenomena affect the crew of one of the shuttlecraft by spending 2 Threat or as the result of a Complication, or if the initial Task fails.

- **Sudden Storm** – A sudden, powerful storm springs up almost out of nowhere (a threat response by the oceanic entity), making navigation dangerous. While still in the storm the Difficulty for all ship related actions is increased by 1 and the Difficulty is increased to 2. To get out of the storm, the pilot must attempt a **Daring + Conn** Task with a Difficulty

of 3. Each turn the shuttle remains in the storm it takes 4▲ damage. If only the ship's sensors are being used a sudden ion storm appears in orbit. The storm affects the crew's ship as described above but inflicts 8▲ damage for every turn they remain inside the storm.

- **Mild Hallucinations** – One of the Player Characters experiences mild hallucinations. This is an effect of the life-form that is the ocean reaching out and trying to make contact. The effect is fairly mild, visions of bright lights, distorted vision, etc. but the Complication range for the affected character increases to 4. This is an attempt by the entity to reach out and make contact with the Player Characters, but it is too unfamiliar with their minds to be successful. This phenomenon should occur before a Reverie occurs.

- **Reverie** – A Player Character experiences a sudden and powerful flashback from an event in their past. This event should be a first meeting or encounter that significantly impacted the character's life: a first contact, or a first love, or maybe the person who inspired them to enter Starfleet. The flashback only lasts a few seconds, but the effects are a lingering sense of unease and distraction lasts the rest of the scene. The character who experiences the reverie has the Complication range for any actions increased to 2. (The Gamemaster can play out this flashback as a short scene to create more dramatic impact.) This is another attempt by the entity to make contact.

The life-forms of the missing workers are in the deepest part of the planet's amethyst ocean at approximately 30,000 meters (more than twice the depth of Earth's deepest ocean). The depth in the ocean is too deep, and there is too much interference to use transporters (due to the electromagnetic interference at the location as well as simply the ocean depth), so they will need to devise a means of reaching the bottom of the ocean trench. The crew could conceivably modify a shuttlecraft. It would have to be a non-warp shuttle since the warp drive of a shuttle would be too heavy for safe operation under the sea. They could also modify space suits to descend to the location. The Gamemaster will need to determine the Difficulty or hazards depending on the approach used by the crew. The depth under the sea will result in immense pressure, most likely requiring the crew to make modifications to existing gear such as shuttlecraft or space suits. Modifying existing gear to operate on the bottom of the trench requires a **Reason + Science** Task with a Difficulty of 1 (to determine the exact pressure resistance requires) followed by a **Reason + Engineering** Task with a Difficulty of 1 that has a base time of 3 hours. The time can be reduced by spending Momentum with each point halving the required time.

If asked, Lishka does have two additional (4-person) submersibles that can be used. The submersibles are unarmed but are equipped with cutting and excavation tools. She will loan them to the Player Characters if they wish, though she will make it clear that she expects to be reimbursed for any damages. If the Player Characters wish to leave the submersible, they still have to modify space suits to withstand the pressure.

The missing workers are all clustered in the same area at the bottom of the trench atop a magnificent growth of glowing crystal. Numerous crystalline formations are clustered in the area. The workers are all encased inside a shell of crystal material that appears to be the same substance as the crystalline formations. A Player Character can scan the encased workers and attempt a **Reason + Medicine or Science** Task with a Difficulty of 2.

Anyone attempting the Task learns that inside the crystalline cocoon there is a liquid that appears to be similar to the seawater but with some different mineral content. The miners themselves appear to be alive, though in a coma and are somehow able to breathe the water. The cocoons are connected to the surrounding crystal, but it appears that they can safely be broken away.

THE ABASSAN SEA

The Abassan sea might appear to be a normal, if somewhat mineral rich, ocean, but it is a living entity. In fact, the sea and the crystalline formations that form the land masses on Abassa are all alive, though perhaps not in a manner understood by most people. Even Federation scientists would be baffled by the life cycle of this entity. A lifetime could be spent understanding its secrets.

The ocean entity's life-cycle begins as a liquid, which over time hardens into crystal, which in turn crumbles into nutrient that forms more liquid. It is sentient, although its form of sentience is completely alien to the humanoid mind. It has more in common with some cozmozoan life-forms than it does with humanoids such as Humans or Klingons. Some might theorize that it is related to the Founders or the Silver Blood (encountered by Voyager in the Delta Quadrant) and this is certainly possible.

The oceanic entity had not encountered humanoid life before the arrival of Lishka and the refinery workers. At first, it was curious, but once the refinery started processing the sea water, it began to feel a sensation it had never felt before and barely understood – pain. This pain continued to increase as the refinery grew larger until it became intolerable. It was at that point that it released it's cry for help. The entity exists in multiple dimensions and at least partly in subspace. There may have been others of its kind in the same region of space, but they are all long gone. Perhaps they have all vanished into another dimension – the others may exist entirely in subspace or some other dimension. When it began suffering pain, it cried out in the only way it knew how: by blasting a tetryon wave out into subspace. The same tetryon wave that the Player Characters' ship encountered.

The entity has been trying to understand the creatures that are causing it harm. It has some understanding that they have intelligence and it is trying to learn how to communicate with them. To this end, it captured several workers from the refinery. The ocean can manipulate itself to form tendrils and even create basic shapes and images. Its best means of understanding the captured workers is to essentially absorb them. When the workers are discovered this process is only partly completed.

A Player Character who succeeds at the Task realizes that the liquid inside the cocoons appears to permeate the bodies of the workers down to the cellular level and appears to be keeping the workers alive. Just breaking the cocoons will likely kill them.

The Player Characters can also spend Momentum to learn additional information:

- Not only has the liquid penetrated to the cellular level but it also appears at the subatomic level, especially in areas of the brain and nervous system.

- The glowing crystalline formation where the cocoons are found is emitting low-level energy patterns that are similar to the electrical patterns in the Human (or humanoid) brains. The crystal may be alive in some sense.

Cutting the cocoons free of the crystalline structure is not difficult and requires a **Control + Security** (or **Medicine** or **Engineering** if a scalpel or cutting torch is used) Task with a Difficulty of 0 (assuming a phaser is used). However, soon after someone begins cutting anyone who did not receive a Reverie in the previous scene receives one now (at no Threat cost). This Reverie is very different though. This time the characters all experience a memory of a time they were badly wounded. Each of the characters who experience the Reverie also suffer 4 ▲ damage. If a Player Character who was cutting one of the cocoons free experiences a Reverie they must succeed at a **Daring + Security** Task with a Difficulty of 3 or either break the cocoon or hit someone nearby. The remaining crystals break free at this point.

If a Player Character with psychic abilities, such as a Vulcan or a Betazoid, attempts to communicate with the crystal, then it is achievable (see the Sidebar on the Abassan Sea in Act 2, Scene 1). They can, however, communicate that they want to free the workers at which point the cocoons will break free from the surrounding crystal, seemingly on their own.

SCENE 3: STUDYING THE COCOONS

The workers can be taken back up to the ship, or there is a full medical facility at the mining facility. As described in the previous scene, if the cocoons are broken open, the workers inside die almost instantly as the fluids inside them cause their bodies to break apart at the subatomic level.

EXTENDED TASK: SAVING THE WORKERS

Discovering a safe means of removing the workers from the cocoons requires an Extended Task that has a Work track of 15, Difficulty 3, Magnitude 3, and Resistance of 2. The following special rules apply:

- If a Player Character already discovered that the liquid inside the cocoons is affecting the workers on the subatomic level, the Resistance for the 2nd Breakthrough is reduced to 0 and the Difficulty to 1.

- If a Player Character uses **Reason + Science** to assist the Resistance and Difficulty for all Tasks are reduced by 1.

- Each Task attempt is one interval of time, and each interval is 30 minutes.

  There are two-time factors that push the Player Characters to proceed as fast as possible:

  1. The storms caused by the entity are going to destroy the refinery (and kill everyone inside) in 6-8 hours.

  2. No matter how well the Player Characters negotiate with her, Lishka will only wait so long before she attempts to retaliate.

- **Breakthrough 1** – Any cut, but a phaser or other cutting tool, is likely to cause the crystalline cocoon to shatter. Applying a specific sonic frequency causes the cocoon to dissolve safely. This could be done in a small area, allowing the cocoon to be punctured and the internal liquid to be tested. Devising a sonic cutting tool requires a successful **Reason + Engineering** Task with a Difficulty of 3.

- **Breakthrough 2** – The liquid permeates the cocooned workers down to the subatomic level. It seems to be slowly working through them, most likely analyzing them. The workers also have traces of tetryon particles.

- **Breakthrough 3** – A cure is devised. A modulated thoron pulse while the workers immersed in a nutrient fluid should rid the workers of the subatomic particles and allow them to survive the process. To modulate the thoron pulse properly, a Player Character must make a successful **Reason + Science** Task with a Difficulty of 2. Creating a properly balanced nutrient fluid requires a successful **Reason + Medicine** Task with a Difficulty of 2.

At Breakthrough 3 the Player Character conducting research also realizes that they may be able to communicate with the entity if they can bring one of the workers out of the coma. Bringing a worker to consciousness, without harming them requires a successful **Insight or Reason + Medicine** Task with a Difficulty of 2. (See **Act 3, Scene 3** for information about communicating with the entity in this state.)

A CRY FROM THE VOID
ACT 3: NEW LIFE

SCENE 1: REPERCUSSIONS

Soon after the workers are recovered, the oceanic entity responds. Massive waves begin pounding the shoreline placing the refinery at risk. The return trip to the surface becomes difficult, requiring the pilot of any craft to make a successful **Control** or **Daring + Conn** Task with a Difficulty of 3 to avoid the massive eddies and upswell of debris from the ocean floor. Failure means that the shuttle (or other craft) takes 3 ▲ damage. Everyone inside the craft must attempt a **Control** or **Daring + Security** Task against a Difficulty of 2 or take 2 ▲ damage from being buffeted about during the ride (this increases to 6 ▲ if the Piloting Task is failed.

Once back on the surface, a Player Character can attempt to determine how long the refinery will last against the onslaught by making a **Reason + Engineering** or **Science** Task with a Difficulty of 2. If successful, they know that the refinery will last 6-8 hours before the structural integrity fails.

SCENE 2: REACTIONS

Lishka immediately enacts plans to protect the refinery and the workers as best she knows how. Even if the Player Characters offer to beam all of the workers to safety aboard the ship, Lishka and about a quarter of the workers refuse and attempt to solve the problem on their own – a solution that proves to be deadly to the life-form that is Abassa's ocean.

Mining deuterium requires scientists, so upon realizing that the oceans of Abassa are alive, Lishka sets her best and brightest to working on a solution to neutralize the oceanic entity. Having already been suspicious that the ocean was a life-form of some kind they had already done some preliminary work and they quickly determine that the easiest and most effective approach is to modify their ship's weaponry to generate nadion particle waves that would likely disrupt the creature.

Lishka announces her plan to the characters. Most likely, they do not approve of this plan (remind any Players that Starfleet would not approve of killing or severely injuring a new life-form). However, if the crew decide to go along with Lishka's plan, she provides them with the necessary information to adjust their weaponry. One of the crew must make a successful **Reason + Engineering** Task with a Difficulty of 1. Then proceed to **Encounter: Firing the Nadions**.

A Player Character can negotiate with Lishka to convince her to hold off the attack, but she argues that her workers are in danger. Convincing her to stand down requires using the Social Conflict rules. The initial attempt may be a Negotiation Persuasion Task to convince Lishka to stand down and has a Difficulty of 4. If the Players effectively role-play their argument, give them an Advantage. If the initial Persuasion Task fails, the Players can use Social Tools to change the dynamic and allow an additional roll:

- They could use intimidation (giving them an Advantage reducing the difficulty by 1 to 3 steps, depending on how forceful their actions).

- They can show evidence that the entity is sentient and that causing it more harm might cause it to release more tetryon waves, likely destroying Lishka's ships. This gives them an Advantage reducing the difficulty by 1.

- They could use deception and lie to Lishka about some unseen danger. The Advantage here depends upon what the Player Characters make up.

If Lishka yields to the characters' wishes, Vol acts on his own to protect the refinery and orders some of the ships to begin the attack on the oceanic entity. The Gamemaster can send in one freighter for free and spend Threat for additional ships to join the attack (3 Threat for each freighter and 1 for each interceptor). The ships are at various locations in orbit around the planet and require one turn to get into position. The captains of the ships shut off their comms and do not respond to hails.

ENCOUNTER: FIRING THE NADIONS

Lishka has six interceptors and three freighters. These ships do not attack the characters unless they try to interfere with their attack on the ocean entity. As soon as the first nadion particles strike the ocean, the entity responds by emitting tetryon pulses at the offending ships. This includes the Player Characters' ship only if they are part of the attack. Empathic characters who have attuned to the entity feel overwhelming waves of pain emanating from the entity. The Gamemaster may wish to require Tasks for such characters to avoid becoming overwhelmed.

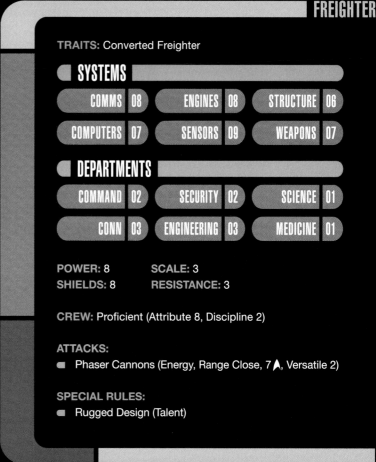

TRAITS: Converted Freighter

SYSTEMS

| COMMS 08 | ENGINES 08 | STRUCTURE 06 |
| COMPUTERS 07 | SENSORS 09 | WEAPONS 07 |

DEPARTMENTS

| COMMAND 02 | SECURITY 02 | SCIENCE 01 |
| CONN 03 | ENGINEERING 03 | MEDICINE 01 |

POWER: 8 **SCALE:** 3
SHIELDS: 8 **RESISTANCE:** 3

CREW: Proficient (Attribute 8, Discipline 2)

ATTACKS:
- Phaser Cannons (Energy, Range Close, 7▲, Versatile 2)

SPECIAL RULES:
- Rugged Design (Talent)

The tetryon bursts affect up to 2 ships every turn and cause 8▲ damage that ignores shields. Destroying the entity is an Extended Task with a Work track of 10, Difficulty 2, and Magnitude 3. After the first Breakthrough, the oceanic entity can only attack one ship per turn. The second Breakthrough reduces that damages to 4▲. After the third Breakthrough, the entity dies.

SCENE 3: COMMUNICATIONS

This scene or parts of this scene may take place earlier in the story but lays out all of the possible means of communicating with the entity and how it responds.

Mind-Meld or Telepathic Communication – When in liquid form, the "mind" of the entity is too alien for a character with psychic abilities to detect or interact with. However, once a telepathic character discovers that the glowing crystals are actually some form of living entity, they can attempt to attune themselves to its psychic wavelength. This requires a successful **Insight + Command** or **Science** Task with a Difficulty of 4. Once properly attuned to the entity's mental frequency, a telepathic character can use their powers as normal.

The crystalline formations have a rigid mental structure. They cannot be communicated with in full sentences or even complete thoughts, but rather only a single concept or thought. How the entity reacts is up to the Gamemaster to decide based on what the Player Characters try to communicate to it. Overly complicated thoughts and ideas only confuse and maybe even anger it, and it should be noted that the Player Character does not have complete control over the ocean entity. Rather, it is more like a relationship between a parent and child. If it has been provoked, the child may continue to act on its own.

Visions and Images – The oceanic entity can communicate through visions. These visions are symbolic and manifest in the form of memories. If it is attempting to greet someone, a Player Character might have a flashback of their first time meeting someone important. The oceanic entity can also form rudimentary shapes and create images on its surface. If some level of contact has already been

made, a Player Character walking to the shoreline might experience this as a hand seemingly reaching out of the water in greeting. It may also mimic actions taken by the Player Characters.

The Workers – The most effective way to communicate with the entity is to awaken a worker from their coma before the process of purging the invasive liquid is complete. The Gamemaster could also decide to have one or more of the workers awaken during the purging process (which could make for an eerie scene). In this stage, the entity has complete control of the worker and is able to speak through them. Their language should be stilted and communication of some concepts might prove difficult, but a full conversation is possible, though any awakened worker always communicates in their native language. After any communication is complete, the entity removes itself from the host bodies, leaving them weakened, but otherwise in good health.

A CRY FROM THE VOID
CONCLUSION

The ultimate conclusion of this story is making first contact with the oceanic entity and coming to some resolution as to the fate of the refinery. Lishka is not necessarily the villain of this mission; that role is reserved for Vol. In fact, though she suffers from typical Ferengi greed, Lishka could be viewed in a sympathetic light since she is trying to break with the Ferengi patriarchy that controls and demeans its women. If the refinery fails, she will be destitute and may even be forced to return to Ferenginar.

If the characters prevent the oceanic entity from being attacked or at least killed, they can awaken the workers and speak with the entity and may be able to work out a compromise. The entity can separate itself and could form a reservoir in the vicinity of the refinery where it deposits any of its waste. This waste material is ten times richer in deuterium and contains twice as much latinum. Feel free to play out these discussions or leave them to happen later, off-camera. And of course, there

is the matter of Lishka officially registering her operation with the Federation.

CONTINUING VOYAGES...

This mission leaves a couple lingering questions. Who was the oceanic entity trying to contact? Are there more of this species or another allied species out there somewhere? Do they receive the message and if so how do they respond? This could be the seeds for a future mission or series of missions. If the Federation allows Lishka to continue her refining operation, especially of latinum, how does the Ferengi Alliance react? Perhaps Lishka starts a movement and uses her newfound wealth to help smuggle other female Ferengi offworld and offers them positions in her organization. Perhaps she even enlists the aid of her old friends, the Starfleet officers who helped her before.

CHAPTER 09.00

DARKNESS

BY SAM WEBB

572821400412
3985104697936745

DARKNESS
SYNOPSIS

This mission takes place on the frontier of explored space, in response to a distress call from a Vulcan Expeditionary Group on the planet of Trax Epsilon I. The Players' vessel arrives in the Trax Epsilon system to find the Class-H planet the Vulcans were studying is now a black void in the sky, with an atmosphere that absorbs all but 0.04% of light. With the distress call no longer transmitting, an away team should investigate.

Initial scans suggest that the atmosphere appears unbreathable, so EV suits will have to be worn. Down on the planet, the thick black atmosphere that surrounds the crew proves intimidating, limiting their vision to barely a meter or so away. Once the away team locates the Vulcan's base camp, they find the shell of an outpost, void of power. By repowering and repairing its systems, they may be able to find more about what happened to the expedition, while the Players' ship can try to cut through the atmosphere and the geomagnetic anomalies of the planet.

While searching for the now-dead Vulcan team, the away team finds an alien ship crashed and decomposing. Clues lead the away team to discover the ship was bioengineered and contained hibernation pods that now lie empty. Suddenly, the dead Vulcans reawaken, possessed by a vast alien mind trying to mind-meld with the away team to make telepathic contact.

What follows is a race to make first contact on both sides: an alien mind contained in the planet's geomagnetism attempts to make telepathic contact with the Player Characters, while they in turn make discoveries about the aliens terraforming the planet and determine how to make first contact. The Krilins colonizing the planet are a hive, telepathically guided by the mind that has moved to this planet's magnetic fields, the new atmosphere having been created by them through bioengineered terraforming techniques.

DIRECTIVES

In addition to the Prime Directive, the following Directives apply:

- It is Starfleet's Duty to Respond to Distress Calls
- Recover the Vulcan Science Team

The Gamemaster begins this mission with 2 points of Threat for each Player Character in the group.

OTHER ERAS OF PLAY

This mission can work in all eras of *Star Trek* with only an adjustment to the stardate required.

SPECTRAL ABSORPTION ANALYSIS

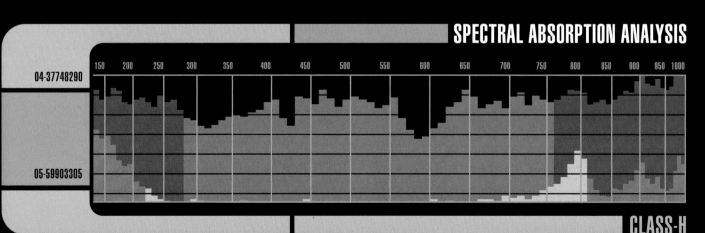

04-37748290

05-59903305

CLASS-H

ACT 1: INTO THE DARKNESS

SCENE 1: THE DISTRESS CALL

Once the captain's log has been read or paraphrased as an introduction, the Players' vessel enters the Trax Epsilon system. From here the Players can make initial scans of the planet either from the edge of the system, or from orbit (either way the result will be the same).

A **Reason + Science** Task with a Difficulty of 1, assisted by the ship's **Sensors + Science**, will reveal the first planet in the system is displaying strange, yet unseen characteristics: the planet is covered in a black atmosphere, reflecting all but 0.04% of light. The viewer shows an incredible sight against its bright blue-white sun, a dark void in the center of the viewscreen. The sensors don't detect much else, and nothing of the planet's surface upon which the Vulcan team had their outpost. The planet's magnetic field is also anomalous – its poles moving and fluctuating, causing interference to sensors and communications.

Momentum spent to *Obtain Information* may reveal its current atmospheric composition as predominantly a silicate molecule. Any further questions from *Obtain Information* Momentum spends will need further analysis, but the Gamemaster can give basic information, covering Traits and any other information from the sections below.

TRAX EPSILON I

Trax Epsilon I, in the Kepler sector, is registered by long-range probes as a Class-H planet, marginally habitable, with arid conditions and very little surface water. The Vulcan Expeditionary Group came here to study the planet's atmosphere, as they'd never encountered a Class-H atmosphere so close to its sun – just 0.03 AUs away. Since they landed, the planet has undergone an incredible transformation into the hellish, light-absorbing globe on the viewscreen.

On the surface, Players will find these incredibly difficult conditions:

- *Darkness 2* – The atmosphere of the planet absorbs almost all light, and some of the infrared and ultraviolet

CAPTAIN'S LOG

Captain's Log, stardate 47253.6. We are responding to a distress call from a Vulcan Expeditionary Group on Trax Epsilon I. We lost the signal one day ago, but are still en route. The distress call read: "We require immediate assistance, atmospheric conditions have proven too hazardous to the expedition to continue. One team lost, their coordinates are enclosed. Two members of the expedition remain here at base camp T'Vral. We request the nearest Starfleet vessel make contact and extract us. Message repeats.

THE STATE OF THE PLANET

The atmosphere is now composed of a thick silicate gas. The silicon ions, having bonded with oxygen, has rendered the air unbreathable so environment (EV) suits must be worn. Not only that, at a quantum level these silicate ions absorb light waves, which means all but 0.04% of light that hits the planet from its parent star is absorbed. Without this, the planet has reduced in temperature significantly over the course of several days, and without an EV suit people on the surface would have to endure subzero temperatures.

spectrum. This Trait is enough to render all visual perception beyond about 1-2 meters impossible. It also increases all Tasks that involve visual detection within two meters by 2. Any Threat spends to increase the Difficulty of related Tasks only need 1 Threat, not 2.

- *Geomagnetic Anomalies* – The magnetic field of the planet is in a state of flux. Any Tasks to scan the planet, or scans while on the surface, are increased in Difficulty by 1.

- *Hostile Atmosphere* – The planet's atmosphere has undergone a huge change in chemical composition, rendering it unbreathable and very cold. Any humanoid that breathes a Class-M atmosphere exposed to this atmosphere suffers 3⚡ of Stress per round, as they suffocate, or if left without thermal insulation may freeze to death.

LOCATING THE OUTPOST

A **Reason + Conn** Task with a Difficulty of 2 should allow anyone to find the Vulcan Expeditionary Group's research outpost, using library records of their landing site compared with current telemetry.

Player Characters can either beam down to the planet or use a shuttle to travel to the surface. Transporting down from a transporter pad is a **Control + Engineering** Task with a Difficulty of 3, due to the **Geomagnetic Anomalies**, assisted by the ship's **Sensors + Engineering**. Travelling down by shuttle will introduce the scene below. Regardless of which choice the Players make, the characters will need to wear EV suits, which normally have an Opportunity cost of 1 for each character; but, because they could not operate without them, the cost is reduced to 0.

OPTIONAL SCENE: A SHUTTLE RIDE

Players wishing to take a shuttle to the surface will need to succeed with a **Control + Conn** Task with a Difficulty

WHAT HAPPENED TO THE VULCANS?

The two deceased Vulcan scientists are the two members of their team who lasted the longest. Unfortunately, they (like the rest of their group) were attacked by the Krilian Pods, hungry creatures looking for electrical power to feed upon.

Menos and V'Lar had not heard from the rest of their team for three days, and when the thick black atmosphere rolled in they decided to send the distress call. As soon as they did the creatures attacked.

As their prefab buildings were breached, life-support failed and they quickly made their way to an access panel and put on their EV suits. They made some attempt to defend themselves, with phasers, but were clearly unsuccessful. They were ripped from their prefab buildings, and picked off by the huge creatures. An important distinction to make is about the EV suits that are the most damaged, with only mild blunt force trauma suffered by Vulcans due to impacts from the pod creatures. The Krilian Pods effectively sucked the power from their suits, while the smashed visors depressurised the suit and exposed the Vulcans to the hostile atmosphere.

of 2, assisted by the shuttle's **Engines + Conn**. Spend Threat to increase the Difficulty based on the incredibly limited visibility, but let the Players Succeed at Cost of a Complication, which can be the shuttle crashing or a System on the shuttle being disabled before landing.

You may, if you want to get to the heart of the mission or add some immediate action, introduce one of the aliens in an attack on the shuttle. Spend 2 Threat to introduce a Krilian Pod, about the size of a shuttle, using it to try and knock the Players out of the sky. It attacks because it perceives the shuttle as prey, trying to ground it so it can feed on its engines.

Use its NPC stats as comparable to a Scale 1 Small Craft, and use the rules for *Ramming Speed* attacks from Starship Combat (***Star Trek Adventures*** core rulebook, page 222) even if it defeats the Krilian Pod. During their turn, a Player may want to scan the creature, which is a **Daring + Science** Task with a Difficulty of 3 due to the **Darkness** and the **Geomagnetic Anomalies**. You may also limit their ability to target the creature due to the location Traits, unless they've completed a *Sensor Sweep* Task.

The Players may be able to get information about the creatures from scanning it in this encounter, or from killing the creature in self-defense and locating the Pod's body. This is good if you want a shorter game, or you want to ramp up the danger immediately, but does introduce the aliens very early on, reducing the suspense of Act 1.

SCENE 2: THE OUTPOST

When the away team arrives at the Vulcan base camp, EV suits on, they discover a darkness the likes of which they've never experienced. The only light produced is from their own head lamps, and even that light only extends a meter wherever they go.

Operating on an away mission with an EV suit increases the Difficulty of all Control Tasks by 1, due to the suit's restrictions. The **Geomagnetic Anomalies** also increase the Difficulty of hailing the ship, or each other at a distance, by 1. You may want to allow the characters to Succeed at Cost when trying to communicate with their ship, with a Complication limiting what kind of information they can get across due to the interference or being cut off.

Read or paraphrase the following:

Stumbling across the arid ground, your EV lights barely illuminating a meter in front of you, you finally find walls, cabling, and closed hatches. The Vulcan outpost lies abandoned, void of power. Prefab buildings have been torn up, with breaches and tears all along their alloy-plated

sides. *None of the doors open, and with no emergency power, will take some effort to open manually. The consoles lie dead and tricorder scans show that not even life-support functions inside the buildings.*

Let the Player Characters investigate the prefabs, emphasising the difficulty they are having in their EV suits and the sheer darkness all around them. If you think any investigation is particularly difficult, ask for a Task with an increased Difficulty due to the location Traits. Any Complications from Tasks here, or a particularly evil Threat spend, could start a psychological episode in a character because of the darkness.

They find the following:

- No members of the Vulcan expedition are present in the prefabs.

- All power has been drained from the outpost, even emergency power and batteries. If the Players want to get power back online, they will need to complete Key Tasks of the Challenge below.

- All the Vulcan's EV suits are gone from their locker.

- Outside, two Vulcan scientists lie dead, with smashed EV suits. Power has been drained from the EV suits too.

An investigation of the dead Vulcan expedition members (an **Insight + Medicine** Task with a Difficulty of 2) will confirm they are dead, their bodies frozen inside their non-functioning EV suits. Their likenesses register as two scientists of the Vulcan Expeditionary Group; two confirmed deaths (Menos and V'Lar). Any *Obtain Information* Momentum spends could reveal the following:

- The Vulcans themselves died of asphyxiation, not wounds or blunt force trauma.

- The suits breaches expose key power points, cabling, and batteries.

If the Players want to get the base camp up and running again, they're going to need a new power supply, and complete the first Key Tasks of the Challenge:

- **Acquire a new power supply:** This can be accomplished through jury-rigging or engineering improvisation, or by communicating with their ship. A Task should be required for any option.

- **Get power back online:** The electro-plasma system overloaded due to a massive unregulated transfer of power, and the team needs to integrate their solution with the Vulcan prefabs. This is a **Control + Engineering** Task with a Difficulty of 3, due to the EV suits and the *Darkness*. Any Focus in Power Systems would apply here, particularly Electro-Plasma Power Systems.

- **Recover computer systems:** (Locked) Once the power is back online the crew can attempt to recover computer functionality. This is a **Reason + Engineering** Task with a Difficulty of 2. A Focus in Computers applies.

Once certain Key Tasks have been completed, the characters can attempt the following Tasks around the base camp:

- **Research the logs:** (Locked) Once the computer system has been recovered, the away team can research the logs of the expedition group. This is an **Insight + Conn** Task with a Difficulty of 0. You can either read the log to the Players without asking for a roll, or let them roll, read the log, and let them spend the Momentum they gain to ask questions using *Obtain Information*.

- **Re-establish Life Support:** (Locked) Once the power systems are back online, the away team can try to reestablish life support to the prefabs. This is a **Control + Engineering** Task with a Difficulty of 4. Anyone assisting this Task cannot help with other unlocked Tasks, depending on how you are managing the group's time.

The away team can recover the locations of several impact craters all around the planet, recorded by the Vulcans' sensors, the nearest being about 1,000 km away. These serve as points of interest in the following act for Players to investigate.

THE EXPEDITION LOGS

Menos' logs are matter of fact, even dull in places, but the following excerpts are the most pertinent.

"Stardate 47197.4. Establishing base camp we have deduced the planet's semi-major axis as 0.03556 AU, orbital eccentricity of 0.0018, Orbital period of 2.47063 days, a rotational period of 6.125 hours, and an orbital inclination of 83.57. The day/night period will take some adjustment."

"Stardate 47248.1. This morning, several unidentified objects fell and impacted the surface of the planet, producing substantial shockwaves, which has impaired some of our equipment – most notably sensors. While first thought of as large meteorites, scans detect life signs, and as such an exploratory team has been selected to investigate the phenomena. The nearest impact sight is a day's travel by desert flyer... I have not been selected."

"Stardate 47249.9. We have not heard from the exploratory team today. We will attempt to reestablish communications by transmitting every 3 hours, with the standard call and response procedure."

"Stardate 47250.5. A storm has begun to move in on our position – an intensely thick, black storm. The sensors are measuring sudden electrostatic discharges from its strange composition. This weather was not detected in orbit by initial surveys, so I must continue to try and gain telemetry – though as noted in my previous log, the sensor equipment has been functioning at 37.51% efficiency since the impacts."

"Stardate 47251.7. The atmospheric phenomenon is all around us now, having entirely replaced the composition of the Class-H atmosphere of the planet previously. No contact has been made with the exploratory team and I am uncertain our communications have been penetrating the atmospheric phenomenon. We have decided to activate a distress call to alert Starfleet to our situation."

A supplementary log follows the final log, with the strained voice of Menos: *"Expedition log, supplemental – we are under attack from an unknown alien species. They have inflicted breaches to the structure of the buildings and main power is offline. Environmental controls are failing, I have ordered V'Lar to prepare the EV suits."* A pause is followed by phaser fire and an alien scream, as well as the sounds of an EV suit pressurising. *"This log will be our last here. We will –"* Menos' voice cuts out with a crash, and an incredibly uncomfortable pause follows, with the muffled sounds of crunches and alien screams before the computer closes the log.

DARKNESS

ACT 2: FOLLOWING THE FIELDS

SCENE 1: INVESTIGATING THE PLANET

Either in orbit or at base camp, science and engineering characters might be working to cut through the thick atmospheric interference, and investigate the phenomenon, guided by the Scientific Method.

WHAT IS THIS ATMOSPHERIC PHENOMENON?
THE SCIENTIFIC METHOD

The Scientific Method is outlined in the **Star Trek Adventures** core rulebook, p.157, but is also explained here, made relevant to this mission.

STEP 1: OBSERVE

Since the characters have observed the anomalous atmosphere in the previous act, they can know immediately the lead Discipline is Science. Characters with a high Science Discipline should become the Research Lead, with others assisting if they feel they can have a positive influence on progress.

STEP 2: HYPOTHESIZE

Ask the Players to choose 3 to 5 Focuses that might apply to the phenomenon, as Hypotheses of why the atmosphere has changed so dramatically. They don't need to possess the Focus, and can choose freely. The correct Focus, or "The Right Way" is *Terraforming*, but do not inform the Players. If none of the Hypotheses put forward fit the problem, immediately gain 1 point of Threat and tell the Players to start this step again. Players don't need to be precise; if they're reasonably close with suggestions like *Alien Technology* or *Climate Change*, Step 3 can proceed and they can be informed on how they can refine their thinking.

STEP 3: TEST

Investigating the phenomenon is the 'testing' involved with this particular scientific method, accompanied by an Extended Task. As the group uses the computer to simulate their Hypothesis and compare the result with the readings of the atmosphere, each Breakthrough they achieve will give them more information about the phenomenon. It's important that these Breakthroughs are interesting to the Players if there isn't a deadline

or some jeopardy alongside its completion. If you are managing two separate groups of characters, let those testing their theory attempt one Task before moving back to the away team for part of a scene. If the away team is investigating from base camp, or if all characters are aboard their ship, then continue this Extended Task until it is completed.

EXTENDED TASK
> **Work Track:** 20
> **Magnitude:** 4
> **Difficulty:** 4
> **Resistance:** 2

With a Magnitude of 4, the Players need 4 Breakthroughs in their research to effectively recalibrate the sensors and communications systems to provide them with an Advantage to cancel out the **Geomagnetic Anomalies** Trait.

- **Breakthrough 1** shows the researchers the atmospheric composition is now dominated by a rare silicate gas. It has never been recorded naturally, and was not present on the planet during initial scans. This Breakthrough also informs the Players that *Terraforming* is the Right Way, or that they need to refine their thinking if the Focus they have picked is a stretch. As with all Extended Tasks, reduce the Difficulty of further Tasks by 1 for each Breakthrough.

- **Breakthrough 2** proves there is a link between the **Geomagnetic Anomalies** and the **Darkness** of the silicon substance in the atmosphere. It seems the silicate acts as a kind of catalyst for the fluctuations in the magnetic field, though it is unclear why the fluctuations are occurring. It also shows them that the gas is concentrated at several sites around the planet (but leave the Players to link this observation with the impact sites in the Vulcan logs).

- **Breakthrough 3** shows the characters that, at the quantum level, the silicate gas absorbs the visible light spectrum, and is affecting subspace communications down to the planet in the same way. This invites the Players to apply more of their Focuses to their Task rolls, such as *Quantum Mechanics*.

Breakthrough 4 maps the shifting magnetic poles and electrostatic energy in the atmosphere to a degree that the sensors and communications can be easily calibrated to compensate. This provides the Players with an Advantage **Geomagnetic Mapping** that cancels any Difficulty increase to **Sensors** Tasks due to the **Darkness** or **Geomagnetic Anomalies** Traits.

Any Complications, or Threat spends, here can increase the Difficulty of Tasks or the Resistance of the Extended Task if the characters are not making the right assumptions from the information gathered, but be careful to provide rewarding obstacles to their research rather than just blocking their progress.

FURTHER SCANS

With the sensors now calibrated, the Players may now try to get more information on the planet overall, or focus their attention on particular areas of the planet. Here's what they can ultimately find out, but consider pacing these discoveries with the away team's progress:

- Several fresh impact craters dot the surface all over the planet, about 100 in all. *Obtain Information* Momentum spends can reveal more (see *Scene 2: Looking for the Exploration Team*).

- Large life-forms can be detected across the planet. Five meters across and twice as long (Scale 1), these creatures are flying with long tentacle-like tendrils. *Obtain Information* Momentum spends can reveal more (see p. 110).

- The remaining Vulcan expedition bodies can be found by searching for the specific EV suit materials or Vulcan DNA, but as they are dead, no life-signs can be found. This is a **Control + Science** Task with a Difficulty of 4 due to its specificity. Success can pinpoint the team's

REVERSING THE PROCESS

The Players may wish to figure out a way to completely reverse the effects of these beings on the planet, or at least stop the decay of the alien vessels. Encourage them to use the Scientific Method as the basis of their research and implementation, with a Good Way related to **ions** or **electrolysis**, with even an *Outside the Box* theory if presented well enough (see p.159 of the **Star Trek Adventures** core rulebook).

Reversing the atmospheric change is impossible for the crew and their vessel, however, without the help from the huge climate control systems used by the Federation to colonize and terraform.

location at a crater 1,000km from the Vulcan base camp (see *Scene 2: Looking for the Exploration Team*).

SCENE 2: LOOKING FOR THE EXPLORATION TEAM

On the search for the expeditionary group, the crew should make their way to the crater contained in Menos' log from Act 1. If they do, then move onto *The Vulcans* encounter on p.115. The team could try transporting to a crater with a base Difficulty of 2 (with the help of their vessel), or they could try and pilot there in their shuttle. If the journey matters, then a Task is required; otherwise, begin framing the scene below.

If investigating another crater, or if you need the away team to stumble upon a discovery, then you can use this information to provide some progress to the mission. Likewise, you can use it to ask any questions that the Players may have after *The Vulcans* encounter.

Around a large crater, approximately 1 kilometer in diameter, a kind of alien craft, around Scale 3, has seemingly crashed here – its hull is thick and composed of a silicon-based alloy, fizzing and evaporating to form the thick atmosphere all around. If any members of the away team touch the hull, it's incredibly hot – the EV suit only just protecting them from burns, with the hull crumbling away to any kind of applied force. Inside the vessel is even stranger than its exterior. The inside of this vessel looks closer to some xenobiological diagrams than it does the interior of a starship. **Reason + Science**, **Conn**, or **Medicine** Tasks, with a base Difficulty of 2, can begin to unravel this enigma:

- The vessel contains organs, similar to some large alien entities encountered at this scale, but based in silicates. Further study or questions indicate that if it was once alive, it is dead now. It has been dead since impact, the most probable cause of any post-mortem investigation by the scientific or medical members of the away team.

- The craft does not use warp drive, but can propel itself to sublight speeds thanks to a state of quantum mechanics. Characters with a Focus in *Quantum Mechanics* would likely be the only people who could put the pieces together to theorize such a thing, while those with more rounded Focuses in Warp Technology or Methods of Interstellar Travel can tell it is not a warp-capable vessel.

- Inside, chambers like berths or larvae pods lie cracked open and empty. Further investigation can confirm that beings were inside, from some residual organic-silicon based evidence, serving as a kind of embryonic gel or water to a creature inside – it could have birthed these creatures, around Scale 1, or (as is true) whatever was inside was hibernating.

- There is a direct chemical correlation between the erosion of the hull and the atmospheric change. A massive, catalyzed chemical reaction is forming the thick silicate gas from the huge creature, stealing the oxygen from the atmosphere to produce rare silicon-oxygen molecules. The whole being, inside and out, is showing signs of this reaction. If allowed to continue, the being here would fully 'decompose' within about two standard weeks – all its matter expressed into the atmosphere.

ENCOUNTER: THE VULCANS

Inside and around the giant dead beast, members of the Vulcan science team lay dead – their EV suits smashed and cut up, with zero residual power signatures. All of them bear the same blunt force impacts that breached their suits and exposed them to the unbreathable atmosphere. They also all show the evidence of rapid electrical power transfer (from the alien's harvesting the electrical energy in their suits).

Once the away team has some answers to what is going on inside the alien vessel, quietly the six Vulcan scientists wake up, altogether not being themselves. They are dead, that is medical fact, but an alien consciousness has taken them over as they seemingly attack the crew. The alien consciousness, having once been connected to the Vulcans through a mind-meld with one of the alien creatures, is aware of the minds of the dead Vulcans and is manipulating them with electrical energies.

If you can catch one of the away team members off-guard, or provide a 'jump scare' for the Players, then take the first turn; otherwise, let the characters react first to the deceased Vulcans returning to their feet. Use six Vulcan Scientist Hosts for an away team of 5, and make Non-lethal Unarmed Strike attacks as normal, but the Vulcans are not trying to harm the away team – they're trying to mind-meld with them, taken over by the alien intelligence the Vulcans themselves connected with, that's yet to present itself (see **Act 3**).

If you inflict an Injury to one of the Player Characters, instead of inflicting an Injury, smash the visor of that character's EV suit, exposing them to the silicate air. If you can, spend 2 Momentum to attempt a *Swift Task* to mind-meld with the character. This is an Opposed Task, **Reason + Command** with a base Difficulty of 1 for each character (unless they are incapacitated, in which case it isn't opposed.) Complications here can result in pain for the Player Character, including disorientation, or lingering emotional damage from trying to resist.

When the Vulcan scientists were attacked by the Krilian Pods as a last-ditch attempt at survival they mind-melded with the aliens. Instead of calming one creature, they connected with a vast consciousness. This alien consciousness gained an incredible new perspective on the universe, one of vision, communication through language, and society based on individuals. Since their exposure and death, the consciousness has been able to keep a link to the Vulcan brains, and as such cumbersomely control them. Without the fine control required for speech, the consciousness tries to do what it can to communicate with the away team – by tactile telepathy.

TRAITS: Vulcan, Psychically-Controlled

VALUES: Use Any Means to Communicate

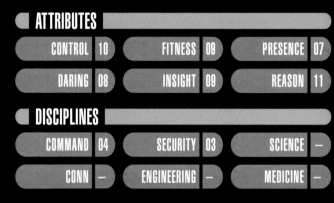

ATTRIBUTES

| CONTROL 10 | FITNESS 09 | PRESENCE 07 |
| DARING 08 | INSIGHT 09 | REASON 11 |

DISCIPLINES

| COMMAND 04 | SECURITY 03 | SCIENCE – |
| CONN – | ENGINEERING – | MEDICINE – |

FOCUSES: Tactile Telepathy

STRESS: 12   **RESISTANCE:** 1

ATTACKS:
- Unarmed Strike (Melee, 4▲ Knockdown, Size 1H, Non-lethal)

SPECIAL RULES:
- **Immune to Pain**
- **Immune to Fear**
- **Deathly Resistance:** Hosts can only be defeated by Lethal attacks, ignoring any Non-lethal Injuries, and gain +2 Resistance to Non-lethal attacks.
- **Mind-Meld:** The hosts are able to initiate the melding of minds through physical contact. This will always require a **Reason + Command** Task with a Difficulty of at least 1, which can be opposed by an unwilling participant. If successful, the host links the minds of the alien consciousness with the participant, sharing thoughts.
- **A Vast Alien Mind:** The host can re-roll 1d20 when attempting to mind-meld with another humanoid.

DARKNESS
ACT 3: CONTACT

From here, the Players will most likely want to seek shelter from the harsh environment, or if they have done well in defending themselves from the dead Vulcans, to recover the bodies. They may also have serious questions about the alien mind. The following scenes may be attempted in any order, but the real climax to the story comes with an attack by the pod creatures, and the attempted first contact

With this Trait, the geomagnetic fields of the planet begin to fluctuate wildly, searching for other humanoid magnetic fields. In actuality, the alien consciousness is the magnetic field, and exists here, in and around the planet. It is trying to cut off any energies it can comprehend, including scans or beams directed to and from the Players' ship in orbit, so that it can search for the away team through its Krilian

SCENE 1: DECIPHERING THE GEOMAGNETIC

Whether aboard the ship or at the base camp, the characters may wish to make contact with the Krilian Mind, or further investigate the geomagnetic anomalies. The two things are irrevocably linked and so attempting one will also make progress in completing the other goal.

Depending on the tools at their disposal, the Players may attempt to decipher the geomagnetic fields or may have brought back the Vulcan bodies that have been telepathically controlled by the Krilian Mind. By attempting some initial Key Tasks in the following Gated Challenge, the Player Characters can make contact with the Krilian Mind:

- **Observe the Magnetic Fields:** By observing and interpreting the magnetic fields of the planet with an **Insight + Science** Task with a Difficulty of 2, assisted by the ship's **Sensors + Science**, the characters can conclude they are being changed by an intelligence. *Obtain Information* Momentum spends here may reveal more about the Krilian Mind, even detecting its pod creatures if they haven't been already.

- **Test the Fields:** The characters can then attempt to manipulate the magnetic fields by interacting with it using their deflector, with a **Control + Engineering** Task with a Difficulty of 1, assisted by the ship's **Weapons + Engineering**. Success will prove a correlation with their deflector emissions and the reaction from the magnetic field of the planet not found in nature; the changes they are making are being reacted to, like a creature or person reacting to a touch or a push with a response.

- **Make Contact:** Using the ship's deflector dish, the crew can attempt to communicate with the Krilian Mind by modifying the communications systems and succeeding at a **Presence + Command** Task with a Difficulty of 5 assisted by the ship's modified **Communications + Conn**. A Focus in *First Contact Procedures* would apply, as would some sort of Focus in the Communications Systems.

- **Observe the Vulcan Hosts:** By performing a **Medicine** Task to examine the dead Vulcan scientists, a medical officer can deduce that they are controlled by something or someone else – their brain patterns register strange readings not normal for a Vulcan, their neurons firing almost randomly at times. *Obtain Information* Momentum spends here can hint that the Krilian Mind is controlling these people, and is finding it difficult and does not have control of their full faculties.

THE KRILIAN MIND [MAJOR NPC]

The Krilian Mind is a huge electromagnetic being of planetary proportions capable of manipulating magnetism and electrical charges in its native atmosphere of silicate particles. It has been carried here in the bioengineered electromagnetic field of the Krilian ships, the terraforming of the planet by its pod creatures a means to create a new home for the Krilians. As a hive mind it communicates to its pod workers by manipulating the geomagnetism of the planet – its own method of telepathy. When it learned of the Vulcan minds here, due to their mind-meld, it searched for more minds, and now searches for more humanoid creatures to understand and initiate some kind of first contact.

TRAITS: Electromagnetic Creature, Hive Mind, Telepath

VALUES:
- I Am The Krilian
- I Must Become a New Home to My Pod
- To Find Other Minds, To Understand Humanoids

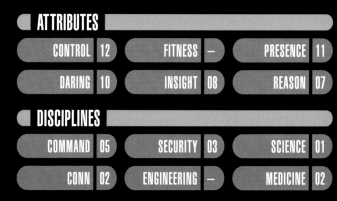

ATTRIBUTES

CONTROL	12	FITNESS	–	PRESENCE	11
DARING	10	INSIGHT	08	REASON	07

DISCIPLINES

COMMAND	05	SECURITY	03	SCIENCE	01
CONN	02	ENGINEERING	–	MEDICINE	02

FOCUSES: Bioengineering, Magnetism, Telepathy

STRESS: 20   **RESISTANCE:** 2
MAGNITUDE: 5

SPECIAL RULES:
- **Electromagnetic Being:** The Krilian Mind exists as the geomagnetic field of Trax Epsilon I, and as such cannot be affected by any physical effects. If the electromagnetic being would be targeted by some other effect from a starship, treat its 20 Stress as the Work for an Extended Task, with a Magnitude of 5, Resistance of 2, attempting Opposed Tasks using **Control + Science** with a base Difficulty of 1.
- **Environmental Manipulation:** The Krilian Mind can create a localized ion storm in the atmosphere by succeed at a **Control + Security** Task with a Difficulty of 2, which introduces a location Trait **Ion Storm** with a hazard: (6 ▲ Area, Intense, Deadly)

It's conceivable that a strong telepath, such as the Betazoids or highly-trained Vulcan, would detect the linked-consciousness of the Krilians. If you have a such a Player you can introduce the matter of telepathy or even the idea of a large alien consciousness as soon as they experience the planet – but for the sake of the story and the enjoyment of the other Players only hint to them the truth of what's going on, so there is as much for the other Player Characters to investigate as they have.

They might attempt some Insight or Reason-based Tasks to learn more, but by the sheer scale of the mind involved, make this either difficult or strenuous for the Player Character, with Complications or Success at Cost having an impact on their mental health.

- **Mind-Meld with the Vulcan:** A telepathic character can attempt to make psychic contact with the Krilian Mind via the Vulcans, by attempting a **Control + Medicine** Task with a Difficulty of 3.

- **Make Contact:** Using the Vulcan brain as a telepathic conduit, the crew can attempt to communicate with the Krilian Mind, by succeeding at a **Presence + Command** Task, with a Difficulty of 5, assisted by the character who holds the telepathic link if they are not the Task's leader. A Focus in *First Contact Procedures* will apply.

SCENE 2: THE HUNT FOR CONTACT

Now that the Krilian Mind is aware of the away team, it is searching for them in order to learn more. This may be easy if any surviving Vulcans have been recovered by the away team, as it can see and hear them through the Vulcan's senses. If not, it will send its pod creatures to look for them, using their highly sensitive EM spectrum receptors, from the electrical activity of the Player Characters' bodies.

As the Player Characters traverse the landscape, or maybe having spent some time working on their findings at the Vulcan expedition base camp, introduce a pod creature into the scene, flying around the thick silicate atmosphere like a squid through inky water. The pod will have one objective: to sense the away team and tear open their suits to initiate tactile telepathy.

The following encounter assumes the characters have returned to the base camp, with life-support functioning, but not having yet completed the Challenge to make contact with the Krilian Mind. If this isn't the case, then frame the encounter relevant to your circumstances. If the away team has returned to the ship, then forego this encounter and integrate the information learned from it in scans of the planet in the Challenge above.

ENCOUNTER: KRILIAN PODS

The Krilian Pods, at first, attempt **Insight + Medicine** Tasks with a Difficulty of 2 to detect the Player Characters at range, and are then guided to attack the away team, to break through their EV suits so that the Krilian Mind can make tactile telepathic contact. Like the encounter in Act 2, if you injure a Player Character, then instead of inflicting an Injury, smash the visor of that character's EV suit, exposing them to the silicate air. If you can, spend 2 Threat to attempt a *Swift Task* to mind-meld with the character. This is an Opposed Task, **Reason + Command** with a base Difficulty of 1, for each character. Complications here can result in pain for the Player Character, including disorientation, or lingering emotional damage from trying to resist. If you are successful, then proceed to *Scene 3: First Contact*.

During this encounter, if timed right, other staff aboard the ship or members of the away team can attempt the Challenge to make contact with the Krilian Mind in a safe way, using the deflector dish of the ship or by jury-rigging the systems of the Vulcan base camp, attempting to use the universal translator to communicate with them – though it is not easy since their language manipulates the EM spectrum. The away team must try to communicate with the alien creatures, as the aliens try to crack open their EV suits, with the darkness all around them.

THE CHALLENGE: MAKING CONTACT

If the away team alone is trying to make safe contact with the Krilian Mind, then you can replicate the Challenge from Scene 1, but substituting the work on the deflector with jury-rigging communication systems at base camp:

- **Test the Fields:** The characters can then attempt to manipulate the magnetic fields by interacting with it using the base camp's communications systems to prove this theory, with a **Control + Engineering** Task with a Difficulty of 2. Success will prove a correlation with their communications signal and the reaction from the magnetic field of the planet not found in nature; the changes they are making are being reacted to, like a creature or person reacting to a touch or a push with a response.

To continue, see p.117.

SCENE 3: FIRST CONTACT

If the away team can break through the language barrier and effectively communicate with the creatures, or if they mind-meld with a Vulcan or Krilian Pod they can learn a great deal, sharing thoughts with the Krilian Mind.

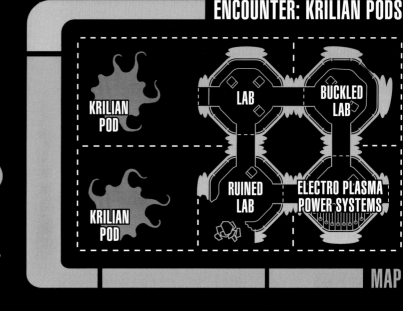

MAP

KRILIAN POD [NOTABLE NPC]

Krilian Pods are intelligent but controlled and guided by the Krilian Mind's magnetic fields. They are biological engineers, rather than electromechanical; the larger carcasses the away team found were actually inter-planetary hibernation pods that transformed the planet into a host for their hive mind consciousness. The thick black gases now polluting the atmosphere are in effect the atmosphere for the Krilian, and when the Krilian Mind's consciousness expanded into the planet its magnetic fields changing irrevocably as the Mind inhabited it.

The Krilian Pods feed on electrical energy, sensing their surroundings by detecting magnetic fields and homing in on electromagnetic fields. They are also telepathic within their species, due to this sense. Only with the revelation of telepathic contact with the Vulcans can they form a conduit to the Krilian Mind.

TRAITS: Krilian, Hive Worker, Telepathic

VALUES:
- We Must Engineer a New Home

ATTRIBUTES

CONTROL	08	FITNESS	13	PRESENCE	07
DARING	09	INSIGHT	09	REASON	08

DISCIPLINES

COMMAND	–	SECURITY	02	SCIENCE	01
CONN	03	ENGINEERING	02	MEDICINE	01

FOCUSES: Aerial Motion, Krilian Bioengineering

STRESS: 15   **RESISTANCE:** 4

ATTACKS:
- Unarmed Strike (Melee, 4▲ Knockdown, Vicious 1, Size 1H, Non-lethal)
- Consume Energy (See Special Rules)

SPECIAL RULES:
- **Consume Energy:** As an attack the Krilian Pod can consume electrical energy from any source of power. It drains 1▲ point of Power from an object within reach. If the object doesn't have any Power points then it is drained of power and is now useless until repaired.
- **Flying Creature:** Krilian Pods can either propel themselves through the air or use their tentacles for ground-based movement.
- **Night Vision:** The Pods have highly sensitive organs that can detect minute variations in the magnetic fields around them, and this is how they orientate themselves and perceive the world.
- **Scale 1:** Pod creatures are about the size of a shuttlepod, increasing their maximum Fitness, Resistance to 4, and their Unarmed Strike by 1 and granting the Vicious 1 Damage Effect.
- **Tentacles:** The Krilian Pod has several tentacles as limbs, functioning as both arms and legs. If the Krilian Pod spends Threat to perform a *Swift Task* that is either *Sprint* or an attack, the cost is reduced by 1.

Ultimately these aliens didn't take them for intelligent life, focusing only on the EM signature of the power source inside the EV suits (masked behind that signature the minute magnetic fields of the away team were not perceived by the aliens).

- These aliens are colonizing this planet as they know best, hibernating for centuries of sublight travel and emerging from their bio-ships to terraform the planet.

- The Krilian Mind is, in effect, the 'queen' of a hive; the pods are her workers.

- They are not overtly hostile, but they did not know of humanoid life and wish to understand more.

A mind-meld may prove hazardous to any Player Character forced to take part, while their body is exposed to an atmosphere they can't respire in. They will need to persuade and educate the Krilian Mind of how they need oxygen with a **Presence + Command** Task with a Difficulty of 3, and that the link must be

severed if they are going to make prolonged contact. This scene may also be the first time that the two parties have actually made contact, and therefore the above Challenge to modify communications systems either at base camp or aboard their ship may be attempted at this point, so that the Player Characters may speak on more comfortable terms.

FIRST CONTACT PROCEDURES

It's Starfleet's duty, recorded in several of its Directives, to respect intelligent life throughout the Galaxy. With that in mind, the first exchanges between the Krilian Mind at the away team will be careful. The Krilian Mind is eager to learn more about them too, however, and so the exchange that takes place should focus on the relationship Starfleet may have with the Krilians in the future, once the Krilian Mind understands the nature of humanoid life. The away team may have to convince the Krilians that they need to recover the Vulcan Expeditionary Group here, as their mission dictates, with further *Persuasion* Tasks with varying Difficulty, depending on how much the Krilian Mind now understands about Federation society.

CHAPTER 09.50

DARKNESS
CONCLUSION

The Krilian Mind are a unique species, a sublight civilization with intelligence enough to travel the stars and terraform other planets with bioengineering. Now that first contact has been initiated, Starfleet is free to recover the Vulcan expedition, but what about future relations with the Krilian?

CONTINUING VOYAGES...

- Perhaps a follow up mission could be to begin diplomatic talks with the Krilian, focusing on their

preservation as a species and protecting their new claim on Trax Epsilon.

- Where did they come from? Perhaps the Player Characters can negotiate for that information and learn more about the Krilian, their society, and their technology. Do more Krilian Minds exist?

- Perhaps the Krilians aren't as independent as one might think, and the Vulcan Expeditionary Group was targeted somehow by the Tal Shiar, who found the bio-ship and directed it towards Trax Epsilon.

CHAPTER 10.00

THE ANGSTROM OPERATION

BY JASON BULMAHN

470559022042
2411046259399101

THE ANGSTROM OPERATION
SYNOPSIS

The mission begins while the Player Characters are on a routine patrol near the Cardassian Demilitarized Zone. They are contacted by Starfleet ordering them to the Dran'Ankos system. An unremarkable brown dwarf, the star has only one planet, a small tidally locked body in close orbit, home to a small research facility called Angstrom Base. The base sent out a disturbing distress call just four days ago and has not been heard from since. The Players are ordered to go to the base, restore it if possible, but to retrieve the research at all costs.

Arriving in system, the star is giving off very erratic readings, and appears to be in the process of losing stellar mass. In just a few hours, it will become dangerously unstable. The base, which straddles the terminator of the planet, looks like it has taken damage to both the night-side operations area and the day-side research facility. The characters can scan the base to learn the extent of the damage, but must travel there by shuttle due to solar radiation. Arriving, they find the place in disarray, with dead crew littering the base. Through careful investigation it becomes apparent that the crew went mad and turned on each other. Worse still, the crew that are still alive in the lower levels attack when approached.

The nature of the problem becomes apparent when the characters encounter parasites responsible for the terrible neck and back wounds on some of the crew. Some of these foul neural parasites still lurk on this side of the base, mostly in engineering, and they attack the characters whenever they draw near. The characters gain control over some of the base, and restoring power and the main computer goes a long way to making exploration easier. They also learn that V'Tol, the Vulcan commander in charge of the base, is still alive, but has gone completely mad. He is operating an experimental inversion drive that is destabilizing the nearby star. To make matters worse, the Characters' ship reports that there are Cardassian ships entering the system.

The Players must try to subdue or otherwise neutralize the V'Tol and shut down the inversion drive. This does not save the star, but it buys more time. They must also find a way to get the technology off the planet, or they must destroy it to ensure it does not fall into Cardassian hands. They also have a chance to save some of the crew. If the plan falls apart, the characters might be forced to destroy the base before the Cardassians arrive.

OTHER ERAS OF PLAY

For games set in the *Enterprise* and The Original Series eras, the conflict with the Cardassians should be replaced with a threat more appropriate to that era. Consider using the Andorians for the *Enterprise* era and the Klingons for The Original Series era. The only other complication for these eras is the lack of knowledge about the neural parasites (although this can be avoided if the events in this mission take place after the events depicted in "Operation: Annihilate!"). In such cases, any attempts to pull up research on the creatures fails, but the knowledge of their weaknesses might be contained in the medical files of the base, as the chief medical officer tried to study the creatures just before the base went mad.

DIRECTIVES

In addition to the Prime Directive, the Directives for this mission are:

- Retrieve the stellar research data at all costs.

- Prevent the base from falling into enemy hands.

The Gamemaster begins this mission with 2 points of Threat for each Player Character in the group.

THE ANGSTROM OPERATION
ACT 1: ORDERED INTO CHAOS

SCENE 1: A CRYPTIC MESSAGE

The mission begins with the Players in the middle of a routine patrol mission along the Cardassian Demilitarized Zone. For the past week, they have been shadowed by a pair of Cardassian Galor-class cruisers on the other side of the border.

The ship receives a priority one transmission from Starfleet Command, ordering them to proceed at maximum warp to the Dran'Ankos system. Once there, they are to secure the Angstrom Research Base and recover its data at all costs. Seeing as the system is in dispute with the Cardassians, they are also to ensure that none of the base's research falls into Cardassian hands.

Included with the message is the final transmission from the base and technical information on the facilities and its staff.

FINAL TRANSMISSION
Along with the orders, the message from Starfleet also included a recording of the final transmission from the Angstrom Research Facility. A transmission four days earlier showed nothing out of the ordinary. The transmission, which is audio only, has been identified as coming from Senior Stellar Researcher Amelia Adams. In the recording, she can be heard crying out in agony, the only words that are intelligible are "the mutiny failed… they're everywhere now".

ANGSTROM RESEARCH BASE
While en route to the Dran'Ankos system, the characters have plenty of time to look up data on the research base and learn what they can about its crew and mission. The information in the sidebar is readily available from the ship's archive.

CAPTAIN'S LOG

Captain's Log, Stardate 45641.2. We are one week into a patrol of the Cardassian DMZ. Our Cardassian friends continue to trail us on their side of the border, but there has been no sign of hostility. Being this close has the crew on edge, but I have no reason to believe this will be anything other than ordinary.

Captain's Log, Supplemental. I may have spoken too soon. We have received a priority one message from Starfleet ordering us to the Dran'Ankos system, just on the edge of the DMZ, to lend assistance to a research base that has gone silent after sending out a disturbing message. Looks like our routine patrol is going to be anything but.

ANGSTROM RESEARCH FACILITY

Located on Dran'Ankos Prime, the base is located on both sides of the tidally locked planet. The majority of the structure is on the "night-side," including housing, recreation, and operations areas (including the shuttlebay). The "day-side" contains the research labs. Two surface tubes, just under 5km long, connect the two halves by a tram system.

Staff: Base Commander V'Tok, total compliment 64 (55 researchers, 9 support staff)

Base Specifications: Accommodations for up to 75, Type 2 Solar Shields, 2 shuttles (Scale 1, no warp capabilities).

Primary Mission: Research into the deuterium potential in low mass brown dwarf, such as Dran'Ankos. Phase 1: Limited photosphere agitation and gas sampling. Phase 2: Inversion testing for coronal mass capture and refinement. Phase 3: CLASSIFIED.

SCENE 2: DRAN'ANKOS

Under maximum warp, it takes 7 hours for the characters to reach the Dran'Ankos system, but the moment they come out of warp, it becomes apparent that there is something wrong.

Dran'Ankos is a Class-T Brown Dwarf. The magenta substellar object has only a single planet in orbit. Files on record note that it is very stable, with an average surface temperature of 940K, but sensor readings are terribly erratic. The brown dwarf's temperature has risen to 1,100K and it is unleashing strong bursts of X-ray radiation throughout the system.

There are a number of Tasks that the Players can perform before attempting to enter the Angstrom Research Base. Sensors are hampered by **Stellar Emissions** from the brown dwarf, which is giving off a number of unusual readings. As a result, many of these Tasks (which would normally be Difficulty 0) are instead more challenging to perform.

Scan the Angstrom Research Base: Getting an idea of what is happening in the base requires a **Reason + Science** Task with a Difficulty of 1. The basic scan reveals that that there are life-forms, but the number varies between 24, 47, and 942. It also reveals that main

power is down, but that the solar shields are still engaged at maximum (which prevents the use of transporters). In addition, the base has minimal life-support, and everything appears to be functioning off the battery.

Damage Report: A **Control + Engineering** Task with a Difficulty of 1 reveals that the base has taken extensive internal damage and that one of the tram lines between the two parts of the base looks like it has taken heavy damage. There is a fire contained in that tram line and emergency bulkheads will hold for no more than 24 hours. Spending Momentum reveals that the damage was caused from the inside, possibly through the use of a mining charge.

Stellar Observation: The brown dwarf is giving off strange readings, which can be analyzed with a **Reason + Science** Task with a Difficulty of 3. Success reveals that the star is steadily gaining temperature, increasing its convection currents, and its surface is starting to destabilize. Spending Momentum here reveals that this process will increase over the next 12 hours, at which point it will start throwing stellar mass into the system, which would be very dangerous to any ship in the vicinity.

With the Angstrom's stellar shields up at maximum, transport to the base is impossible without a working pad in the base or pattern enhancers. The main shuttlebay is open, and one of its craft is missing.

SCENE 3: BOARDING ACTION

With the main power down and no crew onboard to guide them in, the characters must fly a shuttlecraft down to the base. Landing the craft without damage requires a **Control + Conn** Task with a Difficulty of 3. This Task is performed with **Success at Cost**, and failing can result in damage to the shuttle, preventing it from being used to escape. This damage can be repaired with a **Control + Engineering** Task with a Difficulty of 2, but this is hampered by the **Main Power Down** and **Main Computer Down** location Traits, which make it significantly more difficult to repair the shuttle (bringing the Difficulty up to 4).

Once they have landed, it is clear that there has been fighting in the shuttlebay. There is a dead ensign, with a phaser burn to his face lying near the door. Scanning the ensign allows a **Control + Medicine** Task with a Difficulty of 2. Success reveals that although he died from a phaser set to kill, there was something else seriously wrong with him. Spending Momentum reveals that he has a puncture wound on his back and his nervous system looks like it has been all but destroyed.

SCENE 4: EXPLORING THE LOWER DECKS

There is a lot to be learned from exploring the lower decks on night-side part of the Angstrom facility, but with **Main Power Down** and the **Main Computer Down** Traits, there is not much the characters can learn from the panels in the shuttlebay. There is a simple base diagram posted next to the door leading out of the bay. This floor contains mostly storage space, but they have access to the Jefferies tubes that connect the floors of the base. The 2nd floor contains the mess hall, crew quarters, and medical, while the 3rd floor contains main operations. The 3rd floor also connects to engineering, transit, and life-support, all of which are currently sealed off by emergency bulkheads.

Details of each section follow.

STORAGE

There is not much to be learned here. It looks like many of the supply crates (all of which are filled with scientific instruments and basic supplies) have been rummaged through without care. Of particular note, there is a security crate that was forced open. It contained eight hand phasers (type-1), of which all but one is missing. If the away team is looking for a specific piece of equipment, spending Momentum here might allow it to be found.

CREW QUARTERS

Most of the scientific crew have quarters on the second floor of the facility, with the only exception being the department heads and support leads, who have larger rooms on the third floor. There are 14 dead scientists in this part of the base. Eight of them looked like they were killed in their sleep by phaser blasts at point blank range. The other six bodies are located around a barricade near the mess hall. Two outside were killed by phaser fire and bear wounds on their neck and back similar to the crewman in the shuttlebay (with the same internal trauma). The other four are on the inside of the barricade and appear to have died from blunt wounds to the head and body (with no sign of the strange wounds). A **Control + Medicine** Task with a Difficulty of 1 reveals that the fight happened about 6 days ago (those in their quarters died at around the same time). An **Insight + Reason** Task with a Difficulty of 1 uncovers that the fight was between those with the mysterious wounds and those without them, and that the unwounded were overrun and killed.

MESS HALL

Beyond the barricade is the mess hall, where the uninfected scientists who were off-duty when the trouble started made their last stand. The room itself is in total disarray with tables and benches knocked over and tossed aside to create hasty cover. An odd squelching noise can be heard coming from inside this room. When the characters enter, in the flickering light, they can see an Andorian writhing in the shadows. A flat irregular disk detaches from his back and flees through a ventilation shaft just as the scientist, driven mad by pain, charges with a crude club. There is no negotiating with him; his mind is too far gone.

If the characters manage to subdue the scientist, he falls into unconsciousness, his body wracked by convulsions. A **Reason + Medicine** Task with a Difficulty of 1 uncovers that even though he is unconscious, the pain centers of his brain are very active. Spending 1 Momentum on this check detects foreign cells located all throughout his nervous system, especially clustered around a puncture wound on the back of his neck. There is a slimy residue there as well. Spending an additional Momentum determines that the nervous system is starting to degrade, and that the cells themselves are starting to form a cyst around the wound site. This cyst appears to be made up entirely from nervous system cells that are undergoing some sort of metamorphosis. Nothing else can be learned without a medical bay.

There is no sign of the creature that flew off through the ventilation, though anyone listening at the damaged grate can hear echoes of that strange squelching noise.

MEDICAL BAY

Located at the end of the floor, the medical bay is modest, but functional. In the center of the room is a tall specimen jar that contains what appears to be a gigantic flesh-colored cell. This is a Denevan neural parasite, the

PAIN-CRAZED SCIENTIST [MINOR NPC]

Most of the scientific staff of the base are either dead or driven mad by pain. They still have some limited control over their faculties, but they sputter nonsense and scream incoherently.

TRAITS: Human, Crazed

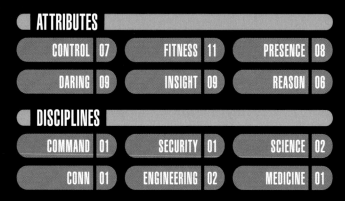

ATTRIBUTES

| CONTROL | 07 | FITNESS | 11 | PRESENCE | 08 |
| DARING | 09 | INSIGHT | 09 | REASON | 06 |

DISCIPLINES

| COMMAND | 01 | SECURITY | 01 | SCIENCE | 02 |
| CONN | 01 | ENGINEERING | 02 | MEDICINE | 01 |

FOCUSES: Hand-to-Hand Combat, Stellar Science

STRESS: 12   **RESISTANCE:** 1

ATTACKS:

- Unarmed Strike (Melee, 2▲ Knockdown, Size 1H, Non-lethal)
- Club or pipe (Melee, 3▲ Knockdown, Size 1H)
- **Escalation** Phaser Type-1 (Ranged, 3▲, Size 1H, Charge, Hidden 1)

---

only one that was killed by the security staff before they overran the base. Unfortunately for the staff, they had no way to identify the creature, as their database contains no information on the events that happened on Deneva. Once power is restored, the characters can access the medical officer's log, which describes the process by which the creature was surgically removed from the host, (Mr. Myroki) who died during the procedure from extreme shock. The creature was catalogued for further study, but the base descended into madness before any work could be done. Using the medical bay's scanners allows a **Reason + Science** Task with a Difficulty of 2 to determine that the creature appears to be most akin to a gigantic neural cell. Spending Momentum uncovers that although it is dead, parts of it still seem to be alive, responding to stimuli from another source, likely through some sort of connection to others of its kind. If the scans from the medical bay are uploaded to the ship, the crew can identify the creatures for what they are, although this might take a few hours to dig through all of the records.

In addition to the creature, there are also three bodies here. One is Mr. Myroki, a maintenance operator, who has a terrible wound on his back, and two other members of the operation staff, both of whom were killed by asphyxiation. There is a padd with the bodies that includes an open report stating that Mr. Myroki and the others were outside the base performing maintenance on an intake that had become closed with "biological matter." Myroki was injured during the work and somehow turned a laser drill on the other two, breaching their suits.

ENCOUNTER: CRAZY SCIENTISTS

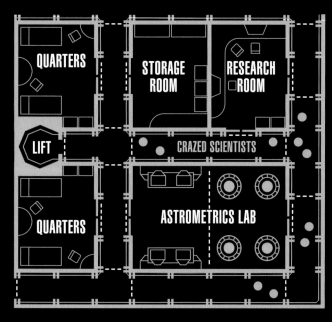

MAP

ENCOUNTER: CRAZY SCIENTISTS

As the characters move about the base, they might run into a small party of crazed scientists, roaming the halls in a pain-induced haze. Place this encounter whenever makes the most sense during the flow of the mission. The crazed scientists are far from subtle, charging and stumbling wherever they are encountered. During the run up, they scream and yell at the characters, telling them to leave this place, and never come back, although these threats are mixed in with cries of agony. Each of them has terrible wounds on their neck or back, punctures that lead directly into their nervous system. The first group should have just two scientists, but each subsequent attack includes one additional scientist, almost as if there is an intelligence behind the attack.

ACT 2: RESTORING ORDER

SCENE 1: GRIM OPERATIONS

Arriving at the third floor, the characters will make their way toward operations. If they skipped the second floor entirely, the first group of crazed scientists attack just outside the doorway to ops.

Operations is a large room, with a view of the crater dominating one wall of the room. The room itself is a nightmare. There are two dead bodies here, a lot of damage from phaser fire, and very little appears to be operational.

One of the operations officers is sprawled over a console in a pool of dried blood. Another is severely burned by phaser fire near the window. The window itself looks like it is not entirely stable, as it took numerous phaser hits. Looking at the body on the console reveals the cause of death to be a slice through her abdomen, caused by a large bladed weapon. She shows no other wounds and she has a phaser in her hand. The burned officer is impossible to identify, having taken a phaser blast to the face. He has multiple other hits, and an **Insight + Medicine** Task with a Difficulty of 2 uncovers that they started out as stun hits, but increased in severity, and any one of them should have incapacitated the man. He also has a puncture wound on his shoulder and a severely damaged nervous system.

Although **Main Power is Down**, there is still emergency power to many of the terminals in this room. These terminals report that the **Main Computer is Offline**, but they still report the status of the base's main reactor, which is approaching critical. Without the main computer, learning more requires an **Insight + Engineering** Task with a Difficulty of 3. If successful, the terminal states that main power failed after the primary research holding tank failed, causing an environmental breach in engineering. Protocols shut down the reactor and put the base on backup batteries. This occurred 3 days ago. Spending Momentum reveals that the research tank ruptured due to it being overpressured, listing the supply source as the "Stellar Inversion Drive."

Finally, the characters can discover the operations logs. All entries are dated 7 days ago from Operations Commander Elora Welgin. They are all routine until 10 days ago. A log

CAPTAIN'S LOG

Captain's Log, supplemental. The base is in chaos. The dead litter the halls and roaming bands of crazed crew are clearly responsible. A madness has taken hold of the Angstrom Research base, caused by an unknown pathogen. Unless we can restore power, there is little chance of getting the situation under control.

HORROR ON THE ANGSTROM

Until the characters gain control of engineering, the environment should feel oppressive. Nothing is working and the dead litter the halls of the research facility. Make sure to play up the gloomy environment, lit only by flashing red emergency lights, dancing shadows, and the occasional odd noise (such as a door that keeps trying to close on a dead body, or a strange squelching noise coming from the ventilation). Even once main power is restored, much of the base is simply not functional. Firefights have damaged systems throughout the facility. The Gamemaster should feel free to spend Threat to add Complications from damaged equipment and malfunctioning systems.

mentions that maintenance is needed on the exhaust manifolds, due to some sort of biological contamination from the surface (odd, because the planetoid is lifeless). A log from several hours later reports that Mr. Myroki, who was assigned to the task, was involved in some sort of accident, which claimed the lives of two other operations staff and that he was taken to medical for emergency treatments for some sort of parasite. The log then notes that another crew is being assigned to complete the original maintenance work. The final log is panicked, stating "It's all those damn scientists' fault. They've cut off comms. They are coming." The woman on the logs is the dead woman draped over the console.

Surrounding operations are the quarters for all of the department heads and important operations staff members. While most of these are unremarkable, filled with personal effects and mementos, there are a few things of note.

Commander Welgin's Quarters: Although there is no sign of struggle here, it is obvious that someone forced their way into this room and attempted to get into the security locker but failed to do so. The locker can be opened with a **Reason + Engineering** or **Security** Task with a Difficulty of 2. Inside are three type-2 phasers and a single type-3 phaser rifle.

Researcher Amelia Adams' Quarters: The quarters of this senior stellar researcher are a mess, as if a fight took place here. This is also the location where the last message from the base was sent, but there is no sign of Adams in the room (she can be found in Environmental Control).

Chief Researcher V'Tol: The head of stellar research has quarters just outside operations with a beautiful view of the crater. For a Vulcan, V'Tol's quarters are incredibly chaotic, with furniture, research dossiers, and sculpture tossed all about. In the center of the bed, stained by sweat, is a research tunic, the back of which has been torn off and stained with Vulcan blood. Scanning the bed and tunic with a **Control + Medicine** Task with a Difficulty of 1 uncovers the presence of the strange foreign cells found in the bodies of the dead.

V'tol's logs are all encrypted, but they can be accessed with an **Insight + Engineering** Task with a Difficulty of 2. The logs are orderly and regimented, made once per day at almost exactly the same time every morning, but all that changed 10 days ago. There is a log from the evening on that day, mentioning only "Due to the accident, work on the drive has been halted for the day. I have requested a specimen so that I might try to catalog this creature that seems so suited to this environment."

Logs from the following day are erratic, talking first about the "samples" and the "incident," while mentioning great pain and an attempt to maintain logic and focus. All of this is interspersed with Vulcan chants and bits of ritual that are easily identified by anyone who speaks Vulcan. A log from 2 days later states only, "They know and they must

TIMELINE

Logs and duty reports can be found in the main computer and with about an hour's worth of work, a rough timeline can be constructed. The following are only approximate times, usually corresponding to when the log was filed, not exactly when the event occurred.

10 Days ago: A malfunction in the exhaust system results in three maintenance workers going out to clear what was being read as a biological contaminant. The report describes hundreds of "cell-like organisms" crowding around the intake and exhaust manifolds. The report also notes that there was an accident with a laser drill, resulting in the death of two of the workers. The third was injured by the biological contaminant. Samples were brought inside, and some were collected from inside the environmental systems.

9 Days ago: V'Tol, the chief of stellar research, asked to examine one of the creatures, curious about how it could survive in such a hostile environment. Surgery to remove the contaminant from the worker resulted in his demise.

8 Days ago: Reports of the cells infiltrating the base came from all decks. There was a recorded log of V'Tol accessing environmental control, but the log of what he did inside the system was erased. All research logs from the day-side base ends and work there was put on hold.

7 Days ago: Panic took over the base, with fights breaking out all over. Crew were kidnapped or beaten by others and taken to the day-side facility. Commander Welgin sent operations personnel to the facility via the tram, but all were lost in an explosion that appeared to be deliberate.

6 Days ago: Order broke down. Adams sent the final message. Crew barricaded themselves from each other. V'Tol locked out communication and scrambled all of the base's security codes.

From this point onward, there are no further logs, only records of what happened to base systems.

5 Days ago: One of the base's shuttles departed with two on board. They flew into the Dran'Ankos star and were destroyed.

3 Days ago: The holding tank ruptured in engineering. Main power and the computer were shut down. There are no further entries.

be made one with us." The final log is from only 4 days ago, and states "The pain is clarity. The clarity is purpose. I know what I must do."

SCENE 3: POISONED ENGINEERING

Emergency bulkheads seal off all access points to engineering, due to the stellar gas leak that has contaminated the chamber. These can be overridden with a **Fitness + Engineering** Task with a Difficulty of 2, but doing so begins a timed encounter.

All of engineering is flooded with stellar gas collected from the Dran'Ankos star using the inversion drive located on the day-side base. The tank was never meant to hold a great deal of pressure, so when V'Tol turned the drive to maximum, the tank ruptured. Emergency cut-offs took over, but the damage had been done. Engineering was flooded with stellar gases which caused the computer to go into shutdown and place the entire night-side base on battery. The moment the door is opened, the gas begins to escape, which causes bulkheads all around the base to slam shut, trapping characters in engineering. Unless all of the characters are wearing environmental suits, they have a limited amount of time before they are overcome by the toxic gasses.

This is a timed Gated Challenge. The characters have a total of 9 intervals (each one representing a minute) to complete this Challenge before they risk harm from the toxic gasses (taking 1 ▲ Stress per additional interval). The Tasks are divided up into three groups: before startup, startup, and after startup. Characters can attempt various Tasks simultaneously, but no more than one additional character can assist on any given Task. The Tasks are as follows:

- **Before Startup:** Seal the Ruptured Tank* (**Daring + Engineering**, Difficulty 3), Prime the Reactor* (**Control + Engineering**, Difficulty 2), Adjust Environmental Flow (**Insight + Science** or **Medicine**, Difficulty 2, performing this Task reduces the Difficulty of all other Before Startup Tasks by 1). Distribute Emergency Breathers (**Daring** or **Presence + Command**, Difficulty 1, increases the total number of intervals before taking Stress damage to 12). Tasks marked with a * must be completed before the Startup Task can be done.

- **Startup:** Bring the Reactor Online (**Control + Engineering**, Difficulty 3).

- **After Startup:** Restart the Main Computer (**Control + Science**, Difficulty 2), Purge Environmental Contaminants (**Insight + Medicine**, Difficulty 3). Both Tasks must be completed to succeed at the Challenge.

SCENE 4: FIRST CONTACT

Once the characters have secured engineering, they can explore the remainder of the night-side of the facility. With the main computer back on-line, they can also learn the exact timeline of what happened and they can attempt to contact the day-side of the base. They can explore the transit center, which connects the two parts of the base, and the environmental controls, which are infested with neural parasites.

Using the Main Computer: The facility does not have the sort of high-tech internal sensors and recording devices possessed by most starships; as a result, the characters can only learn limited information. The base has a count of the life signs aboard, but these are just as confusing as they were from the characters' ship. Not counting any casualties since they arrived (or the characters), the computer thinks that there are 24, 47, or 942 life-forms aboard the base (this malfunction is caused by the sensors not knowing how to count the neural parasites). The computer reads the vast majority of the life-forms in the day-side base.

There is an open comm line to the day-side base, but it shows something rather confusing. There is a padd propped up in front of the comm line, showing an active reading of the Dran'Ankos star, but it is difficult to make out due to the odd symbol drawn onto the surface in green blood. It is the Vulcan symbol for "The End." Any other attempts at communication fail, and if the attempts repeat, the comm line is cut off from the source.

Characters can use the main computer to establish a timeline of events over the past 10 days (see previous page). The main computer here is the primary core for the base and its operations, but it does not have access to the research data, which is kept in secure drives in the day-side of the base. A **Daring + Engineering** Task with a Difficulty of 3 establishes a link, but it is very slow and will take at least 8 hours to download all of the research data (time the Players do not have once the Cardassians arrive).

Transit Center: Located near the rim of the crater, the transit center is a small building that houses the night-side end of both tram lines that lead over the surface of the planet to the day-side base. These trams are tubes of metal to shield travelers from the stellar radiation on the surface.

When the characters arrive, they discover four more dead bodies, one of which was killed with a long slice, down across the chest, while the other three died of exposure to the gases vented in engineering. One of them looks like he was badly burned before he died, and the wound is bandaged. Two of them have puncture wounds on their neck or back, but the effect on their nervous system does not appear to be as severe. An **Insight + Medicine** Task with a Difficulty of 1 reveals that the crew with the puncture wounds must have died before the effects of the wound could occur. The Task also reveals that whatever bladed weapon killed the crew here, it is likely the same weapon that killed Commander Welgin. There is a tricorder next to one of the bodies. There is only one file of note to be found on the device, and it appears to be readings of trace elements of an explosive compound. A successful **Control + Science** Task with a Difficulty of 1 reveals similar trace elements that rise in concentration close to tram tube 1.

Tram tube 2 is sealed by emergency bulkheads. Even now, the metal of the bulkheads is glowing slightly and is too hot to approach. The system reports a "malfunction" and that fire suppression systems are offline. A **Daring + Engineering** Task with a Difficulty of 3 can get the system to vent the tube to space. While this does not make tram tube 2 functional, it does put out the fire.

Tram tube 1 appears to be functional, but the tram is at the other end. This tram tube is trapped just like the other with explosive charges. Simply calling the tram will set them off. See Act 3 for details on the trap and other ways to reach the day-side of the base.

Finally, there is an airlock here that leads out onto the surface (although still shielded by the crater wall from the star's harsh radiation). Inside the airlock is the only survivor in the night-side base not totally driven mad with pain. Hiding inside a locker, using reserve oxygen to stay alive, Senior Stellar Researcher Amelia Adams is barely conscious. Reviving her is a simple matter, but the moment she regains her senses, she cries out in pain. She has a scratch running up her neck where a parasite grazed her during the initial attack. Even this brief contact was enough to put her in agony, but it never gave the parasites complete control, which allowed her to send that last desperate

NEURAL PAIN

In addition to the normal rules for the neural parasites found on page 342 of the core rulebook, consider adding the following: Anyone who takes 2 or more Stress damage from their attacks gains the **Pain** Complication that hinders any Tasks that rely on **Control**, **Insight**, and **Reason**. If the creatures attach to a character, and is later removed (because it is killed or it flies away), that character gains this Complication twice. Diagnosing these conditions requires a **Control + Medicine** Task with a Difficulty of 2. With the Starfleet files on hand, curing these conditions requires a burst of intense UV light, which can be performed with the gear in the medical bay. Without the files, coming up with the cure requires a **Reason + Medicine** Task with a Difficulty of 4.

message. Getting her to calm down enough to talk requires a **Presence + Command** Task with a Difficulty of 2.

Amelia does not know what the parasites are, but she knows they came from the surface of the planet and that they may have been stowaways on the hull of the previous vessel that supplied the base a few weeks ago. She can relate what happened up to the environmental breach, although she spent most of that time hiding in her quarters, and then ultimately in here. She does know one thing of vital importance. V'Tol has gone mad and has killed more than one crew with his *lirpa*. Worse, he has turned on the stellar inversion drive, which might result in the destruction of this entire system (see the Stellar Inversion Drive sidebar for more information). She stresses that they must find a way to stop him before the Dran'Ankos star loses its cohesion and destroys the base and everyone on it.

Environmental Control: The original source of the outbreak inside the base, environmental control is the only place that still has neural parasites in the night-side, with most of them fleeing with the crazed infected to the day-side. The parasites are hiding in the ventilation system and do not emerge until after the contamination is cleared. Once this is done, a swarm of the neural parasites infest this room and anyone who draws nearby can hear the alien squelching noise they make coming from inside. The parasites attack anyone in the area, but they do not pursue outside engineering. Once on the loose, anyone traveling through this area risks attack.

SCENE 5: CARDASSIAN TROUBLE

At this point, after the characters have explored the majority of the night-side of the base, it should become clear that V'Tol and the neural parasites are the true danger here. The madman is using the equipment in the day-side of the base to destabilize the star. As soon as the characters begin to formulate a plan for solving this problem, they receive an urgent message from their ship.

Long-range sensors have detected two Cardassian *Galor*-class cruisers approaching the Dran'Ankos system at high warp. Their signature matches the ships which shadowed them at the start of the mission. They also received an audio message that they can relay to the away team.

"This is Gul Anvok of the Sixth Order. Your presence in the Dran'Ankos system is clearly in violation of the treaty. By order of the Cardassian High Command, we order you to leave this system immediately. Warning one of one delivered, Anvok out."

Sensors indicate that the cruisers will enter the system in a little over 2 hours. Proceed to Act 3.

THE ANGSTROM OPERATION
ACT 3: MADNESS

Time is running out and there are many ways that the characters might try to resolve this problem. They can travel to the sun-side base and subdue or try to reason with V'Tol. If successful, they can grab the data cores and leave before the Cardassians arrive. This solves the primary objective, but it does leave the base infested with deadly parasites. Alternatively, they can try to stall the Cardassians and get the information through a slow data link, but V'Tol might destroy the Dran'Ankos star before they can finish. Finally, there is the matter of dealing with the neural parasites, which is no easy task, but is possible once the characters control the entire base.

SCENE 1: GETTING TO THE DAY-SIDE

Simply getting to the day-side of the base is no simple task. Walking across the surface is a 5 km trek across a harsh environment, blasted by deadly radiation. Tram tube 1 works, but is rigged with mining charges set to explode if the tram travels through it. Transporters cannot beam through the shields on the base and lowering them would be deadly. Finally, a shuttle could be used, but this requires careful piloting with no room for error.

Fixing the Tram: If the bomb is not defused, when the tram is called in, it explodes. The shockwave deals 2 ▲ of Stress to everyone in the transit center. If the bomb is discovered, it can be disarmed. This requires a character to crawl about 200 meters into the tram tunnel. Once there, they must make a **Fitness + Engineering** Task with a Difficulty of 2 to disarm the bomb. The Task takes 30 minutes to complete.

Flying to the Day-Side: Without the tram, the only reliable way to reach the day-side is to fly a shuttle to the base and quickly enter through its airlock (it has no shuttlebay). The radiation is so dangerous here that flying to the day-side base is best done very close to the surface, hiding as much as possible behind ridges and craters. Reaching the base requires a **Daring + Conn** Task with a Difficulty of 3.

Transporting: It is risky to use the transporters to reach the day-side, but doing so requires the stellar shields to be brought down for a moment during beaming. Timing this just

CHIEF RESEARCHER V'TOL [MAJOR NPC]

The Vulcan head of the research team here at the Angstrom base was driven mad by exposure to the neural parasites. When they could not control him, more and more attached to him, driving him into a deep psychosis. He now believes that the only way to free his mind is to unleash the full power of the Dran'Ankos star, purging himself of any impurities.

TRAITS: Vulcan

VALUE: We Must be Cleansed

ATTRIBUTES

CONTROL 09	FITNESS 12	PRESENCE 09
DARING 10	INSIGHT 09	REASON 07

DISCIPLINES

COMMAND 02	SECURITY 02	SCIENCE 04
CONN 01	ENGINEERING 03	MEDICINE 02

FOCUSES: Experimental Engineering, Hand-to-Hand Combat, Stellar Science

STRESS: 14   **RESISTANCE:** 1

ATTACKS:
- *Lirpa* (Melee, 5 ▲ Vicious 1, Size 2H)
- Unarmed Strike (Melee, 3 ▲ Knockdown, Size 1H, Non-lethal)
- **Escalation** Phaser Type-1 (Ranged, 4 ▲, Size 1H, Charge, Hidden 1)

SPECIAL RULES:
- **Intense Scrutiny:** Whenever V'Tol succeeds at a Task using Reason or Control as part of an Extended Task, he may ignore up to two Resistance for every Effect rolled.
- **Studious:** Whenever V'Tol spends one or more Momentum to *Obtain Information*, he may ask one additional question.

right requires a **Control + Engineering** Task with a Difficulty of 3. This Task is made with Success at Cost, with each character taking 1 ▲ of Stress for each missing success.

SCENE 2: THE MADNESS OF V'TOL

The day-side part of the Angstrom research facility is a relatively small place. There is a small transit center leading directly into the main research area. Off of this are a few private offices and storage lockers. When the characters arrive, V'Tol, who is covered in neural parasites, is in the center of the research area, operating the controls of a device that is unleashing a stream of highly charged particles into the Dran'Ankos star, destabilizing its surface and causing the star to lose its cohesion. This is the Stellar Inversion Drive and it has been the subject of the team's research for the better part of two years, as they tried to determine if low mass stars could be "mined" for their precious materials. Unfortunately, the device is not stable, and it is causing serious damage to the Dran'Ankos star.

V'Tol is hostile to any interruption of his work. Worse, he sees strangers as interlopers bent on preventing his work. He becomes terribly violent whenever anyone enters the room who is not under his command. If the characters

have brought Adams along, and have cured her of the pain, she can convince V'Tol to hear them out. This allows the characters to attempt to reason with V'Tol, making a **Presence + Command** Task with a Difficulty of 4 to get him to listen. This can be aided by any Vulcans in the group. Once calmed, V'Tol can be convinced to turn off the Stellar Inversion Drive with a **Reason + Command** Task with a Difficulty of 3. Characters might try and point out the damage it is causing, aiding with an **Insight + Science** Task.

If diplomacy fails, V'Tol attacks, grabbing his *lirpa* and charging the nearest character. With the neural parasites making him resistant to pain, and the deadly *lirpa* in his hands, V'Tol can be a difficult combatant. In addition, once he takes any wounds, neural parasites might emerge from the ventilation shafts to attack other characters and other crazed scientists might emerge from labs to attack as well. You are encouraged to spend threat to call on additional foes to raise the stakes of this fight.

SCENE 3: CARDASSIAN PROBLEMS

Two hours after the transmission, the Cardassians arrive in the Dran'Ankos system. They immediately go to high alert if the characters' ship is still in orbit, but they do not move to attack right away. Instead, they stand off and launch their own shuttles to the base. This can add significant complications to matters going on inside the facility.

Characters on the ship can try to stall the Cardassians or bluff them into holding off any exploration, but only for a short while. A **Control + Conn** Task with a Difficulty of 2 places the ship in orbit over the base, making it risky to send shuttles down without leaving them defenseless. A **Presence + Security** Task with a Difficulty of 2 can be used to impress upon the Cardassians the dangers of entering the base. The Difficulty drops to 1 if the Players explain the neural parasites. Finally, the characters might resort to hostilities if any shuttles are launched (see pages 263-264 of the core rulebook for statistics of a *Galor*-class cruiser).

If allowed to enter the base, the Cardassians send a six-person exploration team, led by Gul Anvok himself. They are soon attacked by hostile scientists and neural parasites alike. By the time they encounter any of the characters, they treat anything moving as hostile. That said, they make their way directly to operations first, closing out all

STELLAR INVERSION DRIVE

Research at the Angstrom Research Base centers on low mass stars and the gasses they contain, some of which are relatively rare. The goal was to find a way to harvest these gasses, even if that comes at the cost of the star itself. The stellar inversion drive works by creating a disturbance in the star's photosphere, creating a fountain of gas, not unlike a controlled solar flare. The thought was that a capture device could be created to harness these gasses before they fall back into the star or dissipate. Unfortunately, the research never made it that far. Although it is not part of the research, Starfleet is concerned that this technology could be weaponized, used intentionally to destroy stars.

remote access and locking out comms. This might force the characters into a fight with them back in ops, in which case, use the statistics on page 328 of the core rulebook.

THE ANGSTROM OPERATION
CONCLUSION

This mission can end in a number of ways. If the characters are entirely successful, they can calm T'Vol, cure him and the other remaining crew, destroy the neural parasites and evacuate the base and its research before the Cardassians arrive. Such a victory might earn several commendations for the characters and a note of gratitude from the survivors for their personal records. T'Vol, should he survive, retires soon after he is cleared of charges for his role in the event.

Settling for a partial success might not save the crew, but it could still save the research. A failure might result in the destruction of the Angstrom Research Facility and maybe even the Dran'Ankos star system. The only thing worse would be if the inversion drive also somehow fell into Cardassian hands. Such a catastrophe would be a serious black mark on the service records of all involved.

CONTINUING VOYAGES...

The fate of the Stellar Inversion Drive is a classified secret for Starfleet to determine, but it could show up again, in a different kind of research.

More insidious are the Neural Parasites. Some of these horrifying creatures might find their way onto the character's ship, travelling to the next starbase or planet they visit, only to start their plague all over again. The life cycle of these creatures is not fully understood and it might be revealed that they harvest neural cells from their hosts as part of their reproduction. Such a truth would certainly lead them to more inhabited worlds to conquer.

STAR TREK™
ADVENTURES

A FULL RANGE OF BOOKS & ACCESSORIES

NCC-1701-D Limited Edition Corebook	Gamesmaster Screen
Away Team Edition Corebook	Command, Operations & Sciences Dice Sets
Command Division Book	The Next Generation Miniatures
Operations Division Book	The Original Series Miniatures
Sciences Division Book	Romulan Strike Team Miniatures
Alpha Quadrant Book	Klingon Warband Miniatures
Beta Quadrant Book	Borg Collective Miniatures
Gamma Quadrant Book	Starfleet Away Team Miniatures
Delta Quadrant Book	Star Trek Villains Miniatures
These Are The Voyages: Missions Vol.1	Starfleet Geomorphic Deck Tiles
Limited Edition Borg Cube Box Set	Starfleet Landing Party Miniatures

AVAILABLE FROM MODIPHIUS.COM/STAR-TREK
OR VISIT YOUR FRIENDLY LOCAL GAMING STORE

MODIPHIUS™
ENTERTAINMENT

2d20™

BECOME A HERO OF BARSOOM

THE HYBORIAN AGE AWAITS YOU

OTHER CONAN TITLES
Conan the Thief
Conan the Mercenary
Conan the Pirate
Conan the Brigand
The Book of Skelos
Conan the Wanderer
Conan the Adventurer
Conan the Scout
Conan the King
Nameless Cults
Ancient Ruins & Cursed Cities
Conan Monolith Boardgame Sourcebook
The Shadow of the Sorcerer
Horrors of the Hyborian Age

ACCESSORIES
Gamemaster Screen
Geomorphic Tile Sets
Doom & Fortune Tokens
Q-Workshop Dice
Card Decks
Stygian Doom Pit
Fabric & Poster Maps
Character Sheet Pad
Conqueror's Bag

MODIPHIUS™ ENTERTAINMENT

2D20™

CABINET

ROBERT E. HOWARD™ OFFICIAL LICENSE

HYBORIA™

modiphius.com/conan

VAMPIRE

THE MASQUERADE

ORIGINS AWARD WINNER

VAMPIRE: THE MASQUERADE is the original and ultimate roleplaying game of personal and political horror. You are a vampire, struggling for survival, supremacy, and your own fading humanity—afraid of what you are capable of, and fearful of the inhuman conspiracies that surround you.

NEW RELEASES COMING SOON

☥ THE FALL OF LONDON V5 CHRONICLE

London is burning. As the Second Inquisition put the city's Kindred to the torch, your characters wake from torpor. The sensible thing would be to flee now, but before you can leave the capital, you have one last job to do. This campaign is perfect to bring your Vampire players up to speed on the plot developments in Vampire: The Masquerade 5th Edition or as as a gateway for new players.

☥ V5 PLAYERS GUIDE

A guide to playing different styles of Vampire: The Masquerade to help you play the way YOU want to play, from gritty street level drama to romantic blood opera, complete with advice, new rules, and guidance on using the 5th Edition system to play previous editions of Vampire.

MŌDIPHIÜS™
ENTERTAINMENT

WHITE WOLF